Doing Daily Battle

FATIMA MERNISSI

Doing Daily Battle

Interviews with Moroccan Women

Translated by Mary Jo Lakeland

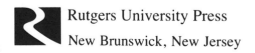

Rutgers University Press
New Brunswick, New Jersey

English translation first published in the United States of
America by Rutgers University Press, 1989

English translation first published in Great Britain by The Women's Press, Limited,
1988

First published as *Le Maroc Raconté par ses Femmes*, 1984

Copyright © Société Marocaine des Editeurs Réunis, 1984; copyright
© 1986 by Fatima Mernissi; English translation copyright © 1988 by
Mary Jo Lakeland; copyright © 1989 by Rutgers, The State University

Contents

1
Introduction: Women's Morocco

The dialogue between the sexes, even if it takes place, is likely to end up in a monologue, according to Omar Ibn al-Khattab the Just. [1]

Why? Answering that question would launch us into an exposé that would explain why the silence of women is one of the bases of Moroccan civilisation, and that is not the objective of this book.

Its objective, on the other hand, is to break that ancestral silence, whatever the reasons for it.

How does Morocco appear through the words of its women? Is it a familiar Morocco (that is, the same as that described by men), or is it an unknown Morocco? What are the benchmarks, the reference points of the female view? Are they the same as those of the male view? What are the problems and struggles that emerge from the female view, the crucial struggles that justify life and structure it? According to the most pervasive male discourse, echoed by the media, the problems and struggles that motivate women and structure their lives are supposed to be the problems and struggles associated with being loved and desired – obviously by a man with the means to pay for the woman-as-body that, in this male discourse, is something to be bought and sold. Beauty and sexuality (in the narrow sense of seductiveness) are supposed to be the major poles around which the life of a woman revolves.

However, it seems that women's Morocco is actually a territory where the struggles and problems are quite different. With women's words, the people who have been immersed in this woman–beauty–seduction discourse are going to find one surprise after another. They are going to find themselves in unfamiliar territory. Only a minority of women – and one that is disappearing – still lives in a harem. For all the others, life is played out around the struggle for food, for wages, for some income, however minimal. In the Morocco of women, earning one's living is the essential

1

concern and purpose in life. Women exist above all as economic agents, as sources of income, energy, and work, ceaselessly struggling against poverty, unemployment and insecurity. In this collection of interviews there is a single exception: Batul Binjalluna, raised in a harem in Fez during the twenties and married into another harem on the eve of World War II. But there are no more Batuls. Her counterpart today would be a women equipped with university degrees and fired by fierce ambitions for salary and professional status. Today a middle-class woman of Fez or Casablanca views the quest for an education and a profession as an intrinsic facet of her 'beauty', just as the harem woman would regard a golden belt. Even in the class where a woman's earning potential can be left unused without great damage to the family – that is, in the class where the husband earns enough to support his wife and children – one finds a strong assertion of an economic identity by women. The era of secluded women is truly over. The men and women who preserve it as a model or project it as an ideal for women's lot are to be pitied, because they are confusing history and fantasy.

They are all the more pitiable because non-productive secluded women only existed in Moroccan historical reality as very exceptional cases. It should not be forgotten that the history of Morocco until very recently was the history of a country undermined by famine, epidemics, and internal dissensions.[2] In Moroccan historical reality the women of the peasant masses constituting the majority of the population did not have the option of being supported by their husbands, but had to work very hard.[3] Article 115 of the Moroccan Family Law, which stipulates that 'every person provides for his needs through his own resources with the exception of the wife whose upkeep (*nafaqa*) is incumbent on her husband', reflects not reality but the wide gulf that separates women's experience and the principles inspiring the article. In this regard it is interesting to note that the Moroccan Family Law was drafted solely by men. At the dawn of Moroccan independence, the nationalist leaders, who had undergone torture in prison so that equality and democracy could reign, designed the future Moroccan family without consulting the central element of that family – women.

These interviews reveal that in fact in low-income families the husbands are often physically and economically absent, with unemployment and migration in search of work making them totally unable to take responsibility for their children.

The interviews contribute to our knowledge about Morocco on two levels. The first is that of perception. The lack of correspondence between men's perception and women's perception of the world has always been impossible to get a grip on in our society because of women's silence. The monopoly enjoyed by the male view in Muslim society weighs very heavily on the future of democracy, which presupposes a multiplicity of views. Just as a three-year-old child, seeing an unequal relationship between father and mother, learns to relate to another person in terms of the negation of the right of women to express themselves, so this same child, grown to be an adult, will fix elections in order to prevent others (men or women) from expressing themselves.

The second contribution of these interviews is on the level of reality. They identify the changes that have occurred in the situation of women in recent decades. According to the views of women, what are the dimensions now of a woman's life, where the changes have been so profound and irreversible, and what have been the consequences of these changes?

It is in access to public space, employment, and education that women's lives have undergone the most fundamental changes. Space, employment, and education seem to be the areas where the struggles which agitate society (especially the class struggle) show up in the life of women with the greatest clarity.

I am going to limit myself in this introduction to reflecting on the changes that have been produced (or have miscarried) in the relations between the sexes solely in terms of perceptions. I am doing this not because this is more important than viewing it in terms of reality, but because the problem of the access of women to employment, education, and space cannot be overlooked by even the most closed minds. But I am doing this above all because I believe that the problem of 'what-is-perceived' –which may escape even the most alert minds – is the key problem of cultural revolution and one of the causes of its failure in our society.

In this introduction I intend to argue that, for a woman, the famous hierarchy that is maintained between infrastructure (economics, experience) and superstructure (ideology, perception) is an absurdity. In a society where change is viewed as an external attack and where tradition occupies a pre-eminent place in the so-called strategies for 'the future' and for 'development policies' (as is the case in the Muslim countries), ideology and perception have an over-determining influence. The problems confronting Morocco in its difficulties with development are ideological before they are economic. The problems our society faces today are not technological (which machine should be manufactured) but perceptual: what are the urgent problems that require a priority solution? The ability of the planner, the politician, and the intellectual to perceive, identify, and deal with national priority problems depends on their openness to the ideas of the masses and their applying these ideas – that is, their ability to transcend their own subjectivity, their own 'perception-of-reality'.

One fact that the planners, politicians, and intellectuals often forget is that the 'masses' are sexed, and that women constitute half of them. We will see that the neglect of this fact has radical implications for the perception of, and decision-making about, the problems that ravage our society and sap its energies, as well as for the required solutions.

The gap between female perception and male perception

The world that emerges through the words of women is a world fundamentally different from the world prescribed as ideal by the 'pervasive' male discourse, the discourse that reverberates in legislation and the state-operated mass media. I prefer to use the word *pervasive* rather than *dominant*, because to say *the dominant discourse* would imply the existence of other discordant, contradictory discourses. However, in present-day Morocco, although there exist various other male discourses (in particular the discourses of progressive intellectuals often in conflict with the dominant discourse), they are scarcely 'heard'. One hears one bell alone ringing, that of the pervasive discourse. It rings so loudly and has such powerful means at its disposal that it renders the progressive discourses inaudible. Besides the means that the dominant male discourse commands, there is another factor that frustrates progressive discourses, and that is the quasi-terrorist pressure put on them by the official discourse. The way, for example, in which very serious problems, such as polygyny, repudiation, sexual inequality in inheritance, and contraception, are dealt with by the progressive parties is strictly determined by blackmail and the fear of being accused of atheism by the dominant ideological apparatus for any challenge they might pose.

We know that in the logic of the dominant Islamic ideology, any change is considered to be innovation (in Arabic, *bid'a*), and innovation is errant behaviour (*dalala*), whence the danger for parties with progressve views on women of being labelled heretical. So, when I speak of the gap between the male view and the female view, I am referring only to the pervasive male discourse. These interviews show that there is a total divorce between the female view and the male view, at least in the perception of three phenomena: sex roles, the marital couple, and contraception.

Sex roles: according to women, the 'weaker sex' is the male sex

According to the 'pervasive' male discourse, the sexes are not equal: there is a strong sex, man; and a weak sex, woman. In their own view, women see themselves as a race of giants doing daily battle against the destructive monsters of unemployment, poverty, and degrading jobs. One extreme case of this self-valorisation of women as economic agents is the interview with Aisha al-Hyaniya. This ten-year-old child was torn from her native province at the age of seven to be hired out as a maid in a family in Fez. Aisha remembers her rural childhood as a period when she was able to create almost mythical economic wealth. She could grow plants, take part in the olive-pressing, fetch water and firewood, go fishing, hunt birds, make bread, and care for the animals.

In the view of women, men play no role at all in the daily battle that women wage to earn a living. Not only do men not support them and their children according to the concept of *nafaqa*[4] in Article 115 of the Moroccan Family Law, but they are not even capable of acting as a buffer between women and the social forces that torment and assail them.

All the women interviewed, with the exception of Batul Binjalluna, who was imprisoned in a harem, see themselves as participating actively in the economic life of the family, independent of the income and social standing of the husband. The teacher Rabi'a, wife of a doctor, explains that at the time of her marriage her husband demanded that she work, and that once the household was set up, it was she who was careful to continue working. After the failure of her marriage, she linked her decision to get a divorce to her ability to earn a living. For her, the right to self-expression and having an independent income go hand in hand: 'We have gained the right to tell a man what we think, something my mother could never do, and the possibility of demanding a divorce, even if we have to bear all the consequences and disadvantages.'

Nazha, the only woman interviewed who had had a university education and who came from a modest urban background, began very young to work to earn her living. While still in secondary school, she looked for work that would allow her to earn money during school vacations to cover part of her expenses.

For women who are illiterate or have only a few years of schooling, their working life begins in childhood. Most of those belonging to the underprivileged classes begin to work at the age of five or six. In the countryside they take part in work in the fields and in animal care, as well as in the drudgery of fetching water and firewood. In towns, they are 'placed' in other families or 'apprenticed' to a *mu'allima*. Men, whether husbands or fathers, do not manage to protect women against premature entry into the work force, or migration to the city with all its risks, or unemployment, or sweatshop exploitation by employers. The hardships of the agricultural sector, the peasants' ever-losing battles for land and for protecting it from exploitation, always rebound on the lives of women, in their view. Men are seen as anti-heroes, overcome, just like women, by the destructive forces that destabilise the rural world. Drought and the steady loss of families' lands reduce men and women to resorting to migration to the cities as an individual or group solution at some time or another in their lives. In the case of Dawiya al-Filaliya, migration was an individual decision. In other cases, a woman migrates as a partner in a couple after marriage. In still others, she migrates alone, but by decision of the family, as in the cases of little girls placed as 'maids'.

In short, in these interviews one doesn't find a single case in which a woman describes a man as a strong, protective person and a woman as a weak person expecting protection and largesse from a man. It seems that here we encounter one of the gravest distortions in perception, a distortion which moreover has repercussions on the way in which the state, the decision-maker in matters of planning and legislation, takes a position and acts: namely, the fact of perceiving man as the pillar of the family, the provider, and the only working member of it. Because of this, all job-creation policies, whether in the rural or urban sectors, are focused on the creation of jobs for men. This has been the case, for example, with two projects that have played a very important role in the national economy: the projects for agrarian reform and for national development. This male fantasy (that Moroccan women do not support themselves) also explains the failure of the policy for the education and professional training of women. The rare projects for the advancement of women are designed for a 'homemaker' who doesn't exist in the poor classes that are the target of these programmes. So it was that for years the objective of the training programmes of the Ministry of Youth and Sports and the Ministry of Social Affairs and Mutual Aid was to teach women house-wifely skills, especially sewing, knitting, cooking, and embroidery. These programmes were directed toward a phantom woman, since the 'home' had been deserted by women in search of paid work since child-hood. One final consequence of the male fantasy of the 'husband pro-vider', who supports his wife and children and who is the sole model for Moroccan legislation and economic planning, is the senseless discus-sion, which has been going on since 1975, on the need 'to integrate women into development', as if development had already taken place and women were sitting on the sidelines twiddling their thumbs. Women see perfectly well that they are deeply involved in the economic struggle, in the struggle for survival, in the struggle for a paid job, and in the struggle against the insecurities of a job when they get one. So it seems that at the level of perception, the divorce between the 'pervasive' male discourse and women's view is total. Now, what is the situation with regard to the perception of the marital couple?

Perception of the marital couple

In the 'pervasive' male discourse, the marital couple does not exist, if one defines it as an entity formed by two persons equally involved in the quest for life, and in which there is a pooling of economic resources and not merely the contribution of just one of them. The marriage model, operative in law and in the values affirmed by this discourse, is an unbal-anced and totally asymmetrical relationship in both economic and affec-tive terms.

On the economic level, the conjugal entity is formed by a dependent person, the wife, and a rich and generous husband, who sees to the total satisfaction of the needs of the former. On the affective level, the disequi-librium is just as obvious. Faithfulness is demanded only of the wife. The man can have other partners: polygyny officially allows him to 'share' himself among four women, and repudiation allows him to replace these by others as often as he wants – and this he does by unilateral, independent decision. His caprice is the sole law and judge. When polygyny and repudiation are instituted as laws in a given society, it is clear that that society has opted against the existence of the marital couple as an entity in which economic and affective relations will be based on equality.

We discover from the words of women that they have a totally subversive approach to the subject of the couple. They insist upon a conjugal couple based on economic and affective equality as the sole viable model and they are completely dedicated to creating it.

On one hand they demand fidelity, and, on the other, they show through their daily struggles that a poor man is worthy of being loved. The lives of the women interviewed here destroy by their mere example the key fantasy of the 'pervasive' male discourse: namely, that only an economically powerful man is worthy of being loved. In their own words, the women reveal that they love men not because they are rich and generous, but because they can be loving. The women love the men not for what men can give them in the way of money and material resources, but for what they can give in the way of affective resources. They demand to be loved, to have a privileged, exclusive relationship with their husbands; material support is secondary since they are able to support themselves.

> I laid down certain conditions to my husband before having my first child. I told him: 'I can accept hunger and destitution; I can live with you in a dilapidated house, a house of corrugated metal, a tent if necessary. But if I see you doing – if I see you with another woman – or even if, for example, you decide to stay out late and come back to me afterwards, even if you have done nothing (and how would I know?) – that I would not put up with.'

This was the determination of Tahra Bint Muhammad, who was torn away from her mountain home by migration and ended up in a shantytown outside Rabat after her marriage.

The marital couple seems to hold together miraculously despite the grave problems which menace the family, especially unemployment, which not only causes the man to be incapable of fulfilling his role as provider of *nafaqa*, but also makes his intermittent absence a fact of life in the modern family. In the case of Habiba the psychic, her second marriage is a success in her terms not because her husband is rich and generous, but because during her attacks by the *riah* he rolls around with her on the ground in the puddles of water and mud. Habiba's husband is not only unemployed, he is *ma'dhur*, as she calls him. In fact, he is a legless cripple.

The stubborn determination of these women to create a family based on a strong couple is shown by their persistent refusal of the partner chosen by their parents. Almost all of these women refused the 'fiancé' offered to them by their parents and claimed for themselves the right to choose another man who better met their tastes and desires. Here also women seem to be making a break with another institution of the Muslim family incorporated into the Family Law – the institution of the *wali*, or system of matrimonial tutelage, which prevents 'the woman herself from concluding an act of marriage, but which has her represented by the *wali* whom she has chosen to do it for her' (Article 12 of the Family Law).

Legally speaking, a Muslim marriage is not a marriage concluded between a man and a woman, but a deed signed between two men, for the law specifies that the 'female legal guardian must delegate a male representative to contract marriage in the name of her ward'. So the *wali* (the mandatory representative) can only be a man. It can be argued that the institution of matrimonial tutelage does not confer on the man who represents the woman during the conclusion of the marriage contract the right to choose her husband. However, you only have to look at what happens in reality, as it pours from women's accounts, to see that fathers and brothers do not respect the subtlety of Muslim law and usually arrogate to themselves the right to choose a husband for their daughter or sister, who finds herself obliged to reject that choice in order to assert her own will.

Once again one sees how women, with their desires and wishes, come into conflict with the male laws that rule the world for them. But another subject on which there is total conflict between male laws and choices and the wishes of women is contraception. The laws and debates on this subject in political and religious circles reveal a total disjunction between these circles and the needs and wishes of women.

Contraception: the gap between political and religious positions and women's wishes

These interviews teach us that one of the crucial problems confronting a woman in Moroccan society is her inability to control and plan her pregnancies. The interviews reveal first of all that a large part of a woman's life is devoted to giving birth to children who die at a young age. Infant mortality seems to be one of the calamities that drain women's energy.

The women interviewed also disclose that, faced with the economic problems that threaten and destabilise their families, they often have recourse to abortion, by any possible method whether traditional or modern, in order to space their births. This spacing seems to be a constant, compelling problem, a necessity posed by the threat that repeated pregnancies make to their own health and that of their children. The problem of the control and spacing of births emerges in the words of these women as a source of great distress. If it were resolved, it would permit women to face and deal with the other logistic problems they confont every day in their efforts to support their families with insufficient and irregular resources.

If Moroccan society were a society in which the dominant ideology (the priority objectives for the survival of the group) reflected the problems and needs of the masses without distinctions of class or sex, birth control would figure among the priority concerns. However – and it is here that one can measure the negative and paralysing gap between male and female views on the possibilities for a real development of the country – a problem which seems to have been a constant worry of Moroccan women for centuries (since they have evolved a whole pharmacopoeia and medical practice to solve it) has only been dealt with by the state and its officials very tardily and only then under international pressure. And it is still being disputed by politicians and planners – all of the male sex – as a foreign import imposed on the Muslim countries by the imperialists. [5]

In fact, the Moroccan state, which in the enthusiasm of the dawn of independence tried to identify the crucial problems which should have priority and legitimacy as national issues, not only made no effort to tackle the problem of birth control, but only agreed to make an about-face ten years later under the pressure of international capitalist organisations. It did not base its analyses and decisions on the views of Moroccan women, but it let itself be guided by the Ford Foundation, the Population Council, USAID, and the International Planned Parenthood Federation (IPPF).

In 1965 the Division of Statistics of the Secretariat of State for Planning drew the attention of the government to the dangers represented by demographic increase to the economic and social development of the country. The Ministry of Health then contracted with the Ford

Foundation, the Population Council, and the IPPF to send a group of doctors to visit family planning centers in London and Brussels. In 1966 the first consulting centers for family planning opened as part of the public health services. In the same year a family planning seminar was held in Rabat. [6]

This document also informs us that 'Morocco has received since 1966 around one million US dollars in aid for its demographic program.'

Among the organisations which financed the programme were the Ford Foundation, the Population Council, USAID (which alone gave around $400,000 for family planning programmes), the IPPF, the Swedish Development Agency (SIDA), the Canadian International Development Agency (CIDA), and finally the Technical Cooperation Services of the French Ministry of Foreign Affairs.

Many of the demographic studies used by the country have been financed by foreign agencies. One example is the public opinion poll on family planning carried out in Morocco in 1966-7 by the Ministry of Health and the Secretariat of State for Planning, which was funded by the Ford Foundation in its programme of 'technical and financial assistance'. [7] The American government aid programme also contributed technical assistance in the preparation of the census and various demographic studies. USAID covered part of the funding for the Centre of Demographic Studies and Research of the Secretariat of State for Planning. [8]

International organisations have also contributed generously to the financing of seminars and conferences, at which religious authorities were brought from the four corners of the Muslim world to discuss Islam and birth control. One of these was the conference on 'Islam and Family Planning', which took place in Rabat in December 1971 and which was funded by the London-based IPPF. The latter also took part in the creation of the Moroccan Family Planning Association.

So the interest of Moroccan officials in birth control was not in any way generated by listening to the mass of ordinary women. It was strictly conditioned by the concerns of the organisations that financed demographic programmes in the Third World. And these concerns are purely strategic, particularly concern for the demographic imbalance between the capitalist countries (where the population scarcely reproduces itself) and the satellite countries (which have a 'galloping' birth rate).

The strategic aims which inspired the international financing of the family planning programmes in the Third World not only conditioned the institutional approaches and techniques adopted by the officials of these countries, but also had a strong determining influence on the attitudes of the progressive forces in these countries toward this problem.

Thus for a long time progressive forces in Morocco have criticised and rejected family planning programmes on the grounds that they were financed by imperialist organisations. And they did this without ever asking about the desires and needs of Moroccan women in this matter. Their analysis of the question seemed to focus only on the objectives of the international agencies as the determining factor. The voices of women, expressing their desperate need to control births, which manifested itself in their equally desperate recourse to traditional methods of abortion, seemed to have no impact on their calculations.

Ironically, birth control was also rejected by the forces of the right as an imperialist conspiracy against Islam. The interviews with these women reveal that during the period when the progressives, in the name of revolution, and the forces of the right, in the name of Islam, were condemning the family planning programme set up by the Moroccan government according to the inadequate models of the Ford Foundation and the Population Council, Moroccan women were trying every day to space their births, often through abortion in cruel and inhuman conditions.

The question of birth control, which has been handled by the technocratic leadership, where decisions are made exclusively by males and are haggled over by the political and religious leadership, illustrates very clearly that imperialist objectives succeed only with a leadership which does not listen to the masses, half of whom are women. The funds invested by the Americans in the Moroccan family planning programmes would have had a completely different impact if they had been administered by people responsive to the urgent needs of the majority of women. Perhaps women would have preferred to take part in the development of contraceptive techniques based on an analysis of the traditional heritage on this subject, instead of just having to accept the mechanical importation of pills and IUDs manufactured by American companies.

If Moroccan officials had listened to the voice of women, they would have adopted a birth control programme as far as back in 1956, for the pure and simple reason that that would have been the desire and need of the mass of women, who alone are capable of carrying out a task that men delegate to them: nurturing children while getting by on resources not only scarce but also constantly reduced by galloping inflation.

If the progressives had listened to the mass of women, they would have hesitated to condemn the family planning programme simply because it was advocated and financed by 'imperialist' agencies. They would have had to support the principle of a demographic policy and fight for the participation of women of the poorer classes in the development and implementing of it.

It is easy to see the absurdity of the arguments for and against development, as long as they remain limited to a male elite, whatever its ideological base. A progressive leadership only energises a society to the extent that it is the transmitter of the life force of the people, and the people are 50 per cent female.

Scientific method and terrorist actions

In this conclusion I want to speak as a Moroccan woman who uses writing and analysis – two tools which are exclusively male in our culture. And let no one tell me that 'in our heritage there have always been women scholars'. Our heritage, as I have experienced it as a child, adolescent, and adult, is an obscurantist and mutilating heritage. I was born in 1940 in a middle-class home in Fez, the 'capital of science' and 'centre of civilisation'. I was born exactly 500 metres from Karaouin University. One could not be better situated to benefit from our heritage and its advantages. Well, I was born there and I was raised by illiterate women, who were not only physically confined but intellectually mutilated in the name of honour and a female ideal cherished by the male bourgeoisie, who immerse themselves in this heritage to the point of drowning.

My father adored me. He used to take me on his mule to the mosque for Friday prayers, and he kept me by his side during long hours of reading or discussions with his friends. The books that he loved and regularly pored over were histories of Muslim civilisation, which was his passion. Nevertheless, my father, who adored me, who was immersed in our heritage and impassioned by our civilisation, bought me a *djellaba* and tried to force the veil on me at the age of four. For him there was no contradiction between civilisation, refinement, and immuring alive, physically and mentally, a child of the female sex.

As a Moroccan woman who has had access to writing and an advanced education (for very particular historical reasons which have little to do with any free choice of our bourgeoisie), I have learned to distinguish the varieties of terrorist tactics that men, who monopolise the symbolic values of our society, use to stop me from expressing myself, or to denigrate what I say – which comes to the same thing. I have thus had time to develop a sixth sense to detect the kind of man who, in the middle of a professional or 'social' conversation with me, slips into the terrorist mode. I can describe this type of man in minute detail to help others to identify him. But, alas, I believe that he is in fact quite easily identifiable, because he violently opposes all notions of open-mindedness or change whether made by men or women.

His terrorist tactics can be expressed in two sentences: firstly, 'What you are talking about is an imported idea' (referring to access to the cultural heritage); and secondly, 'What you are talking about is not representative' (referring to access to science). What is the meaning of these two sentences so often thrown at any Moroccan citizen, male or female, who puts forward any idea which appears to upset the established order?

The first phrase implies that the person speaking sets himself up as the guardian and legitimate and exclusive interpreter of the cultural heritage and its content, and excludes *you* from access to this national heritage. Not only does he ban your access to it, but he accuses you of the worst crime in his book – treason to the national cause. You are an agent of foreign enemies.

The second phrase – 'What you are talking about is not representative' – refers to science, but the mechanism and the implications are the same. The person speaking sets himself up as the general guardian of scientific truth. He has a monopoly on scientific truth, and it is in the name of that scientific truth (confused by him with representativeness) that he intimates that you should hold your tongue.

As a result of this, I have discovered that the relations between the sexes are always inextricably and unconditionally linked to class relations. I have discovered that, in addition to these 'terrorist men' who try to deprive me of my right to self-expression, there is another group of men, less visible because with less access to the corridors of prestige and power; these men are the personification of the desire for change, for living differently, for progressing toward a more humane society where people would have the right to expression and creativity and equal access to national resources. I discovered that these men were 'castrated' like me of their right to the 'heritage' and to 'science', the monopoly *par excellence* of male power. These men had an entirely different attitude toward me. They did everything they could within the little power they had to give me confidence in myself and to help me to persist in my desire for self-expression. They are colleagues and friends in the Faculté des Lettres at the university. So it was that I learned one small truth, and that was that you should never analyse sex discrimination outside the context of class relations, especially when it's a matter of struggle over the symbolic values of a society. This explains why progressive men are so present in my life and thoughts and why it is so important for men who strongly support change to integrate 'female' values into their theory and practice. Progressive men can do nothing if they don't lay claim to 'female' values. And women who desire change will in no way succeed if they do not persist in breaking through the barriers and walls that withhold 'male' values from us. We must not forget that we have been born and raised, men and women, in a society where class inequalities operate in a sexually segregated field of struggle.

As I remarked above, every time I make a claim to the equality of democratic practice in conversation with Mr Terrorist, he deals me a nearly fatal blow with his weapons of 'the heritage' and 'representativeness'. So I discovered that according to his system of values, any claim of equality and democratic practice is a claim foreign to the cultural heritage and foreign to scientific truth.

I concluded from this that what my Mr Terrorist was claiming as 'the heritage' and 'scientific truth' was, in fact, a very specific interpretation of both the heritage and science, which situates him in a very precise class relationship to the symbolic values of the society. His interpretation of the symbolic values is one which echoes his class interests. And it is obvious that he has class interests every time he confronts me – me, a woman who advocates change through writing – in a seminar, at a reception, or in a government office, in order to strip me of the 'male attributes of power' that I make use of – namely, access to the written heritage and to science.

It took me a long time to understand all this and even longer to begin to be able to smile when I see a Mr Terrorist drape himself in his toga of 'the heritage' or his academic robes of 'scientific representativeness' in order to perpetrate against me a crime that my male ancestors have committed for such a long time against their wives: symbolic castration, remanding them to silence as the essence of femaleness and a key criterion of beauty.

And so I come to the question that Mr Terrorist will not fail to ask when this book of interviews with women appears: 'Are they representative?'

Well, I would like to demonstrate to you that a man who would react to these interviews by questioning their 'representativeness' would immediately be shown up on the very terrain on which he chose to stand – the scientific field, which is the political field *par excellence*.[9]

The confusion between representativeness and science does not happen by chance. It is the product of a very specific history of the development of the social sciences, which my 'terrorist' blindly espouses and which reveals the degree of his dependence on the 'official science' of the West.[10] This is one aspect. The other is that the individuals who maintain that representativeness equals 'scientificalness' thereby reveal their scholarly deficiency and their failure to keep up with scientific practice and the state of universal scientific knowledge.

Representativeness refers to one precise method, the statistical method which is based on a very particular approach, the quantitative approach, and one precise technique, the questionnaire. Therefore, asserting that scientific practice is reduced to the statistical method, the quantitative approach, and the questionnaire technique, is a political assertion, not a scientific one.

But I have the right, as a researcher, to lay claim to another science. I can, for example, assert my preference for the qualitative approach.

All this is in order to say that these interviews do not pretend to be representative, but that does not imply that they have no 'scientific' importance, since one of the criteria of 'scientificalness' is capturing reality.

Reality is too complex to be reduced to statistical units without distorting it. In the Moroccan government survey of household consumption and expenditures based on the criterion of representativeness, the approach used was quantitative, and the technique was the questionnaire. Representativeness was guaranteed by the manner in which the sample was constructed: 6,309 households, of which 2,960 were urban and 3,349 were rural. These 6,309 households were to give us information on their consumption, and 'the field covered by the survey is the whole country'.[11] The information that this survey gives me, in the form of statistical tables, is limited to concepts which are far from informing me about one dimension of reality: life experience. The table giving me 'the budgetary coefficients of the major categories of goods and services' informs me that in urban areas 44.7 per cent of the budget of a family falls into the category of 'food and drink'. This is an important piece of information, but it is far from encompassing or expressing all the facets of the reality of a family. The interview with Tahra Bint Muhammad conveys to me an amount of information on 'houshold consumption' that no statistical table can ever catch. It is absurd that I should be defending the qualitative approach and the interview technique. I am only doing it because 'official science' wants to convince me that only the questionnaire, based on a series of conventions (called concepts) and of more or less inadequate definitions (admitted to be so by the investigator himself), should be used by me as the sole scientific technique capable of capturing reality.

A questionnaire reduces Tahra Bint Muhammad to a statistical unit, that is, to a robot who will merely reply yes or no to the questions chosen by the investigator. The questions that Tahra Bint Muhammad considers as pertinent or as having priority have no place in the process of the collection of data by questionnaire. In the final analysis, the investigator has very little concern for her priorities. Worse still, the way in which the questions are formulated leaves Tahra Bint Muhammad at the mercy of the investigator. For example, when he asks her how much protein (meat, eggs, milk products) she consumes, he forces her to answer yes or no and to identify the amount of each product.[12] Tahra's wishes and their possible frustration are unconsciously excluded; they do not interest the investigator. I am not going to go into the methodological details nor expand on the difficulties that the project officer, an employee of the Division of Statistics (located in one of the residential neighbourhoods of the capital), would encounter in getting Tahra to understand his concept of 'animal fat' so that she could answer in a way that would be translatable into a statistical code. Here I am raising the epistemological difficulty that dooms the questionnaire more to failure than to success in its claim to capture reality in the context of the Third World. I will limit myself to pointing out a few fundamental obstacles:

1. The average citizen's distrust of the investigator. Often Tahra Bint Muhammad perceives this official of the state statistical survey system as an enemy, to whom one should tell as little as possible.

2. The difficulty of real communication between the person being questioned and the investigator. The latter must translate the oral exchange that takes place between him and the person questioned into a code of concepts, variables, and indicators rigidly defined in the offices of the Division of Statistics.

3. The difficulties of translating the collected data into statistical tables. I shall give just one example: the concept of the median. When

Table 1.3 gives me the median expenditure per household – 'that is, 50 per cent of the households spend on an average less than . . . '[13] – I have the right to ask some questions about the meaning of this concept and all the other concepts of the quantitative approach that they are trying to impose on me as the guarantees of scientific truth.

I am convinced that the sole referent for science can only be reality. One method, one approach, one technique is more scientific than another only to the extent that it more faithfully approximates reality. Fidelity to reality is the one and only rule that should guide our attempts to establish a scientific rapport between us and our environment. And representativeness – that is, the quantitative approach – is far from guaranteeing that fidelity to reality. It is not only necessary to increase the approaches, methods, and techniques, but as citizens of the Third World we must encourage *al-bid'a* and *al-ijtihad* – that is, innovation and independent enquiry by the believer, as distinct from *al-ijma'* (the consensus). We must promote the use of free will and innovation and encourage young investigators to test other methods and techniques.

So I can be proud of my interviews in that they give me a feeling of fidelity to the reality of women's experience that no statistical table has ever given me. How and according to what rules did I conduct these interviews? I began by violating Rule No. 1 that I learned at the Sorbonne and at the American university where I was trained in 'research technique': to maintain objectivity toward the person being interviewed. I cannot be objective toward an illiterate woman, because I have a very special affective relationship to her: I identify with her. I was born in 1940, and very few Moroccan women of that generation have had access to writing and still fewer to an advanced education. So I have a very strong feeling of having escaped illiteracy by an almost absurd miracle. For me, trying to give voice to the illiterate woman is to give voice to this self of mine which should have been doomed to the ancestral silence. My relationship to writing and its uses are very strongly conditioned by this fact. In the conferences, colloquia, round tables, and seminars in which I participate at home and abroad and which are usually almost exclusively male, I feel myself in the position of a voyeur, or rather a voyeuse. I have a strong sense of belonging to the world of illiteracy in which I was immersed until the age of twenty. At that time I rented a room near the university campus in Rabat and became part of the milieu of 'knowledge', 'writing', and advanced degrees – that is, the milieu that continues to be male dominated.

Thus the interviews that I have chosen to share with the reader, from a total of about 100 collected since 1970, are interviews with women and children who are friends with whom I have an involvement that goes beyond superficiality and mistrust. It is not easy to establish a relationship of confidence with another person. Are there some special tips and instructions for interviewing? I myself am in the process of working out some. The few rules that have so far emerged dictated the way in which I conducted these interviews. One of these rules is that the interviewer must, as much as possible, cultivate a relationship of equality and maintain an atmosphere in which the personality of the person being interviewed can freely unfold. For this reason it is necessary to give up the cherished technique of control, of controlling the give and take (as I was taught by my French and American trainers), of knowing how to anticipate and codify, especially while in the process of interviewing. I was taught many tricks, particularly regarding the interview that pretends to be non-directive – one of the methods most used by advertising polls. As for me, I have learned that the best rule is to know how to give up control, to take the risk of wasting time and of looking ridiculous. In this way I have learned that an illiterate woman has her own narrative pace, and that a Moroccan interviewer must learn to be sensitive to that pace and respect it.

The interview with Habiba the psychic confirmed my intuition. In this case the personality of the person being interviewed was such that the role of the interviewer had to be limited to that of a mere receptacle, a mere space in which a coherent experience could be unfolded and reflected – an experience that is the fruit of her daily struggle against the attacks of the *riah*.

I also tried to limit my intervention in the preparation of the words of the interviewees for the printed page. But readability did impose a limit. The spoken word is not the same as a readable text. The raw transcription of the interviews (with the exception of Habiba the psychic) was too fragmentary and repetitive to be readable. So I have often intervened at the level of 'editing' to make them readable. Otherwise, I have kept in the transcriptions all the details which show the misunderstandings due to the aggressive interposition of my subjectivity. I am not at all ashamed to show my blunders as an interviewer. On the contrary, it is by showing them that I will succeed in overcoming them. And this is my second rule for interviewing: develop as much as possible an attitude of self-criticism and of continual testing of your subjectivity in relation to that of the other person.

Another aspect of the interviews that I wanted to preserve is the relaxed, often confusing, way in which many of the interviewees relate time sequences and events. An illiterate woman who has virtually no control over her life, subject to the whims and will of others, has a much more fluid sense of time than an educated Western reader, who is used to analysing time in an attempt to control it. One of the charms of the interviews is to confront such readers with these inconsistencies, which give a taste of how confusing a lifetime of powerlessness is.

These interviews do not claim to be an 'exclusive' depiction of the reality of Moroccan women. Such a claim would be contrary to the open-mindedness that must guide our research into Moroccan reality, our desire to be faithful to it. They are merely a very tentative effort to understand the complexities of that reality. I would wish that the greatest number of researchers – men and women – would find here encouragement for their own personal initiatives along the road of understanding of others and themselves.

These initiatives should have multiple approaches, techniques, and styles of presentation. My greatest wish would be to stimulate through these interviews a series of debates regarding our status as guardians of knowledge and so-called legitimate holders of 'scientific truth'. I say this because in our universe, where illiteracy is not only the present reality but the foreseeable future (given that measures to erase it from the world are not carried out as part of a deliberate political strategy), the weapon of knowledge seems to me to be the most formidable weapon of all.

2

Batul Binjalluna and Mariam Talbiya: young girls in a harem

What is a harem?
A fantasy? Real life? An erotic universe?
A prison world? A women's world or a men's world?
Who is happy in a harem?
The men? The women? The children?

According to the testimony of two women, Batul and Mariam, who lived in one of the most prosperous harems in Fez during the 1930s, a harem has nothing to do with eroticism or pleasure. A harem is, above all, a power structure, a system in which oppression and violence work together in the lives of women to turn their daily life into a prison universe. It is the reflection and mirror of the vise of colonialism which held the master of the harem in its grip.

But although the harem is a prison, it crushes the aspirations of young girls in different ways, according to the class to which they belong:

The young girls of the masters are used in the matrimonial strategies that strengthen the group's power and self-aggrandisement.

The young girls of the enslaved class are trapped in other strategies – they travel other roads.

Batul Binjalluna [1]

Masters, slaves, and free wives

Q: *Let's go back to the time of your birth. How many women were there in the household?*

A: As I remember, each of my brothers had four or five slaves. [2] Hajj

Ahmad had five, Hajj Muhammad had four, and Abd al-Razzaq only had one. That would make ten in all.

Q: *What were their names?*

A: Two were named Yasmin, two others Marzuka, two others Fatima, and so on.

Q: *Could two slaves have the same name in the same household?*

A: Yes. We distinguished one from the other by calling one of them, for example, Yasmin Mother of Aisha, and the other, Yasmin Mother of Khadduj. The others were named Fath Azhar, Ghalia, Mabruka, Zaid al-Khair, Sa'ada, Sa'ida, Anbar, 'Ud al-Ward, because there were not only my brothers' slaves. There were also those of my father. Some slaves had children, others didn't. 'Ud al-Ward, for example, was only rebought after I was born.

Q: *Why was she rebought? Did she have children?*

A: No, she didn't have any. There were also two other slaves who were acquired: Um al-Khair and Mubarka. They had been dismissed by their masters.

Q: *So your brothers each had four or five slaves. Did they also have free wives?*[3]

A: I'm coming to that. What I was just telling you was how it was at the time of my birth: there were only slaves then. The free wives came afterwards.

Only my father had a free wife in addition to his slaves. He had married his cousin. It was with her that he had all my older brothers. When she died, my father married her sister, Lalla. Lalla was there when I was born. In the beginning, my father had no slaves. His mother always used to say to him: 'My son, as long as I am alive, I don't want to see any slaves in this household.' But when she died, he began to buy some. I said before that his first wife left him four sons; they are my older brothers, the ones I told you each had four or five slaves. His second wife bore him twelve children, all of whom died. The children of this second wife didn't live long. The first slave he brought was Marzuka, and after that it was a regular parade. And since then, the family has kept on growing. And we must remember my two uncles who live in the same household with us.

The three brothers had the same occupation – they were wholesale cattle-dealers, buying cattle, fattening them up, and then reselling them.

One of my uncles didn't have any children at all. The other, Abd al-Rahman, had two – two boys. It was he who made the household prosper, who expanded it, and all that. He bought the farm with my father.

Q: *He bought the farm?*

A: Yes. They bought a farm, my father and uncle. At that time, there were not yet any French, and people travelled by muleback. One day when my uncle was sleeping in a tent, after he acquired the farm, he was hit by a bullet. Those who had sold him the farm shot him.

And so my father found himself with a large household. He had a lot of children: twenty boys and eight girls, without counting those who had been cut down by death.

As we were growing up, there was always a feast going on at the house. It seemed as though we were constantly celebrating a marriage. The family was expanding. Every year two or three slaves got pregnant. The slaves helped each other with bringing up their children: I'll take care of your child and you take care of mine. And one would breast-feed the child of another. For example, from my earliest childhood I only slept with Dada Rabha. The slaves were more than sisters to each other.

Amusements and celebrations

Growing up was a happy time for me. We were always playing and laughing. Every Friday there was a celebration at our house, and each time people used to think we were celebrating something special. There would be a dancer, a *shaikha*, and the women seated all around.

Q: *Were there only women?*

A: Only women; and my father comfortably seated on a sofa, were there, in the great hall; the women in formal dress, and the *shaikha* performing. All the women wore gold jewellery, including ankle bracelets. My aunt Zaid al-Khair always wore dazzling robes and all her jewellery was gold. Even we children wore gold jewellery. I say this in order to tell you that they didn't wait until we were grown-up to dress us up.

Q: *Were you unruly when you were little? Whom did you play with? Were there fights among the children?*

A: We were always laughing and playing. My sister Rabi'a and I used to play at being a bride. There were also my nieces Hafida and Zubaida. We really used to stir up a storm, especially Zubaida, who was a real devil, very sly and very sharp into the bargain.

Q: *Didn't anyone teach you to read and write?*

23

A: They set up a Koranic school right inside the house, because there were so many of us with my younger brothers and sisters and my little nephews and nieces. The teacher came to our house. But if I start telling you all the foolishness we got involved in, it will take for ever.

Q: *Did your father hold you in his arms and play with you when you were little?*

A: Every evening he took his seat in his private reception room. And there he brought everybody together, the slaves, the daughters, everybody. We had tea with him.

Q: *And you talked with him? You laughed with him?*

A: No, you didn't laugh with him. There was no question of laughing with him or talking with him. You drank your tea. That was all. After that, everybody went back to their work.

Q: *Did he ever happen to spank you?*

A: We had some whippings!

Q: *Did he also whip the slaves?*

A: No, I never saw him flog any of them. Except Sa'ida and Fatima once.

Q: *Why were they flogged?*

A: Because they were quarrelling, but they made it up straight away. Another time, it was 'Ud al-Ward and Fath Azhar who were quarrelling. Fath Azhar was his favourite. Mama al-Anbar waited all evening long to be the first to speak to him about it. She told him: 'Look at what Fath Azhar did to my sister 'Ud al-Ward.' She didn't give him time to hear what Fath Azhar had to say. Actually, it was Mama 'Ud al-Ward who beat Fath Azhar.

Q: *Why did she beat her?*

A: I don't know. She must have insulted her daughter or something like that. I don't remember exactly. So, when Mama al-Anbar spoke to my father about it, he no longer wanted to listen to Fath Azhar. All the slaves loved each other like sisters, except for Fath Azhar. No one loved her because she was the favourite.

Q: *What did you girls do?*

A: We spent the whole day laughing and playing. And at night, while everybody else was sleeping, we often sat up like djinns; we stayed up very late – and how we laughed! My sisters-in-law, the youngest ones, stayed up with us, the daughters of the house. We became very chummy with them; we loved them a lot, and they loved us just as much. We were like sisters. I don't really know what life was like before we knew them.

Q: *Did you have tambourines for your nightly parties?*
A: No. We didn't know how to play them. We just sat and amused ourselves. But Mama Yasmin never left us alone for a minute. Even if the front door of the house was closed, and the terrace door too, she stayed right with us all the time, her prayer beads in her hand. What a lot of fun we had! When someone used to put something aside to eat, we would steal it and make a treat of it.

Q: *And who took care of the household tasks? Who did the cooking, baked the bread, cleaned the floors?*
A: The slaves took care of the housework. They did the cooking for everybody, because everybody in this world I have just described to you ate at the same table. But when the family got larger and there were 'free wives', that all changed. The free wives ate separately from us, and the slaves too. The free wives had their own dishes, their own furniture, and even their own slaves.

Q: *And why were they separate from the rest of you?*
A: Because there began to be quarrels. My father had to put the slaves in one house and the free wives in another. Luckily we had four buildings to house the whole family. At first, there were only three, but with the arrival of the free wives, my father took a fourth house. The men ate separately, the free wives separately, and even the slaves.

Q: *And you little girls, whom did you eat with?*
A: With Lalla, our stepmother, and our sisters-in-law, the free wives. We got along very well with them. As for our mothers, the slaves, they had two tables just to themselves separately.

Q: *Who did the housework then?*
A: The slaves. The free wives didn't do anything at all. The slaves did the cooking, cleaned the floors – they did everything. Each wife had her own slave. When one took a wife, one had to buy her a slave. She accepted the slave and brought her with her on the day of her wedding. It was the man who presented the slave to his new wife. If the slave got ill or died, well, the husband bought her another one.

Q: *And how did the slaves organise themselves for doing the housework?*
A: By taking turns at the various jobs. But not all of them did the cooking. Only my mother, my Aunt Lyaqut, and Mama Mabruka did that job. Each one did it for one month. And each one would have three other slaves to help her for ten days. They were the ones who kept the place clean, washed the great kettles, and lit the fires. But it was the slave in charge of the cooking who prepared the dishes and served at table. After the first

first ten days, she got three other slaves to help, and then three others, until the end of the month. Then she left and her place was taken by another.

Q: *That's for the cooking. But didn't they do other chores?*

A: The slaves who were not in charge of the cooking did the rest of the work. They served the men, prepared breakfast, etc. The wives who didn't have slaves had 'child maids' to do their housework.

Q: *And who did the floors?*

A: The wives cleaned the floors of their house with the help of their slaves. And those who didn't have slaves did it themselves.

Q: *And you, did you take part in domestic chores?*

A: When we 'came of age',[4] we were told: 'You have to learn to do housekeeping.' They began by teaching us cooking. The slaves cut up the meat and onions and we put in the spices: pepper in one dish, saffron in another, the former with chick peas and the latter with onions. Each girl spent one month in the kitchen with the slave who was in charge at that time. I was there with Mama Lyaqut. My sister Aisha was with my mother, who loved her a lot. It all went very smoothly.

Q: *And did you learn crafts?*

A: It was much later when they set us to learning crafts. The older girls, like us, learned at home. Later the younger ones went out to be taught by the *mu'allima* at her place.[5] As for us, it was our stepmother who taught us embroidery. She taught us by beating us. And for that reason I didn't learn a thing.

Q: *And you couldn't say anything about it?*

A: Nobody dared do anything. You couldn't speak up.

Q: *How were you distributed around the house?*

A: The wives lived on the ground floor. Each one had her own sitting room. The slaves lived upstairs, with two sharing a room. Each house had two floors.[6]

Q: *And the master of the house, your father, how did he organise his life with all these women?*

A: My father had his own room. One of the houses was kept for the men, because there were always guests. Sometimes they spent the whole night playing cards. The wife went to bed all alone. He would call for whichever of the slaves he wanted and invite her to his room. He would stay with her for a while, and then he would go to spend the rest of the night with the free wife.

Q: *Did he invite the slaves in turn?*

A: No. He invited the one he wanted. He would call for the one that he desired.

Q: *And were there slaves that he completely ignored?*

A: Yes, there were some.

Q: *Who lived in the men's house?*

A: The men's house was very large. My father had guests all the time. He used to invite the *sharifs*. He never ate alone. There were always two tables at dinner. The boys stayed with their mothers, but when they began to grow up, they also went to the men's house.

Q: *They didn't spend the night in the same house with their sisters?*

A: No. They slept by themselves. During the day, they could come into the women's house. They came and played, but at night they had to go to their own rooms. The men stayed up until one or two o'clock in the morning playing cards. When the guests left, my father locked up the boys until morning. In the morning they went to school. At the time when there wasn't any public school, they went to the Koranic school. It was much later that they went to public school.

Q: *When people fell ill, who took care of them?*

A: In my time, there was a doctor who came to the house. He was called Tamsamani. He was an old man, not like those who studied in France. If a woman was sick, he came to examine her and prescribe medicaments.

Q: *What kind of medicaments? Herbs?*

A: I don't remember any more.

Engagement and marriage

Q: *How did your older sister get married?*

A: Some people saw her and then came to ask for her hand.

Q: *But where could they have seen her? Did you get to go out?*

A: No, never.

Q: *Not even to the Turkish bath?*

A: Yes, to go to the Turkish bath, yes. We went there at night, once a month. At that period, we rented the Turkish bath. But when there were the sisters-in-law, we began to go to the public bath with everybody else. Then people could see us. They tried to find out if my father had daughters. And so it was that they came to ask for the hand of my sister Zainab. She was engaged for seven years.

Q: *Seven years?*

A: Yes, engaged for seven years!

Q: *Seven years with the marriage contract signed and everything?*

A: No. Frankly I don't know if the contract was signed or not. What I do remember is that they came to our house, there was an understanding, and they recited the *fatiha*. My sister was adorned with pearls for the occasion, but the marriage was not consummated. My family tended to celebrate engagements. It was during the marriage feast of my big sister that my turn came to get engaged.

Q: *How was that?*

A: A woman who used to make mattresses for us saw me in my father's house. Then she went to make some at the house of my future family-in-law, and it was she who told them that my father had marriageable daughters. Then they came to ask for my hand. My father refused to marry me off before my sister Aisha. They told him: 'Your word is enough for us while we await the marriage of your elder daughter.' And when my sister Aisha became engaged, they came back for me. I was married right away. I had given birth to Sidi Muhammad and then Sa'ida while my sister was still engaged, and she remained so for five years. Afterwards, it was the turn of my niece and a lot of the others among the young girls of my group.

Q: *Tell me, didn't you ever go out, to the house of another family, for a wedding, for example?*

A: No. We never went to anybody's house, except that of my elder sister. When we wanted to go to her house, my father asked her for the key to her terrace door. She locked it and gave him the key for the time that we were there. Only girls were invited to her house, and we stayed there for ten to twenty days. Her daughters, my nieces, were the same age as us. They also came to visit us. We had a wonderful time – not a care in the world.

Q: *Otherwise, you didn't go anywhere else?*

A: Yes, once a year at the time of the Prophet's birthday, our stepmother Lalla took us on a visit to Mulay Idris. We were young women then, and the wives of our brothers were already living with us. My father only trusted his wife to take us out.

Q: *What did you wear for going out?* Haiks ?

A: My big sisters put on their *haiks* for going out. I, being still young, put on a *djellaba*, one belonging to my brother Abd al-Rahman, and my sister Aisha wore my brother Muhammad's. Soon afterward, when we began to go to the farm, all the women wore *djellabas*. We also wore veils; the veils were very thick.

Q: *While you were engaged, did your fiancé bring you gifts?*

A: For me, it all happened at the same time – the engagement, the dowry, and all the rest. I received a string of pearls and a gold necklace. At the time of my sister Zainab's wedding, my fiancé gave me a present on the sly. The personal slave who came to the wedding also brought a gift to the bride, and my fiancé took the opportunity to send me a brooch. But I refused it. She gave it back to him, and he kept it until my wedding.

Q: *Tell me a little about your wedding.*

A: During the first seven days of the marriage feast, they showed me off all dressed up.

Q: *Nobody accompanied you to the house of your husband?*

A: Yes. Dada Masa'uda and the *gallasa*. Dada stayed with me for some time, until I got used to everything. On the seventh day I went out to greet the men.

Q: *What men?*

A: The brothers and cousins of my husband. They lived in the same house with him. It was traditional to do it. I could appear only before the men of the family. I had to greet them, and each time that I greeted one, he gave me a gift: bracelets, etc. The following day, I performed the fish ceremony. They bring you a fish and place it next to the fountain.[7] The bride has to take the fish and place it on her right foot. Then they take the fish away and the bride washes her hands in view of everybody. What a world it is in such a great house, with the invocations of the Prophet and the ululations! Then they bring soap on a dish and a bottle of perfume for the bride to wash her hands with. After that, she goes back to her room.

Q: *And afterwards?*

A: Afterwards, I became very friendly with my husband's sisters. They were already young women when I arrived. We became inseparable at once.

Q: *Did you do the housekeeping?*

A: No. I didn't do anything for eight years. I ate and slept, that is all. My family-in-law was very large; all the brothers and cousins of my husband, his father, all of them were married, and each had three, four, or five slaves, not to mention those who had two wives. We lived in three houses. It was the slaves who did the housekeeping. I lived like a queen. My father-in-law loved me very much. Every morning, when he got up, he asked after me.

Q: *Did you talk to him?*

A: No. He was a very stern man. He kept the whole house locked up: the main door, the terrace door. You couldn't see anything that happened outside. He stayed in the smallest of his houses. During the day he received his friends for card games, and in the evening he sometimes went to the house of one and sometimes to the house of another. The family never knew any contention or arguments. We ourselves passed the time laughing and playing cards – that's all. The men were very nervous of my father-in-law. No one dared to smoke in his presence, and no one could raise his voice. One day my husband was delayed at the warehouse; he was doing his accounts. When he came in, his father said to him, 'Get out!' 'But I just came from the warehouse', my husband answered. 'I was doing my accounts. You can ask so-and-so.' My father-in-law didn't budge: 'I don't want any explanations. You must be here on time, and that's all there is to it!'

Q: *Did your father-in-law have an occupation?*

A: He had a large fabric business. He was active on the side of the nationalists, and that was why he later went to prison, then into exile, and so forth.[8] Later he was no longer involved in politics, just in his business. He and his brother were in business together. And it was my husband who went to France to buy the merchandise. All his sons and nephews worked with him in the business.

Q: *How long did you continue living with your family-in-law?*

A: Eight years. I had my first three children there, and then we went to live elsewhere.

Q: *Why?*

A: There were problems between my husband and his family.

Q: *Did you go back to visit your family from time to time?*

A: I used to go to my father's farm. After my sister Zainab and I got married, my father bought a farm in partnership with a Frenchman. Later they broke up the partnership, and my father arranged it so that he got the farm. So we used to go there. The favourite slaves who stayed in Fez used to go walking in the garden of Bab Futuh. We used to go to the farm in the springtime. They put on a special reception for us, the young married women. My father-in-law and my husband went along with me. Every year it was a chance for me to get together with my other married sisters. All those who were married made up the party.

30

Mariam Talbiya[9]

From a sharifian family . . .

I am from a sharifian family, but a poor one. My parents did not have enough money to give me all that they would have liked to have given me, so they put me in the care of a very well-to-do family whom we had known a long time. I was then five years old. I stayed there seven years, until the death of my 'mistress', who had a daughter just about my age. She brought us up alike, without making any distinction between us. She sent us together to the Koranic teacher and then to the *mu'allima*; she really treated me like her daughter. When my mother died in childbirth, my mistress said to me: 'I am like a mother to you; I will keep you; you are my daughter now.'

When I was twelve years old, she in turn died. After her death, her husband tried to sleep with me. So I decided to leave. But where to? My father had remarried and didn't have any room for me at his house, so I went to my sister's. Things began to go sour when I felt that she suspected that her husband liked me. We never said anything to each other about it. I was friendly with a neighbour who had a little girl named Mama. I tried to spend as much time as possible at her house, making myself useful. I took care of the baby, I did the heavy laundry. This was the way I tried to escape my sister's husband and to save my relationship with the only person in the family that I loved. Now I am going to start crying. It is impossible for me to remember certain periods of my life without crying. [She is silent for a moment, as she gains control of her emotions.]

Q: *How do you explain the fact that all these men used to hang around you?*

A: At seventeen years old, I had long red hair to my knees. I was tall and well developed – in the bloom of youth. So they were drawn to me like a cat to the canary. I was poor and not from an important family. So I was fair game for them.

One day I asked a friend of the family, Lalla Fatima, to find me a place in another family where I could go and where I could make my services appreciated without being humiliated. And she brought me to the Binjallun family. [10] But before I left the city, I went to see my younger brother. I told him that I wanted my share of the family inheritance. He told me that he had never seen me at the house when he was growing up, and so I was not his sister. He had only one sister, he said, not two. when I insisted and began to shout at him, he threatened me with a knife. I was so frightened that I decided to give up my share, meagre as it was, and to disappear. My sister and my brother thus shared the little that there was, and I joined the Binjallun family 60 miles from Fez. At that time they lived on a farm.

. . . to a secret pregnancy

The man that I worked for, Muhammad, was very ill. His sisters came to get me to take care of him. I served him, mothered him, did his washing, cleaned up his vomit for a period of weeks – he was very ill. Then he recovered and became handsome, elegant, refined, distinguished. That place had an atmosphere so different from what I had been used to in my poverty in Fez! It was a farm in the grand style: I remember the fields, the beauty of nature, the evening parties, gatherings where there was wine, laughter, where people enjoyed themselves.

In time I too took to enjoying wine and pleasure. I was a virgin, and so he deflowered me. After a few months he became vulgar and violent with me. When I wanted to leave him, he threatened to set the police on my trail. He said that he could ask one of his friends to throw a bottle of wine into the street at my feet and to say that I was his mistress. Or, better still, if I left, he would tell the police that I had robbed him, and would set them after me. He belonged to one of the families of Fez that owed their power to the protection of France. The members of these families could steal and kill with impunity; the law didn't apply to them. [11] As for me, I was poor, without any family protection. He could arrange my disappearance, and nothing would happen. So each time I agreed to remain.

One day, when he was about to leave for France for an operation, I told him that I had missed my period for a month and that I must be pregnant. He told me to see about getting an abortion. Then he left for France. Since there were so many people at that farm, his brothers, their wives, their children, his father's slaves, his not yet married sisters, I decided that it would be better to go to a quieter place. So I asked his permission to go to his older paternal brother (they didn't have the same mother), Si Ahmad, in Fez. The people there were less numerous, and, above all, more kind.

How to get an abortion?

Once I got to Fez, I began to ask for prescriptions for abortion, and I tried them one after another. One of the first consisted of drinking the juice of six lemons with a tablespoonful of hot red pepper – which I did early in the morning. By six o'clock in the evening, I felt as though my intestines were falling to pieces. Once I had recovered, I tried another prescription with fresh tobacco leaves. I put them in a little piece of new wool, and then I inserted the whole thing into my vagina. A few hours later I was vomiting so much that I was dragging myself along on the ground – vomiting so hard that it would have torn trees out by their roots. Next I tried other tricks, always of the same type, and always they brought on vomiting and suffering, with no result. Then I went to see a *faqih* and asked him to perform a *thiqaf* for me. He refused, alleging that it was no longer possible at that stage of my pregnancy. But, instead, he could make me an amulet that would prevent people from seeing that I was pregnant: as long as I wore it, no one would notice that I was pregnant. He made it up for me, and I never took it off. As I was always working with my robes tucked up around my hips, and as it was a first pregnancy and my belly was rather flat, no one really noticed anything. The only thing that happened was that my ankles became swollen, and that was seen.

Meanwhile I kept my secret. But one day I confided in Lalla Malika, a friend of the family. She also was pregnant, but she had a husband. I asked her to help me get rid of the child and said that I would do whatever she wanted: I would give her all that I could lay my hands on. Not only did she not help me, but she went around proclaiming that I was pregnant. Now it was known everywhere, but no one ever spoke to me about it face to face – no one.

I was six months pregnant. It was spring, and my host, Hajj Ahmad, left for his farm with his family to enjoy the spring weather and to look after his property and animals. I thus had to return to that whole hostile world that I had left just a few months before.

My master's sister telephoned Si Ahmad and told him that I must not return to the farm, that I was pregnant, and that it was not the child of their brother. I was a whore, she told him, thrown into the street where I had acquired the bastard I was carrying; I was lying when I said that the child was her brother's. In fact, as she was unmarried, she was afraid for her reputation, afraid that people would say that in the Binjallun household there was a whore pregnant with a bastard. But the elder brother was a gentleman. He knew that I was a *sharifa*, and, I think, he knew his brother very well. In short, he held out against her pressure and told her: 'My brother entrusted this woman to me and I will look after her until he returns. If he had entrusted an ass or a bitch to me, I would have done as much; so with how much more reason do I do it for a human being.'

A month later my master returned from France. His sister met him at the airport and took the opportunity to fill his head with her venom to such an extent tht he would no longer speak a word to me. He completely set his mind against me.

Meanwhile, my legs were still swollen. Some people said that I had aborted the child, others that I was still pregnant. Whispering swirled around me, but no one had the honesty or the pity or courage to come and openly ask me if I was pregnant or not. The hostility of his sister grew worse, and she informed her older sister, who then came and got into the act. They stood guard and prevented me from being alone with their brother. They were like furies.

One day one of their father's slaves, a good and pious man, went to them and told them that it was inhuman to treat me like that, that even if I had committed a crime, I should be treated decently. They told him to go away. Then I decided to lock myself away until the child arrived. But where should I go? To whose house? I could certainly take the bus, but to go where? I compensated by working harder than ever; I spent my time washing other people's clothes, cleaning their houses, serving them. At night I was so exhausted that I fell asleep the moment my head touched the pillow.

The stillborn child

One day I felt sick very early in the morning. I felt ill all day long, but I threw myself into my work without thinking about it. In the evening I was racked by great waves of pain in the back. The house was full, children, adults, old people, my master's brothers and sisters, the slaves of his father, who had outlived him – a teeming world. I ran to Salma, a very sweet young slave whose room was at the back of the house. Her door was closed, she wanted to rest, and she told me to come back later. I pounded on her door, desperate. When she opened it, I said to her: 'Keep my secret, and may God protect you! I am a *sharifa*. My ancestors go back to the Prophet. Keep my secret.' She just stood there, silent. I shook her. 'Will you keep my secret?' 'Yes', she whispered, but remained motionless. 'What's the matter? Do you refuse?' 'No. I dreamed all this a moment ago. I came to lie down after work. I dreamed that you opened my door and said to me, "Keep my secret and my ancestors will come to your aid when you are in trouble." '

34

The pains grew stronger. The child appeared feet first. The first foot emerged. I was tearing my hair, clawing the walls, and then came the second foot. I didn't let out a cry despite my terror. Salma was immobilised in front of me. She was terror-stricken and couldn't help me; she just stared at me. I forced the child to emerge bit by bit. It was half out, almost all of it except the head. It was moving, and then it was still. The child was dead. The head emerged, and then the placenta. A fat white baby. Salma, who was still dumbfounded, finally bestirred herself. She began to wipe up the blood. Then I took the child, wrapped it in a towel, and carried it outside in my arms. I walked down to the river and threw it in. I had no choice.

I slept for a few hours beside Salma, until dawn. Then I started again scrubbing other people's floors, doing their laundry, and serving them.

That very evening I heard that my master had had a car accident. [12]

3

Rabi'a: escape from the harem into the middle of the twentieth century

Born in 1940 into the urban bourgeoisie of Safi, Rabi'a should have aspired to become a woman of the harem like her mother, like all the 'young ladies of good family' of colonial Morocco. It was the obligation of her class.

But the nationalist struggles of the fathers were going to overturn a realm to which their fantasies had given a privileged position and defined as immutable, ahistorical, and outside time and struggles: the realm of intimacy; the realm of privacy; the realm of mothers and daughters; the domestic realm.

Among the notables of colonial Morocco, those who were drawn to the nationalist vision did not at all incorporate into it the liberalisation of family relationships. For them, the nationalist struggle was a struggle for a political redistribution of the cards among the male elites. These notables sent their daughters to school – wearing veils. The schools were called 'schools for Muslim young ladies'. The nationalists worked to bring about 'the beloved Muslim Morocco in which are preserved all the traditions that I respect'. The 'I' here is that of the French Marshal Lyautey, the author of this phrase.

The nationalists dreamed of a new Morocco, industrialised, educated, democratised, where young ladies would continue to be veiled, to be secluded, to watch the course of history from behind the grillwork of arched windows.

Rabi'a, a young lady of good family, longed for something else: she dreamed of self-realisation, of education, of the right to self-expression and reflection. Rabi'a dreamed of living.

Decidedly, the nationalists who had hoped to shatter the dream of the colonialists, were totally lost and without an answer when faced with the dream of their young daughters.

Rabi'a[1]

Q: *What is your profession?*
A: I am a teacher. I teach in a *lycée*. I am employed by the Ministry of National Education. In my family there were fifteen brothers and sisters [laughter].
Q: *You were fifteen brothers and sisters from one mother?*
A: Fortunately, no.

A musical and polygynous father

Q: *So, tell me the whole story.*
A: My father had more than one wife. He loved women, like every self-respecting Moroccan man. He was also very successful in seducing them. He was a musician. He used to get married every month. He would quite regularly choose a new bride from a different section of town. In that way he married quite a lot of women. The first one gave him four children, I think. The second, just one, a girl. The third, three. My mother herself produced six, without counting of course those who died before, during, or after birth. If you count the dead ones, you reach forty-five. If there had not been natural selection, yes, there would have been forty-five. My mother came last. She was his favourite. He loved her very much because all his previous wives had been illiterate and of ordinary background. My mother was an only child; her father, who was rather well-to-do, had her taught at home by a *faqiha*. Mama was a very sensitive, very refined woman, and I believe it was that which my father sought in a woman, rather than sexual satisfaction. You know, the others must have given him everything in that domain. She gave him something else; she shared something else with him, and it was because of that that he preferred her.
Q: *Was she younger than he?*
A: Certainly much younger than he. But you know, I don't remember my father. He lived in Rabat while I lived in Safi with my mother.
Q: *Why didn't your parents live in the same city?*
A: My father was a performer. You know how the elite circles can monopolise a musician. We never saw him. The whole family lived in Safi.
Q: *Did you live all together with the uncles and aunts, or just with your mother and the children?*
A: In the beginning, everybody lived together, my mother's co-wives, their children, the uncles, etc. – a huge household. Just imagine! That

house has now become a school. That will give you an idea of how large it was. I was born at the moment when my mother had decided to make a break, to no longer live in the large household. She had decided to be independent and had set up a household with her children elsewhere. We were really cramped for space there, my mother and her six children – three boys and three girls. But there were great differences in age amongst us. My oldest brother, Jawad, was twenty-five years older than me. I was the last child, and I am thirty years old now. I should also tell you that between my oldest brother and me there had been fourteen births. My mother gave birth to sixteen children, of whom ten died, either in childbirth or after birth. I myself was present at the birth of three or four of them. My mother still talks about it, she loved them so much. You see, we are all very close to each other, because we lived cramped together around my mother. My father was for all practical purposes absent. I only saw him perhaps once or twice. He died when I was four or five years old. I know him only from photos, if you know what I mean.

The guardian

Q: *Who became your guardian after your father's death?*
A: My brother Jawad. He is still the head of the family. He gives orders to everybody, not only to us, his brothers and sisters in the immediate family, but to all the members of the exended family. He used to terrorise everybody and still continues to do so to this day. Even at my age and in my situation, I still feel a certain reserve toward him. I couldn't joke or be flippant in front of him. I have too many bad memories of his violence.
Q: *Did he strike you?*
A: Of course, while my mother never struck us. She was very gentle.
Q: *Did he strike you for just anything?*
A: No, not for just anything. He was a person who knew why he hit us. He chose the occasions. He used to strike my brother Hamid particularly. He would strike him repeatedly with studied violence because he was the intellectual of the family. He felt a special animosity toward Hamid. It must be said that Hamid was something of a devil. He really used to raise hell. And the more his brother struck him, the more disobedient Hamid was.

It was the early days of the cinema, and my oldest brother used to decorate his room with posters of famous actors and actresses of the period, Americans, I think. And young Hamid would come with a needle and poke holes in the eyes of the stars on the walls of Jawad's room. And on some of them he would paint bushy moustaches. Then obviously out would come the cane.

Q: *Was it he who supervised your studies?*

A: Yes, and very strictly.

Q: *The studies of the boys and of the girls, or just of the boys?*

A: I have to make a point here regarding the family and its evolution over time. Don't forget that my oldest sister Malika was twenty years older than me. She is fifty years old now. She got married very young. I was still very little when she was married. We don't share any memories of a common childhood.

When my memories begin, when I began to be aware of what was going on, she was no longer there. On the other hand, I have another sister, Sa'diya, with whom I shared a part of my childhood. I remember her very well. She had a very carefree attitude. They tried to make her learn something. They sent her to the *mu'allima* in the hope that she would assimilate some skill or other that would be useful to her in the future. To learn to make *al-hudub*, for instance. What do you think she got out of those lessons? Coloured stools! She spent her time swallowing the silk threads they gave her to work with, and as a result her stools became multicoloured. She was, and she still is, a riot! I must introduce you to her. So Sa'diya was never sent to school.

Q: *Who then was the first daughter to be sent to school rather than to the* mu'allima?

A: Just a minute. I'm going to explain all that. My sister Malika and the younger one, Sa'diya, were both sent to the *mu'allima*. They were supposed to become experts in cooking, embroidery, lacemaking, etc. But they both were practically illiterate at the end of their sojourn with the *mu'allima*. My oldest sister especially resented that as a terrible deficiency, and later she set herself to acquire the rudiments of reading and writing.

Do you know what she did? After her marriage she set up housekeeping in Meknes, where her husband lived in a new town. She thus had French people for neighbours. This was still during the colonial period. Her children went to primary school. She began to make friends, to visit her neighbours. She exchanged ideas with the Europeans. And do you know what she did? She took up studying again, all by herself, at the same time as her children. She did the primary school work with them, but obviously she didn't go out to do it. She used the exercises that they did at home.

They taught her while they were learning. She was so consumed by the desire to educate herself that she enrolled in the correspondence courses of the Ecole Universelle of Paris. As a result she now reads, writes, and manages very well by herself.

Q: *And her husband, did he encourage her?*

A: To tell the truth, no. You could say that he encouraged her by having teachers come to the house for the children. She took advantage of that to educate herself. She put her mind to it, and in the end she succeeded.

Q: *So, then, who was the first daughter among you to go to school?*

A: It was the third daughter who was the first to be sent to school and not to the *mu'allima*. And the third daughter was me. It was the result of a very special conjunction of circumstances. My guardian, Jawad, though, inclined toward sending me to school. A few rare families in the city were beginning to send their daughters to school. Luckily for me, I was one of that minority. There was another event that was decisive in the story of my schooling. Between my sister Sa'diya, now forty-two years old, and me, at thirty, there is a boy, Hamid, seven years older than me. He was ahead of me in school and was entitled to have a teacher at home, assigned to him by Jawad, to make sure that he had learned what had been taught in class. So Hamid and his young teacher used to pay a little attention to me. While Hamid did his homework, the teacher had me do some reading and a little arithmetic. In addition to school, I also had this help at home. It was a very favourable atmosphere for me. I loved Hamid very much, and he returned my love. We shared many things. That was my good luck.

Q: *How did Jawad encourage you with your studies? Was he easy with you or strict?*

A: I remember receiving quite a few slaps because of my poor marks. And just imagine how all this was organised – each person had his or her own little room and work table, and all this in a huge traditional house. But the separate rooms were solely for working in, because we preferred to sleep all together in the same room. We had a huge house with many rooms, but our favourite way to sleep was together in one room. It was more practical and more fun.

Q: *Did your mother also sleep in the same room with you?*

A: Of course. Everybody did, with the exception of my big brother, who kept to himself.

Q: *Was he married?*

A: No. He never got married. He lived with various European women, but he avoided marriage. Between you and me, he was not entirely wrong.

Q: *Who did live with you in the house then?*

A: My mother, my sister Sa'diya, my brother Hamid, and myself. My big brother left us to go and live by himself. My youngest brother left to go to Meknes to learn a trade, and my sister Malika was married very young, as I told you.

Servants

Q: *And 'maids'?[2] Did you have any?*

A: Naturally!

Q: *Were you brought up by them or by your mother?*

A: By both. Moreover, I regard the 'maid' who brought me up as a mother. I still see her. She comes all the time to my house. We have stayed in contact. You see, she came to our house when she was very young. Her sister used to send her out to beg. That was how she came to our door. My mother was pregnant with me. She asked the older sister to leave her with us. This girl was very young when I was born, and I regarded her more as a sister than a 'maid'. There wasn't a great difference in age between us. I remember very well how she carried me on her back when I had trachoma (I was very susceptible to that malady), with my feet dragging on the floor. Can't you just see it? To soothe me, she would put me on her back and walk round and round the garden. I have another very vivid memory of her. I used to want her beside me when I was on the potty. Obviously she found that a bother. So, in order to frighten me and make me give up this whim, she put some cockroaches under my feet. In any event, she was very young when she came to us; she must have been only eight or ten years old.

The atmosphere at home

Q: *Were you required to do any household chores when you got home from school?*

A: Don't forget that I was the youngest child. I was very spoiled, and they didn't ask me to do anything. But Sa'diya gave me a hard time. She wanted to force me to do housework as she did. She was completely caught up in the traditional household system; she took her turn in the rotation of those in charge of the housework, right along with the 'maids'.[3] There was a great age difference between us.

Q: *And playing? Did your big brother sometimes play with you?*

A: Are you kidding? The minute he appeared, all play ceased. His

41

arrival was announced to us the minute his shadow was seen at the foot of the *darb*. Then we all scattered. The whole family dispersed – my mother, my brothers and sisters, all left in one direction or another. Some went up to the roof, others locked themselves in their rooms, and still others went to get to work in their offices. Jawad was the terror of the family. You see, since my father was dead, he felt obliged to outdo him in strictness. He took his role as supervisor of our upbringing too seriously, to such a degree that when he summoned us, we knew it meant we were to be beaten.

Q: *How did he beat you? With his hand or a cane?*

A: With his hand, good hard spankings and lots of slappings.

Q: *Didn't your mother intervene? Didn't he listen to her a little?*

A: Yes, yes, but all the same . . . My mother was a woman with a lot of common sense. All the members of the family came to her for advice. She was very wise, very unpretentious, and in particular very devout. Every time there was a birth in the extended family, it was she who was asked to choose a name and to preside at the *sab'a*. She was very much loved, but she was still not able to stop my brother. Sometimes he was like a fury, and I have to say that some days we must have got on his nerves. He also worked very hard for us.

Life as a young lady

Q: *When you became a young lady, were you able to go out of the house?*

A: There was no question of that. Moreover, it was because of that that I left home, at the beginning of the first form at the *lycée*, to go and stay with Malika, my married sister in Meknes. I stayed at her house for three or four years; I don't remember exactly now. I did it in order to get away from the pressure my brother was putting on me.

Q: *How old were you when you left home?*

A: Twelve or thirteen. I felt much freer at my sister's house. She lived in the new town, the European part of town. I was able to come and go like a European.

Q: *Did you wear the* djellaba *before that?*

A: Of course I wore the *djellaba*. My brother was intractable on that point. One day – I still remember it – my mother had bought me a piece of pretty navy blue cloth; she wanted to make a *djellaba* for me with it. He made a big scene about it: 'What is this? Your daughter has beautiful blue eyes and very white skin, and you are going to make her a navy blue *djellaba* to make all that stand out even more? You are going to turn her into a prostitute.' He was terrible. He always remained very narrow-minded; he never could loosen up. He did change a lot, but never on that question.

Q: *You stayed three or four years at Meknes?*

A: I left after a quarrel. It was right after independence in 1956. I was at the *lycée* then. We were going to have a little party for our teachers. We wanted to make them understand that independence was one thing and the *lycée* another, that independence was not going to bring about any big change in the running of the *lycée*. So we decided to organise a little party. Each of us bought an admission ticket, and we decided to come dressed in traditional costume. But when I told my sister about the projected party, she dug her heels in and obstinately refused to give me permission.

Q: *Why?*

A: She told me that that kind of a party ended up in an orgy. 'Write to your brother in Safi and ask him for permission to take part in something like that', she told me. I tried to explain to her that there was no question of any orgy, that it was a party organised by my school friends, that everybody could go, that she herself could attend if she wanted to, that all I had to do was buy her a ticket. I told her that it was impossible to write to Safi and get a reply in time. Finally I told her that I absolutely had to go with my schoolmates. Then she slapped me. It became a question of pride for me. I told her that I was going to return home, to leave Meknes, that I couldn't stay with her any longer, that I was a serious-minded, diligent girl and I didn't see anything ill-bred or suspicious in my request.

Q: *Did she also order you around?*

A: Of course. She kept an eye on my schedule. Five past noon, was five past noon. If at five past, I was not in the process of parking my bicycle in the garage, there was a major uproar. I used to find them waiting for me in front of the door, while in other towns, Fez for example, freedom for young girls had made great advances. After independence they had all acquired the right to greater freedom to come and go.

Q: *Didn't you have any little puppy love affair when you were at the* lycée?

A: No, nothing.

Q: *Not even a tiny little infatuation? Didn't anyone write you notes? Not even notes?*

A: Yes, just after my return to Safi. Moreover, that note caused a big scandal. I heard about it for two years. They dinned it into my ears. When I left my sister and returned to Safi, I rejoined the group of my old friends whom I had been with in the first form: Latifa, Aisha, etc. Among them was an Algerian who liked me a lot. He was older than I; he was in the final year, and I had just entered the class studying for the senior high school entrance exam. He was very good at maths, and I was a dud; so he helped me a little. That was in 1956, the time of the struggle in Algeria. The Algerian students were leaving the *lycée* to return home. He had to forgo taking the June exams. He was still in Rabat when he read in the newspaper my name among those who had passed the high school entrance exam. So he sent me a little postcard; you know, the folding kind that you used to buy at the post office in those days. It was just my luck that the postman turned up with the postcard at a time when my brother was at home. So, what a scandal! I was slapped. I was sixteen years old, but none the less my brother made a huge fuss about it.

Q: *What did the note say?*

A: 'I read in the newspaper' – something like that – 'that you have passed. That didn't surprise me, as you deserve to.' A nice gesture. I heard about that postcard for two years. When I was seventeen, they married me off.

Q: *At what age did you begin to think about marriage?*

A: I didn't have time to think about it. Marriage was imposed on me with my first husband. I didn't think about it; they thought about it for me.

Q: *What did you dream about when you were a young girl? What happiness did you dream of?*

A: I wanted very much to get an education. I hoped to be able to become educated in order to liberate myself, to get out from under the thumb of the family. In a way, marriage was for me a sort of liberation. I have told you that I couldn't leave the house, or go to the movies, or receive letters. Frankly, it was very depressing, and so when they spoke to me about marrying my cousin, to me that meant France, the start of another life, the hope of achieving what I wanted. Unfortunately, my stay in France didn't last long enough.

Q: *What idea did you have when you were a teenager of the kind of man who would be able to make you happy?*

A: I imagined him as he was described in the books that I read, the fairy tales, the stories by Countess Segur. But, as I said, the family didn't give me a chance to dream about the ideal man; they imposed one on me in the form of a fiancé. I was very sentimental, I have to admit, very romantic.

I used to memorise poems. I was very influenced by my brother, who used to read a lot. We were very close. He also was very romantic. He was only five years older than me. He lent me novels and books of poems. That was the period of my life when I read more than at any other, between fifteen and eighteen, and it was thanks to him. I learned Musset's *Les Nuits* when I was fourteen years old. It is only now that I realise the importance, the meaning, for me of all that. The rhymes, the symbols coloured my understanding of things, and as a result I remain a romantic. My brother influenced me a lot. It was he who gave me the taste for reading, who talked to me about Europe; he opened many doors for me. We were very close. But that's all over. During my adolescence, he represented the ideal man, the model. He was the Messiah, the perfection one should strive for.

Engagement

Q: *How did your engagement come about?*

A: It was my cousin, the son of my aunt. I had never seen him. We lived in the same neighbourhood, but he was twelve years older than me. But imagine: before marrying him, I was first engaged to his brother. It was during the period when I was living in Meknes. I came to Safi to spend the summer visiting Mama. He saw me and told my family that he wanted to marry me. He brought a lot of pressure to bear. And I was promised in marriage without being present, without being consulted; I had already returned to Meknes.

Q: *They didn't ask your opinion? Were they afraid you would refuse?*

A: No way. I was so terrified by my brother that I couldn't say a word.

Q: *So, then, what happened once the marraige contract had been drawn up? Did your fiancé come to see you?*

A: He used to come to take me out, but I regularly refused. He used to write to me, but I didn't answer. He gave me presents, but I didn't accept them. He was kind, I liked him all right, he was nice – but that was all.

Q: *Did you tell him that you didn't love him?*

A: No, I didn't say anything. I just stayed away from him, I kept my distance.

Q: *Did your brother know that you didn't love him?*

A: He knew it very well.

Q: *Then why did he contract an engagement for you?*

A: Because it was traditional. I had to be married off. My fiancé tried to question me before the marriage. One time he asked if I knew how to cook and manage a house, and he followed me from one room to another asking me that. I told him that I didn't know how to do anything. I really wanted to get rid of him. I was young, very young; I had lots of friends. It was a time of great enthusiasm, the best years, 1950–54, the moment when everybody was seeking something, wanting to achieve something. And at such a moment someone comes to ask you if you know how to cook and make beds! You want to send him on his way rather than marry him. At that time, the attitudes had already changed; a twenty- or thirty-year-old man from Fez would not have come to ask you such a thing. That would have been the last thing on his mind. When my fiancé saw that I didn't respond to his advances, that I kept my distance, he thought that there was somebody else, that I was in love with someone other than him. Of course there was no such person. He had agreed from the start that the marriage would not take place until after I had graduated from high school. He would have to wait until I had finished. So do you know what he did in the meantime? He fixed himself up with a mistress, whom he installed in a house. In his capacity as an *amin* he couldn't chase girls; he had to have a regular one, he said. His father had just died, and he had succeeded to his post as *amin* of the citrus workers – an important job. The 'regular' woman he chose was a notorious prostitute. He supported her officially and lived with her openly while waiting for me to change my mind about him.

When I heard about this, it had just the opposite effect to what he was counting on. I had found a justification for my refusal. I didn't want to hear another word about him, but I couldn't speak about it to my big brother, my guardian. He knew about the official mistress and that didn't seem to pose any problem for him. I had to wait for the return of my younger brother, Hamid, who had gone to Paris to complete his advanced studies. When he got back, I told him that I had always been against this marriage and he knew it. I had decided to end my life in one way or another if I didn't succeed in getting rid of this fiancé whom I had been saddled with. As Hamid was quite friendly with him, he spent the whole summer trying to convince him to give me up, telling him that it was a bad choice, that he would not be happy with me, that he would do better to make his life with another woman. Using a lot of guile and patience, Hamid succeeded in persuading him. I recovered my freedom, and the marriage contract was annulled. He got married immediately afterwards, but not to the mistress he had been supporting. He married a woman whom he had neither seen nor met, a woman chosen for him by his mother and sister.

Q: *Was he quite educated?*

A: Yes. He had reached approximately the fifth year of secondary school. Just imagine! It was the brother of this gentleman that I married.

Marriage

Q: *How did that happen?*

A: Like a bolt from the blue! He was older than his brother, and I couldn't imagine him as a husband. We had diametrically opposite characters. With his strongly developed sense of family responsibility, he used to come to see us, to give advice to my mother on the subject of my education.

I thought he was in love with another cousin of ours. I even thought they were going to be married. Then one day I received a letter, and so did my mother, and my brother as well. He bombarded everybody with letters asking for me in marriage, and he wanted it to take place as soon as possible. We were always quarrelling, he and I. But as I had just refused my first suitor, in the end with the support of my family, it was impossible for me to refuse again. He would have said that I was acting wilfully and consequently the family shouldn't indulge my whims. So I accepted, I let it happen, and I joined him in France.

Q: *He came to get you?*

A: No, not at all. The marriage ceremony took place without him. He had a job in France as an official of the Moroccan government. So he couldn't leave. He sent me two air tickets: one for me and the other for my sister. I left with my sister one month after the marriage contract was signed. We landed one day in France at four o'clock in the morning, and I found myself face to face with my husband. I was eighteen years old.

Q: *How did he behave with you during the first days?*

A: I just felt empty. He was someone I hardly knew. I used to know him in a different context, with different feelings. And now here I was confronted with something else entirely. My sister went back three weeks later.

Q: *Did she accompany you in order to bring back the panties?* [4]

A: No, it wasn't like that! She would not have been able to bring proof of my deflowering because I was so frightened that I wanted it to be done by a doctor. In the end, it was done without a doctor, but at what a price! Just try to imagine the situation: I was embarking on an adventure, I was going abroad for the first time. I was going to join the man that I was soon to start living with as my husband, while for some years previously I had been linked to him by very different feelings. What I felt was not fear but rather a sense of emptiness. My sister was there – that is true – but since our quarrel about the school party, there was still a coldness between us. I no longer confided in her. I couldn't tell her all that was in my mind, except that I didn't love this man at all and that I was very pessimistic about the future. Her response was that one was always fearful in this kind of a situation, but that afterwards one's feelings would change, one would get used to it. You know the sort of thing.

Q: *Did you tell your husband what you thought about him?*

A: I didn't tell him anything, but he was aware of it. He attributed it to 'childishness'. 'You are still a child', he said to me – to me, who had just landed in a strange country. He burbled words that had no meaning for me. He told me that he loved me, that he idolised me, that I was his reason for living – all that stuff at a time when I had just landed, when I was still feeling airsick from my first flight. Most of all I was feeling full of fear at that moment, full of insecurity – I don't know how to describe it better.

Q: *How long did you stay in France?*

A: Around a year. You know, at the beginning, when I joined him in September, he was working on two degrees at the same time. He used to go to study at the Catholic Students Centre. He stayed there very late every night, and I was in a state of panic at being left alone. I was very young; I didn't know Paris, where we were living. I couldn't go for a walk or organise any kind of life for myself. You know, for all practical purposes, I lived in a state of seclusion all the time. I had heard so many stories about the white slave traffic.

Q: *Didn't you have any friends?*

A: No. At that time I didn't know anyone. He knew a few families, because he had spent seven years in Bordeaux before I arrived. But they were families with eight- or nine-year-old children. There was a great gap between them and me. I could only be friends with their children. When we went to visit them, I enjoyed myself more with the children. I was more at ease with them than with their parents.

Q: *And your education? Was that all finished?*

A: No, no. Beginning in October, I enrolled and took courses regularly during that whole year. I stopped just before our return to Morocco. I filled up my time with those courses as it was a very busy, full programme. They were commercial courses, while it was literature that attracted me! Do you begin to get the picture? From one day to the next, I had to change my life, change country, surroundings, studies.

Q: *Why didn't you continue the same course of study that had been inter-rupted in Morocco? Why did you choose to do commercial studies?*

A: I didn't want to. It was my husband who forced me to do it. At that time there was a shortage of good stenographers in the ministry in which he worked. He wanted to make a career in that ministry abroad, a kind of diplomatic career. So, he told me, commercial studies would be very useful to me. What's really hilarious is that, just after that year, he was recalled to the home office and all his projects came to nothing.

Q: *So then, you came back to Morocco?*

A: Yes. We returned to Morocco, and then the social whirl began. You see, in France official life is very limited: one business lunch a month and the national day celebration once a year. The social whirl began in Morocco, where people lead a very hectic social life. There were endless receptions. In France his friends were mostly students, lots of priests, and Catholic families – you know the sort. And you know the customs of that milieu. You are invited, you 'return' the invitation, you get them to try our dishes, etc. In Morocco, it was quite different: I had to accom-pany him and then invite back that whole crowd. That lasted two or three years. Then he moved to another ministry, and the situation deteriorated further. He started drinking, which he had never done before, and visit-ing the *shaikhas*. [5] Then things went from bad to worse. As he had an important job in the administration, people came to ask him favours. Many of them were pushing their own interests. Some were real riff-raff. They used to intrude on us at any time of the day or night, at any time at all. I became those people's *bête noire* because I tried to put an end to it, to prevent my husband from drinking, and to stop the serving of alcohol in my house. The parties at our house gave me an endless amount of work; you know the mess that's created when you invite a whole lot of people. And then, in the middle of all this, I had my little daughter Kenza.

The life of a young couple

I was busy with her for a year, and then I entered the normal school in order to be able to teach later on. At that time, the normal school offered a one-year course with a final exam at the end of the course. When I finished the normal school programme, I began teaching. My husband didn't want me to work. He wanted me to continue my education. At that time, he had begun his internship as a doctor, and, as you know, interns don't earn much; he had a very small salary. So I decided to go to work. As we had bought a house, there were payments to be made. It was absolutely necessary that we both work to cover the household expenses. But he preferred that I continue my education. I enrolled at the Faculty of Law to take the competency courses and get a degree. I did one year and then I gave it up. I wasn't able to do both things at the same time. The homework took a tremendous amount of time, and the classes were terribly crowded those first years of independence in 1958-9.

Q: *When your husband finished his internship, did you continue to work?*
A: Yes.
Q: *Why?*
A: Because I am a very proud woman. I never asked my husband to buy me anything at all. I wanted my work to allow me to buy what I needed, to not depend on my husband. I preferred to keep a certain independence. Sometimes my husband would complain: 'You have assumed too much independence. I know where it comes from. It's from your work, from your car. I'll have to take them both away from you.' But I know how to handle him. I told him that I would hand in my resignation the next day if he was ready to take over supplying my needs. Sometimes I went as far as writing out my resignation and asking him to hand it in himself. Deep down, he wasn't very keen on my resigning. It was a situation that suited him.

Q: *What did you do with your salary?*
A: Well, there, I have to talk in terms of all the household expenditures. You see, we didn't have a definite budget. I didn't know how much my husband earned, nor how much he spent. He spent money in a haphazard way. He never planned anything. We had a very extravagant life style because of the parties we gave. We entertained a lot. I am aware of it now that I am divorced and must live on a small salary. But I didn't realise it before. I did the shopping all at once; I bought supplies by the month. My husband was totally uninterested in household matters. He came to like nice things, to buy silverware, for example, a kitchen range, or gadgets. But as for the little details, the curtains, the trinkets, the little tables, etc. – he never gave them a thought. He would have made an effort if I had not taken it over myself. I used my salary to buy the small pieces of furniture, to buy my clothes and the children's clothes. Sometimes my husband used to say: 'I never know what she does with her money. I don't know if

she's got it salted away in a bank.' He knew perfectly well what I used it for. Our furniture didn't fall out of the sky. He had of course bought some of it, but he didn't have the least notion about prices and didn't at all appreciate how much money I spent. I must say, though, that very rarely did I have to buy food.

Q: *Didn't you ever think about quitting working?*
A: No. I am too active. I am not content just to do housework. I think that someone else can do that, and that it would be a pity for me to devote myself just to that. Besides, it would bore me because I don't like those kinds of chores. I also think that my own work gives me a certain satisfaction: I use my time to do something productive, to teach children. When I come home from work, I have enough time to do my small household chores, the mending, the decorating, and then I have good help. I have a maid who takes care of the cooking and all the rest.

Q: *Do you like your own work?*
A: I must say, I'm not crazy about it any more. I would have liked to be a university teacher, but I would have needed to have graduated from there myself, and unfortunately that was not possible. The evening courses are too demanding. It is an impossible schedule to meet. And then Ramadan, which comes right in the middle of the year, throws the whole programme into disarray. [6] It is impossible to keep up day by day or to make up a whole lost month.

Contraception, pregnancies, childbirth

Q: *Tell me about your pregnancies. Were they unintentional or planned?*
A: The first child arrived just like that. We didn't expect it. We were idiots, the two of us. He was aware of my ignorance in this matter and did nothing about it. Besides, he was in the middle of preparing for his exams. He had a lot of work, and I was enrolled in a special course of commercial studies. We were both occupied with our own work and didn't want any children – that goes without saying. Three months later we found out how foolish we had been. We went from doctor to doctor to try to 'get rid of it'. I had injections, I jumped from high places, I ran up and down stairs, I threw myself on the bed – silliness like that. I knew that in the old days women took great care of themselves for fear that they might abort. So I told myself that doing the opposite would make me lose the fetus. But it was well implanted. When Kenza arrived, she was so

beautiful that we didn't regret that she had arrived in the world. I nursed her for ten months. I had milk to spare. She was a perfect baby.

Q: *At what age did she start speaking? What language did she speak?*

A: She began to jabber away at nine months. I spoke to her in French, and her *dada* spoke to her in Arabic.

Q: *And when was your second child born?*

A: Six years later.

Q: *How did that happen? Did you use contraception or was it by chance?*

A: To tell the truth, I didn't do anything special, but I was being treated for some organic trouble, an inflammation of the cervix. The electrical treatment that I was given hardened the cervix to such an extent that it became impermeable. Naturally I did take some precautions; I used the Ogino method. But when I stopped using that method, when I wanted to have a second child, I realised that the method had in fact been needless. I was only able to get pregnant after I had had treatment to dilate my cervix. We wanted a second child because Kenza began to pick up some bad habits. She was too spoiled; she became too self-centred. And she has remained very much a loner.

The 'dada'

Q: *So Kenza had a* dada*?*

A: Yes. She was a woman who had no children and wanted above all to take care of Kenza. But I used to read books on child rearing and hygiene, and in the beginning I was intent on following them to the letter. I didn't want anyone but me to touch her. When I went out in the evening, I gave orders to let her cry, not to touch her, etc.

Q: *Did she sleep with you?*

A: My husband couldn't stand the noise. He was a very light sleeper. So the baby slept in another room. When she was two years old, she began to sleep with her *dada*. They slept in separate beds, but then they began to sleep together in the same bed. But this was disastrous because the child began to get used to Fatna's warmth and tenderness. She didn't get over it until the age of puberty. She couldn't get to sleep without her *dada*, so that when *dada* left for her village to visit her family, there was a big scene. The child couldn't sleep, she cried the whole night, and Fatna would have to return as fast as possible. I don't have to tell you that Fatna began to blackmail me with this. Every time she wanted a rise in pay, she would leave, preferably at night. The baby would spend the night crying. From her *dada* she had developed needs that I couldn't satisfy for they had grown into certain habits together. For instance, the child would only go to sleep if she had her hand held by Fatna, to the extent that when we were entertaining, Kenza would wait until Fatna had finished working before being able to go to sleep. It became a very worrying situation.

Q: *How did it begin?*

A: It began the day that I went back to work. I stayed at home for a year after the birth of my first daughter. After that, I went to the normal school. It was at that moment that Fatna took on such importance in the child's life. I was not there, and it was she who took care of her. She followed my directions in matters of food and hygiene, but she was very possessive and very prone to take over. As she had never had a child of her own, she totally took over mine – she did the same thing with Aziza, my second daughter. She witnessed the births of the three children. She had a diabolic gift for attaching them to her. The same situation was re-enacted with Aziza, who was born in 1963, six years after Kenza. I had the impression that I was frightening Kenza when I took care of her; Fatna had her own way of giving her the bottle, of bathing her. She had completely transformed her. I felt distanced from my children; I felt there was this woman between them and me. How many times I wanted to get rid of her! But because of them, I let things be. I made concessions and I kept her on. She began to repeat the same tactics with Aziza. She brought
her into her bed at night, secretly. This meant that some of the time she was sleeping with the two girls together.

Death of a child and break-up of the couple

Aziza only lived two years. She was drowned. We were entertaining; we thought she was asleep. Her father woke her up. She was playing around us, and then she disappeared. We found her drowned in the pool in the central courtyard of the house. I don't want to think about it any more because it was so horrible. At nineteen months old she already had a lot of character. It happened when she was struggling to get out of the hands of the little maid who was supervising her, and she fell headfirst into the pool. She was very lively, and already spoke Arabic and French. She behaved like a little adult. And from this time things began to go downhill between my husband and me. After the death of Aziza, my husband, who had started to drink a little, found a real reason to drown himself in alcohol.

Q: *Did he drink alone?*

A: No, unfortunately. He drank with others. But when I voiced objections to their drinking in my house, he began to go to bars, to drink secretly, to bend the elbow here and there.

Q: *What time would he come home?*

A: Late, but he did at least come home. His conscience bothered him. And then he wanted to have another child, to take Aziza's place in some way or other. As far as I was concerned, I thought it would be better to avoid having another child who would be a burden to me in the conditions in which I was living. Afterwards, he insisted so much that I decided that a child might be the saving of him, might perhaps be his last hope. And so I agreed. This is how the third child arrived: it was really an act of Christian charity.

You see, he was not really a man who wanted to have a lot of children; he wanted to have this one because he felt a void, especially because the dead child had borne a strong resemblance to him. And when the new baby was ill at birth, that just about finished my husband off, because he had invested such hopes in it, and on top of that, it was a boy!

Born prematurely, the baby was weak and never gained strength. He didn't cry at birth, and I thought he was dead. The doctor who attended me was an idiot; he didn't even have the skill of a good *qabla*. He wasn't even capable of giving the baby oxygen or massaging it. He left it to come around by itself. The baby soon developed oedema and they thought there was a kidney blockage. He was a month premature and normally would have been put in an incubator. I took him to a Parisian clinic, where a Frenchwoman cared for premature babies. She noticed that the baby was still in the fetal position, his legs and arms drawn up. Finally, he was put into an incubator in that clinic in Paris and remained there for three weeks. The diagnosis was that the baby was not only premature but also jaundiced. The doctors, with whom I was able to speak frankly, told me that there was a link between the baby's condition and the father's alcoholism. So that was really the final blow!

Q: *Did you talk about it with your husband?*

A: I spoke to him in a moment of anger, when I was really pushed too far and when he came to pester me at night. I said to him: 'Isn't it bad enough to have one sick child? Do you want to make some more?' He realised that I was holding him responsible for the child's condition. Naturally he tried to throw the responsibility on to me. My sister had a sick child, but that didn't have anything to do with what was wrong with our child. Hers had been born in perfect health, but its little sister while pushing it around in its pram, had collided with a wall. The baby had fallen out, and the shock had brought on a trauma, a brain lesion. It didn't move, it was critically affected, and remains in a vegetable-like state, if you know what I mean. So my husband never stops repeating: 'It runs in your family; your sister has a sick child.' He doesn't know the facts of the story. He hid behind that accusation, which he constantly reiterated. He did it in bad faith; he lied so well tht he ended up believing his own lie. In order to free himself from his nightmare, he tried to absolve himself. Everybody knows that I enjoy perfect health; we are all very strong. My father was a healthy man; my mother was never ill. She had many children and is in the pink of health at seventy. She lives in a huge house in Safi. You know, I let him think what he wanted to. I did everything I could to help him get out of the mess he was in. I dragged along with him like that for some years.

I knew that he was not a man who would agree to a divorce and that I was condemned to stay in this state for the rest of my life. I adopted a resigned attitude. I tried to organise my life around my work and my children in such a way that I erased him from my life. When I went off to work in the morning, he was still asleep. Sometimes it happened that I came back at noon and found him still in bed or getting ready to go out. Then I would eat with my daughter and take her to school. At three or four o'clock he would come for lunch with a crowd of people. You see, we scarcely crossed each other's path. We no longer had any family life. There were always too many people at the house.

Q: *He would bring people without warning you in advance?*

A: Of course. There were always guests at meals.

Q: *Who did the cooking?*

A: When we were first married, I did it. But when I got pregnant, what with the shopping and the housework, I didn't do it any longer.

Q: *But didn't he realise what he was imposing on you?*

A: No, he never caught on. He often accused me of not wanting to do something because I was afraid of getting varicose veins! He used to keep saying that, because I told him to stop bringing people to the house; I told I was pregnant, I had no help, I was afraid of getting varicose veins. Well, luckily, after that, we got a maid who took care of everything. She was a jewel. She was a very good cook. That was lucky, too, because I was beginning to completely lose interest in cooking.

Q: *Were the people that he invited just men or couples?*

A: In the beginning a lot of couples came to the house, but when things started going downhill I refused to go out with him, and he went out alone, because he always ended up coming home completely drunk. I couldn't stand it. My self-esteem was damaged. I absolutely didn't want to live through such moments. I didn't want to see him get drunk, nor have him involve me in such a spectacle.

Q: *Didn't he wake you up when he came home alone at night?*

A: Of course he woke me up. So then I moved into my own room.

Q: *What did he do about it?*

A: He absolutely had to see me. He put on a big show of remorse and guilt and denials. He knew perfectly well that he was treating me badly, and when he was about to come home, he would often say: 'I don't want to go home. I don't deserve that wife. She is a saint. I don't want to go home.'

Q: *Who would he say that to?*

A: To his friends. It was very difficult for me. When the baby was born and he realised that the boy was going to be ill for his whole life, that did it – that had the effect of completely cutting him off from everybody.

Q: *Didn't you ever think about a divorce?*

A: I thought that it was impossible. He had lots of lawyer friends. I told myself that I would never win a divorce case. So I dragged along.

Q: *Didn't you ever have any moments of peace when he would come home early?*

A: No, he began acting very unnaturally. When he made an effort not to drink, he became unbearable, because he understood that I saw what was happening to him. He was ashamed. He couldn't be relaxed. He was just looking for a chance to go out and begin drinking again. He would no sooner have a few minutes of normal behaviour than he would start looking for an escape – it didn't matter what. He would telephone to some people to come over to give him courage to face me. I became for him someone who was always calm. He used to say, 'She is judging me.' And I think he realised that I was clear-headed. I always tried to save the situation, to keep my dignity no matter what. And because of that, everybody reproached him: 'Look, you have a wife like this, like that; you don't deserve her.' When they talked to him like that, he would sink deeper and deeper into despair. And that was the reason life became unbearable for him when he didn't drink. He became aggressive. Not physically, but talking arrogantly: 'I am going to do you the honour of, give you the gift of, not getting drunk.'

For a long time I waited on him hand and foot. I used to say to myself:

'All right, since he's making an effort, I have to try to help him.' But honestly speaking, deep down inside, I couldn't bear it any longer. I knew that a catastrophe was about to happen. You know, he didn't have a lot of will power. I made appointments with doctors for him to undergo treatment. But he was ashamed to go to a doctor. He wouldn't admit that he was an alcoholic. When I would say to him, 'But you drink!' he would respond with a thick tongue, 'Me, drink?' He could barely get the words out. What was the use of trying to convince someone who was fundamentally dishonest and reckless of the consequences of his behaviour? He wasn't even dishonest, because he was incapable of reasoning clearly.

I ended up by tricking him. I asked some doctors to get him to ask to go on a detoxification programme. I didn't get mixed up in it. I let him believe it was his own idea. When he came to tell me he was leaving on a trip, I knew what he was talking about. I packed his suitcase without a word; I even managed to make him believe that I thought he really was going away on a trip. I told him that I was going to repaint the house and wallpaper my room while he was away, and in fact that is what I did. And so he left. He hid the car because the institution where he was to undergo treatment was in the city where we lived. But he only stayed there for two days and then escaped. I think he came to admit his condition, but he must have felt shamed by the treatment. He is a very complex person. He had been deprived of affection, his mother having died when he was young, his father then marrying the sister of his first wife, who had been living with them. The disappearance of his mother and the sudden installation of his aunt as the mistress of the house was too abrupt a change for him.

Q: *How old was he when this happened?*

A: Twelve or fourteen. He never forgot it. It marked him for life, because he was never happy. He wasn't stupid. He had some good points. After all, he did get to go to France, something many Moroccans weren't able to do at that time.

Q: *How did he get to go to France before finishing his secondary school education? Usually people only go there to attend university.*

A: He went there just for a visit and then stayed on to continue his education. His father helped him of course. He sent him money through some French teachers that he knew. That is how he managed to stay more than ten years in France. He was very well provided for by comparison with lots of Moroccans. But he really squandered it all, and I'm sure his childhood is largely to blame for his wasted life.

Q: *In the beginning of your marriage, did he show you affection?*

A: He was a very sensitive man, but boorish. I was shocked by his way of showing love. I told you that I had never had any flirtations before I was married. When I had my first daughter, he adored her, but in a way that frightened the child. She didn't know how to distinguish between his demonstrations of affection and his roughness. He had very strong feelings, but he expressed them clumsily. He was unhappy because he adored his children and didn't know how to show it to them.

He never succeeded in making those he loved happy. I used to say to myself that he did feel affection for us and I had made my choice. I made a big effort, but I didn't succeed. I was devoted, he was generous, and he thought my feelings were a response to his generosity. He began to chase women quite openly, to become infatuated with one after another, to carry on with them. As long as he was discreet and I saw nothing, it was all right. But when I began to run into him on the corner of the street with another woman . . .

Q: *Did you speak to him about it?*

A: He persisted in denying it until the day I declared that I was not an idiot, that I had seen him, and that lying was not a good tactic. I would have preferred him to say, 'All right, it happened, forgive me.' A man who deliberately lies makes you feel beside yourself. If he had acknowledged his errors, I would have told myself that at least I was dealing with an honest man. So, not only did he drink and make life unbearable, but he chased women – secretaries and the worst kind of slut – and then came home at dawn and lied to me. I found this absolutely detestable.

Q: *In the beginning of your marriage, was there sexual harmony between you?*

A: You know, I had my first orgasm after the birth of my first daughter. To tell the truth, I wasn't at all emancipated on the subject of sexual relations. Nobody had told me about it before I was married. Luckily, a sympathetic sister-in-law had explained to me how things go between a man and a woman. When I got married, I was very frustrated, because my husband was a cousin for whom I felt no passion and who was very clumsy. He had lived a long time in France, while I was a complete novice. I told myself that this must be the way things go, and I felt reduced to a thing. I didn't participate at all; I was his thing.

Q: *Didn't you talk to him about how you felt?*

A: No. He was very shy. He didn't talk at all when we made love.

Besides, we made love in the dark. I didn't feel self-confident enough to start talking to him. He didn't make me feel at ease. He was very reactionary on that subject. And his childhood must have left its mark on him too. He must have had some secret sexual adventures, and some of that stayed with him. And yet, he had lived seven years in France! But he didn't make much progress in that direction.

Q: *Did he continue to have a sex life with you after he began to drink?*

A: No, we didn't have a sex life any more. When he drank a lot, he was tired out. When he met with his first failure, then his second, he couldn't perform any more. We didn't think about it any more.

Q: *He couldn't perform any more or you didn't think about it any more?*

A: He couldn't perform any more, with the result that the breach between us widened.

Q: *What happened the first time? Was it a surprise for him? Did he try to hide it?*

A: Obviously he tried, and that went on for six or seven or eight months.

Q: *How old were you?*

A: It was just after the birth of our second child. I was twenty-four, and he was thirty-five. I remember very well. I had just had the baby. My pregnancy was over. Just after that, I had some problems with nursing the baby, and he would always turn up for dinner with someone and then he had an excuse to go out on the pretext of seeing him home. And he didn't come back until dawn. With the result that for some months he spent the nights away from home. When his impotence continued, I tried to rationalise it: 'You know, it's because of drinking. The alcohol gets on your nerves. Try to stop drinking in order to prove to yourself that you can regain your potency.' 'No, no,' he told me, 'it's just fatigue.' And he went out more than before. He kept out of my sight.

Q: *It never occurred to you that you could leave him?*

A: No, not at all. Moreover, at the beginning, it was he who threatened me with divorce: 'If you don't keep quiet, I'll repudiate you.' And this threat terrified me, you know, I was so young. It was idiotic, but for me it was a humiliation, the end of the world. My husband exploited this tactic to the utmost. I was the first to bend, to make concessions.

Q: *On what occasions did he threaten to repudiate you?*

A: When I remonstrated with him or for something like that. Not for something in the realm of our intimate life, but in the realm of day-to-day life – every time he saw me begin to assert myself, to make a knowing remark. He remained quite feudal, like his father, just a younger version. He knew that the idea of repudiation terrified me, and he employed it to such an extent that he got me used to it. It was he who got me used to the idea of divorce.

The result was that, when we did get a divorce, the idea of divorce had been dinned into me for a long time, for many years. I decided one day to assume responsibility for myself and to ask for a divorce. I couldn't take it any longer. I absolutely had to finish with it. If not, I would have committed suicide. I didn't want to have any more to do with him. I had become allergic to his way of eating, of drinking, of walking, of laughing, of joking. It was on a Friday, I remember. I gave myself until Monday to figure out how to do it.

Q: *Was he surprised when you revealed to him your desire for a divorce?*

A: I said to him, 'Pronounce the formula.'[7] I told him that in my eyes he wasn't worth anything, that he wasn't a man, that I felt only contempt for him, and that, frankly, that was the whole truth. I was able to say those things to him, because they were my real thoughts and feelings.

Age difference in a couple: emergence of will-power in a woman

Q: *How did he react?*

A: It was curious. When we got married, I was eighteen years old. For me he was the image of the perfect man. I put him on a pedestal. Everything he told me was the truth. But suddenly I began to use my own head. I began to think things out for myself and by myself. I began to express some opinions that were sometimes quite sensible. And it was right then that the disaster began. He said, 'A little kid like you is not going to teach me this or that.' He had already begun to be suspicious of me, to no longer be sure of me.

Q: *In what regard?*

A: I don't really know. In all regards. I think that a Moroccan woman develops faster than a man. You know, in the beginning, when I had just arrived in Paris, he warned me, when we were on our way to meet someone, 'This man will kiss your hand, and you must not pull back but let him do it.' When he saw that I didn't need such advice, that I calmly allowed it to be done, he didn't give me any credit. Often he would stress little details: 'Take the number eight bus in that direction, not in the other direction.' He treated me as if I were incapable of working out my way by myself. When I would go to a big department store and wander around, he would get frantic. I would go to the Galerie Lafayette or the Monoprix and stay there for hours, covering all the floors. In the evening, when I returned, I would find him in a panic – he had sent out three or four cars to look for me. He talked to me about the white slave traffic and stuff like that to terrorise me. But he never succeeded.

I would say to him: 'Listen, I can perfectly well take the number eight bus in the other direction, and if I see that it is the wrong direction, I will take in in the right direction. Why do you feel you have to give me so much advice?' He wanted to make me afraid in order to keep me under his thumb. Little by little I began to go around alone, to act on my own initiative. That suited him and at the same time didn't suit him. It is this that creates problems for lots of Moroccan husbands. They are relieved that their wives assume all responsibility, but it really bothers them when someone says to them, 'Your wife is very capable. She handles everything very well. I saw her doing her shopping'; or 'Your house is very nicely decorated.' You see, he himself has never made the slightest effort to arrange the furniture or offered any suggestion for decorating the house. He was flattered that others showed appreciation, but at the same time he was annoyed with me. He would say to himself, 'Well, she is getting cheeky and self-assured with all this flattery', and it must be said that people contributed a lot to that. He was well liked, and his parties went off well, and all that was thanks to me. When I was getting ready to go out and asked him what to wear, he would advise me not to wear a dress that had pleased people, that had been a success, that looked good on me. I don't know what fear . . .

During the evening parties, when he saw me dancing and having a good time, he would call me over and warn me: 'Don't stay too long with that group of people; you've amused yourself enough like that. We're going home.' If I said, 'All right, we'll go', he would answer, 'All right, we'll stay.' He was terrible.

Q: *Did you argue with him about that?*

A: No, I just did what he wanted. He wouldn't admit that he was jealous, no. When he saw that I became friendly with a man or with a couple, he wouldn't allow it. Two couples came often to our place. He had a very bizarre relationship with them. It was he who sought them out – it was never I – but he was distrustful when a friendship developed between us.

Q: *You were never unfaithful to him?*

A: No, never.

Q: *And what about him at that time? Was he already unfaithful?*
A: Yes, but secretly. You know, people contributed a lot to that. They encouraged him to stay out. 'You are afraid of getting spanked', they would say to him when he wanted to leave a party to come home early. They made fun of him.

Q: *Do you think that it is worse for a man to betray his wife than the opposite?*
A: You know, at the beginning, I was uncompromising about it. If my husband should ever betray me, I would commit suicide. Now I find that sort of thing almost normal. But you see, I think that a woman should not do the same thing. If I didn't do it, it was without doubt for egoistic reasons. I love my own person too much, and I wouldn't want to use it just anyhow.

Magic and psychics

Q: *Have you ever known the predictions of a* shuwafa, *a psychic, to come true?*
A: Often.

Q: *Give me their addresses. Tell me, do you go often? Do you go when you have a problem or just for fun?*
A: I know one who is really extraordinary. Everything that he predicted came true. He tells you your past as well as your present and future, just as if he was living with you.

Q: *Do you believe in magic?*
A: No, I don't believe in it. But when I was struggling with my marital problems, people tried to explain to me what was happening by telling me that maybe a woman had cast a spell to make me suffer. I was feeling so helpless that I wanted to believe it. I spent a huge amount of money to be cured by that man. You know, very strange things were happening to me: when I came home from work, I would begin to tremble. I was in a trance. I had cold sweats. They told me it was the effect of the magic spell.

Q: *And what did you think it was?*
A: I couldn't explain it to myself. I was afraid of the dark. I was afraid of my husband. I was afraid of encountering him, because I knew perfectly well that he would come home late in a terrible state, and that he would make me suffer. So, I suffered beforehand, anticipating the night that was going to drag on and on, the insomnia, the horrible scenes. He drank so much that I told myself he wouldn't come home in one piece. I saw

him in pieces. As I now had my own room, my first step was to open my door. Otherwise, he would try to break the lock with a hammer or a screwdriver. He would go outside and bang on my shutters. He rang all the doorbells. They reverberated through the whole house and woke the children up. At two o'clock in the morning he wanted something to eat. He turned on the TV even though there was no programme on the screen. What a racket! I had such a dread of all this! At that period, he had a relationship with a woman who was exploiting him, who maybe did something to him – I don't know what. Maybe it was just a coincidence. What is certain is that I began to hate him, and now I know why. He no longer made me afraid. I realised that I was capable of taking responsibility for myself and the children. I was ready to make any concession to him to gain my freedom. I was ready to make any sacrifice, to accept all the blame. The only thing that frightened me was the thought of leaving my children. I had had as much as I could stand. I had to go see the *qadi*, and the miracle came to pass. My husband decided on a divorce. I think he did it, believing he was teaching me a lesson. He waited a year before remarrying. He used to come to see the children, but there was never any question of our seeing each other again – it was over.

Q: *You believe in magic. Do you believe in djinns?*

A: I know they exist because some sensible people have told me about experiences they have had.

Q: *For example?*

A: I have a friend who is studying at the normal school. One fine day she was entertaining óne of her friends who had just come back from France. She had cooked a rabbit for her. After the meal, my friend took the rabbit's shoulder blade and whiled away the time by reading the future, as we often do for fun. Then she began to hear voices who told her what the person in front of her was thinking.

You know, the psychics were somewhat responsible for my decision to leave my husband, to get a divorce. Some years before my divorce, when I was about twenty-five, I was afraid of the idea of divorce. I didn't realise that I was already taking a lot of responsibility. I told myself that I would never be able to manage all alone. And so I went to a psychic. She told me: 'Your husband drinks, and whatever you do, you are going to divorce him one day. Sooner or later you will get a divorce.' This idea terrified me. I was very, very afraid, and I am still very afraid to go to a *shuwafa*. I took her for the Messiah, even though most of the time she was wide of the mark. The best psychic that I've known was one I went to after my divorce. I went to see her in a different state of mind. Before when I went to psychics, I was always anxious, depressed; I was trying to find comfort, and I came away even more depressed. After my divorce it was different. There was hope, the future, something new in my life. I love it when someone talks to me about the future. I have a lot of hope in the future. Going to a psychic is a diversion nowadays. I don't have serious problems any more. Most of the psychics tell me only optimistic, nice things. Sometimes certain things come true.

Q: *For example?*

A: A man psychic foretold a meeting I would have – with a man whom I knew and who was going to reappear in my life. I really didn't see how that was going to happen and I forgot the prediction. Then one day an old classmate came into my office. He was a colleague and we became very close. We had known each other since we were children. A very deep and close friendship developed between us. After my divorce I was so traumatised that, purely and simply, I just shut myself in. I didn't see anybody any more. I told myself that it was better to learn from the bad experience I had had not to hope for anything. I planned a future for myself in terms of these ideas. But slowly, slowly hope returned.

I became friends with a psychic, a very interesting man. He always told me things that were so true that it became a distraction for me, something to amuse me. He became my friend. I used to go and tell him my little problems, and he would ask me if his predictions came true. You know the kind of thing I'm talking about. Sometimes I just made friendly visits without his predicting for me – just to have news of him. We became friends.

Reflections on male and female roles and the education of a young woman in modern Morocco

Q: *Do you think there is a big difference between men and women, on the psychological plane, for example?*

A: They cannot be the same. A woman is a woman in all that she does and says, in her way of thinking and speaking.

Q: *Do they think differently?*

A: There are certain things that men lack and that women have much more strongly. They have more intuition. In the domestic sphere, a man can't do what a woman does. It's not that he can't, but he would be clumsy. Just as women would be clumsy doing men's work. There are men who change babies' nappies, but they are the exception. Women are more sensitive than men. They feel things more. In Morocco, I know lots of women deserving of praise because they face situations with more dignity than men. A bereavement, for example; a woman bears it with more dignity. She suffers just as much, but she thinks about the consequences, about the rest of the family. She controls herself better. She has more strength of character.

Q: *Do you think that men and women can do the same jobs or not?*

A: I can't see a woman driving a tractor any more than I can see a man with a thimble stitching tiny pleats.

Q: *Then why are the great couturiers and the great chefs men?*

A: Oh, yes, the 'great' ones, I agree. But, in general, I find it difficult to conceive of a man doing embroidery or making swishy skirts.

Q: *What are your plans for Kenza? How are you preparing her for her future, for marriage, for education?*

A: I am trying to direct her, without forcing her too much, of course, toward getting an education. She is intelligent but doesn't always get good marks. She counts too much on her intelligence and that trips her up. She is a child marked by the death of her sister, the illness of her brother, and the divorce. I try to make her understand that languages are a very important thing; I wish that I myself had learned some. With languages, she could get a job in an international organisation, live in the great world, and not remain within the limited perspective in which we ourselves are imprisoned.

Q: *Will you let her go out with someone when she is older?*

A: Yes, on condition that she knows what it's all about. For the time being, I keep the brake on. I am strict with her because she is only thirteen, and I wouldn't want others to give her any wrong ideas.

Q: *For example?*

A: Other children who have lived in other milieux, who have not been supervised, whose education has been faulty, could influence her. I would want to spare her that. But when she is mature enough to understand, I will speak to her about certain things; I will show her her responsibilities. I have already begun doing that to some extent.

Q: *Does she already have her periods?*

A: Yes, she began very early. I came into the bathroom one day, and I saw some stained panties. At first I thought she had sat on something or other, but I quickly realised that it was blood. She was still in primary school. I went to see her and told her: 'Now you have your periods. It is not painful. It is not something bad. Now you have to pay attention and put on a napkin so that it doesn't drip. Don't be afraid. It happens to everybody. I also have my periods and I don't suffer. Now you can have a baby. You have the same possibilities as a grown woman.' She was a little frightened, but when she no longer felt ashamed, she would talk to me about her pain and her sanitary napkins just the way she did about her hair style or her tennis.

Q: *Do you remember when you had your first period?*

A: Yes, I must have been thirteen years old. Nobody had ever spoken to me about it beforehand. I guessed a little about it. We used to see our mothers washing bits of rags, and we suspected a little what that must have been about. The day I got my first period, it was the maids who told me about it. They also pointed out that you must put a little bit of blood on the three legs of the *kanun* in order for your period to last only three days and no longer. They also advised me to throw away my first sanitary napkin any place at all, without watching. In short, a whole mythology. I did the trick about the three legs, and my period lasted eight days! It was the good old days when I believed in all that.

Q: *Have we gained a lot with modernity? I often ask myself that question.*

A: I think we have lost more than we have gained. In the past a woman didn't have all the responsibilities she has now. She just let herself live. She let herself be taken care of. Nowadays, the Moroccan woman wants to have her share of responsibilities. In the past, she was coddled and didn't do anything; I am not sure that she was more unhappy than we are. She at least thought that she was enjoying her life and circumstances.

Q: *Just the same, don't you think that we have gained something? More freedom?*

A: Yes, we have gained the right to tell a man what we think, something my mother could never do, and the possibility of demanding a divorce, even if we have to bear all the consequences and disadvantages. In the past, maybe women nursed this desire but it never came to pass. After all, we do have some pleasures that they didn't have.

Q: *We complain about our lot, but, tell me, if someone asked you to choose another nationality, what would you choose?*

A: I've never thought about that. I'm very comfortable with myself. You know, we are a country that struggles with the problem of underdevelopment, but it's rather a case of mental underdevelopment. I am very optimistic about our capacity for development.

Q: *Do you see any contradictions between tradition and modernity?*

66

A: The contradiction I see is between the individual interest and the collective interest. A country cannot develop if each person thinks first about his or her own little interests – it is not possible. You cannot develop if you think first of all about yourself and then about others. That is the problem. It is there, not somewhere else.

4

Zubaida Zannati and her daughter Nazha: a thirst for education

Zubaida Zannati, born in al-Jadida into a simple provincial family in which the women used to weave carpets, had 'a great ambition to study'. This ambition was temporarily stifled when Zubaida was forced into an early marriage.

But her frustration was only temporary because she was going to realise through her daughters her dream of further education and of the opening up of horizons other than weaving and knitting. Nazha would become a lawyer. Nazha's father, a ship's chef, died under torture in a police station two years before independence.

Zubaida Zannati[1]

Q: *Was your mother the first wife of your father?*
A: No, he had already been married. He only stayed four years with his first wife because she did not give him any children. He separated from her and married my mother, who had eleven children. Seven are dead. There are four of us who survived, three girls and a boy. The others didn't live more than two years. I was married and had my first daughter when my mother was still having babies. I had a sister younger than my daughter, but she is dead.
Q: *Did your family live alone?*
A: No, with my uncle. We lived on the second floor, and my uncle on the first floor. My sister and I lived in this house until we were married.

Schooling, engagement, and first marriage

Q: *How old were you when you were married?*

A: I was thirteen. I had aleady been married for six months when I had my first period.[2] They took me out of school in order to marry me off.

Q: *You went to school?*

A: Yes, they sent me and my sister to a European woman who taught us sewing, lacemaking, knitting, and mending. Then we went to a Moroccan woman from Rabat, who taught us carpet-making. We went in the afternoons, and we had an hour and a half for carpet-making and an hour and a half for schooling. All the men of my family have been educated, and my brother-in-law also went to school. He was thirty years old when he married my sister, who was sixteen. He worked at the Ministry of Youth and Sports. All my cousins went to school. So my sister and I went to school, but when my mother had a lot of children, she kept my sister at home to help her. But I continued to go to school. I was on the point of getting my certificate when they pulled me out. Why? Because they began to have men teachers! My father wouldn't hear of it: 'As long as there were French women as teachers and you were learning a skill, there was no problem. But now that there are men teaching the girls' class, that's the end.' It wasn't just my father who no longer wanted me to go to school; there was also my uncle. And at my mother's school, there was also a *faqih*.[3] He told them: 'It's all right with Muslim women and Christian [European] women, but with men teachers, it is better she should stay home.'

Q: *How did you dress when you went out of the house?*

A: I went without a *djellaba* up to the age of ten. Afterwards I began to wear a *djellaba* and a veil. I was eleven years old when they made me leave school. The principal and my teacher tried to dissuade my father: 'Your daughter is intelligent; let her continue her education.' My father's 'no' was final. So I stayed at home for two years, and then they married me off when I was thirteen.[4]

Q: *How did your engagement take place?*

A: The man who asked for me in marriage lived in the same street as we did. He was a widower and already had two children. In the beginning I didn't want it, but then I had to accept. But it only lasted a year and a half.

Q: *Why so short a time? Did you know him beforehand?*

A: No, I didn't know him, but he knew me. It all happened at the same time – the engagement, the marriage, everything. From the minute I saw him, I didn't like him. I didn't accept him. I never stopped crying. I was miserable. I got pregnant right away. I returned home and stayed there until my confinement. After the baby was born, I didn't want to live with him any more. So I ran away for good.

Q: *But why did you agree to marry him?*

A: I did it for my parents. I didn't want to spoil the wedding for them. I put up with it for six months – against my will. I was just there – that's all. When I got pregnant, I couldn't stand it any longer. I cried all the time. Finally my father intervened: 'The best thing would be for you to let her come home to us', he said to my husband. 'It's being pregnant that makes her act like that. It will be better after the baby is born.' So he waited until then, and he came to our house for the *sab'a*. When it was over, he said to my parents, 'She must come with me.' I flatly refused: 'Take your daughter Farida, if you wish, but I am not going with you. I don't want to live with you any longer.' My father stepped in: 'You can't compel her; the only thing you can do is separate from her.' 'That's out of the question', he replied. He ended up getting the court people involved, and they forced me to return one evening. The next day he came home to lunch, and afterwards I took my daughter and left – but this time not to my parents' house. I went to the house of my maternal uncle, who lived in the same town as we did. I arrived at their place in tears: 'I don't want to live with him any longer.' 'You just stay with us', they told me, 'we'll take care of you.' My husband resorted again to the court: 'My wife has fled', he told them. He went to my father. 'I haven't seen her again', my father said. Finally they found out where I was and came to fetch me by force. But I only stayed one more night at my husband's house. My father had to give some money and move heaven and earth for me to get a divorce. I ceded everything to my husband. But I had the guardianship of my daughter Farida. She would be brought up by my parents in the event of my remarrying.

Q: *And afterwards?*

A: Afterwards, I stayed with my parents for nine months, and then I remarried.

Q: *How did you get acquainted with your second husband?*

A: He asked my uncle for my hand.

Q: *You didn't know him?*

A: I finally got to see him.

Q: *Did you like him?*

A: Yes, I liked him, and we got married. He is the father of my children. We had Nazha, Abd al-Rahman, and Salima. I only lost one daughter, Malika. She was eight months old when she died. We lived together for eight years. He was involved in politics at the time that Ben Youssef was in exile.[5] He was killed in a police station two months before the return of Ben Youssef.

The death of a political dissident

At the time that my second husband died, he was thirty-two and I was twenty-four. I had four children: Farida, from my first marriage, who was nine; Nazha who was six; Abd al-Rahman four years old; and Salima a year and a half. My father had been dead for four years, and my brother Jawad was still in school. He was about to get his school certificate when my father died. He had obtained a scholarship and become a boarder at a secondary school in Marrakech. I also had a married sister in Marrakech; my brother used to spend the weekend at her house, and then he went there to live when my father died. She didn't have any children. In short, my husband died at the police station. They came to tell me, 'Come and see your husband'.

Q: *Did they beat him?*

A: Yes. There had been a fire at the port of al-Jadida, and they suspected him. They took him to the police station about two-thirty in the afternoon, and about seven o'clock in the evening they came to fetch me: a Frenchman and a Moroccan, both from the police. The Frenchman said to me: 'You can come to see your husband. He is seriously injured, at the hospital.' I hesitated a moment, and then I said to him, 'I can't come with you. I can't go out now.' Then the Frenchman said to me, 'If you don't want to come with me, if you don't trust me, there is a Moroccan with me.' I still refused, and I took my son and went to the house of my parents, who were astonished to see me come at that hour. 'Is my brother Jawad here?' I asked. 'He has just put on his pyjamas', my mother replied. It must have been eight o'clock in the evening. I went up to his room and told him all that had happened. 'You mustn't go there', he told me. 'It's surely for questioning about your husband's political activities. It must be that. How long since you've seen him?' 'Since he left this morning', I replied. 'It can only be something political. They want to question you. They are going to mistreat you in order to find out who he goes around with. I myself am going to go.'

He came back in tears: 'My sister,' he said to me, 'you can go see your husband.' 'What happened to him? Did he have an accident? Tell me the truth. Is he dead?' 'They killed him, that's what', he answered. It was terrible. We went to the police station. They didn't want us to see the

71

body. They put it under guard in a room at the hospital. In the beginning they told us that we could see it that night. They didn't want the news of his death to get about. One of us asked when they expected to bury him. We stayed there until midnight. All the family knew what was going on. We left and returned at six o'clock the next morning. We waited there until ten o'clock when the police came to disperse us. They had buried him, and we never found out where his grave was.

Life after the husband's death: Zubaida's brother has to provide for the family

The whole family stayed at the house, and in the evening we put on the funeral dinner. My mother went upstairs to get my brother to come for the *sadaqa*. But he was not in his room. He had left a letter on his night table saying that he couldn't stand to see his sister struggle to feed four children, and so he had decided to leave school and look for work. He had gone to Rabat. He looked for work for three days. Some people gave him a helping hand, and on the fourth day he got a job offer. He had the choice between al-Jadida, Agadir, and Tiznit. He preferred to stay in al-Jadida. He began working at the post office. He rented a house where we all came to live together.

Q: *Who came?*

A: He, my mother, my four children, and myself. Actually, my mother didn't live with me but she often came to help me out. She helped me do the laundry and looked after the children when I wanted to go somewhere – to the Turkish bath, for instance. When she had the time, she came with me, and when I went on a trip to visit my sister, she looked after one of the children.

Q: *And what about their schooling?*

A: I made sure that they learned their lessons. When they were still very small, I helped them with the bits of French that I knew, especially in the evenings when I no longer had anything to do. I let the little one sleep in one room, and I went to join the rest in the other room where they were studying. It filled me with joy to see them studying. I spared no effort. We had a table and chairs; I sat down with them to help them. When I got tired and wanted to go to bed, I asked them to go into the other room where they could keep the light on. They had become used to working very late all by themselves before going to bed.

Q: *Did you go to see their teachers?*

A: I kept in close touch with what they were doing at school

Q: *During the life of your husband, who saw to their schoolwork, you or he?*

A: It was I who supervised their studies; I was friendly with my children's teachers. I used to go to their houses, and I often invited them to come to my house for tea, when they had time. One time the girls told me that the teacher had slapped Nazha. I told them, 'If my daughter deserves punishment, the teacher can kill her if she wants to. My only answer will be to bury her.'

And when the girls reported to her what I had said, she insisted on getting acquainted with 'this Moroccan woman who cares about what her daughter is studying'. She came for tea with me and told me the story of her life. We remained friends until Nazha was moved to another class. In fact, my daughters went to the school that I myself had attended and had been forced to leave. It was the same principal who was now looking after my children. She had accepted Farida and Nazha at the school before the legal age, at four years old. When I went to enrol Nazha at the school, there wasn't any room left, and Nazha started to cry. The principal was very sorry: 'She is still too young.' Nazha was crying: 'I want to go to school and they won't let me.' She could hardly get the words out. The principal wanted to know what was the matter, what the little one was saying. I told her that she wanted to stay at school. They had to put a little mat on the floor for her because they couldn't find a chair. I often went to see the principal.

The children's education

Q: *Whom did your children fear the most? You or their father?*

A: Me. Their father never spanked them. He never refused them anything. It was I who got fed up and spanked them a lot.

Q: *What did you spank them with? Your hand? A belt?*

A: I only spanked them with my hand; I never used a stick.

Q: *Were they very afraid of you?*

A: A little

Q: *Why did you care so much about your daughters' education?*

A: Because I myself had not been able to continue my educaiton. I had a great ambition to study, to reach a certain level. If it had depended on me, I would not have left school at eleven years old; I would have continued my studies in order to be somebody later on; I would have managed to get along better. But my parents were opposed to that. When my eldest daughter got her primary school certificate, my brother went to Rabat, where he knew someone who could get a scholarship for her. He registered her at the girls' secondary school in Rabat. Then when her sister obtained her primary school certificate, she was also admitted to the same secondary school with a scholarship, and they were boarders.

Q: *Did you still live in al-Jadida when your daughters were school boarders in Rabat?*

A: No. After my husband died, my brother worked for only one year in al-Jadida. He was transferred for one year to Beni-Mellal, where we joined him. Then he resigned and signed up for the Auxiliary Forces. When he was training in Casa, we went back to al-Jadida for three months. Afterwards he was posted to Marrakech. We stayed there two years, then three years at Meknes. It was at that time that my daughter failed her final exams; she didn't want to hear any more talk about studying; she had had enough. We came back to al-Jadida for the summer vacation to stay with my children's uncle. He knew an assistant director at the Ministry of Youth and Sports. He telephoned him to ask if he could find summer jobs for my daughters. He told them to come to see him the next day at his office. On the day after that I accompanied them to the Ministry of Youth and Sports, where the two of them were to work.

Q: *What type of work?*

A: Farida worked at the Delegation. Nazha got a job as a typist for only eight days. Farida's job lasted three months. She liked her job a lot and wanted to stay in al-Jadida. So I closed my house in Meknes and returned to settle down with Farida and Salima. We stayed seven months at their uncle's house before we were able to find lodgings. Nazha was still a boarder in Rabat. As for my son, he stayed in Meknes with my brother. Then he accompanied my brother to Nador, where he had been transferred. My son left school in the second year of secondary school. Nazha joined us every summer at the end of the school year. After we had lived there for a year, someone came to ask for my eldest daughter's hand in marriage.

Farida gets married, Salima starts to work, and the son emigrates to France

It was someone who worked with her at the Ministry of Youth and Sports. He came to ask for her hand. After they were engaged, he came often to the house. They were engaged for one year. He had government housing, so Farida left us and went to live at her husband's house. When she had her first daughter, we went to live with her, Salima and I. Afterwards she had a second daughter. It was I who brought up the two of them. We stayed with them until Salima got her secondary school entrance certificate. She had done the fourth year, and then had worked for three months. But she earned very little. Someone who knew her sister Farida telephoned her one day to say that there was a job available and he was looking for a young woman to work with him. He was the director of an agricultural office. He was looking for a young woman of good appearance who spoke a little English. She promised to find him someone and asked Salima if she would rather work or continue her education. 'If it is a well-paid job, I prefer to work', was her reply. When she went to see, they asked her to come back the following Monday, and right then they gave her the job. She earned a good salary. She lived for six months at my sister's house before moving. Her director rented her a house. He was a businessman in addition to his job at the agricultural office. He had an insurance business and a real estate business. We went to live with her and paid part of the rent. My son left for France to look for work. He didn't want to stay any longer in Morocco.

Q: *And then what?*

A: And then – well, that's life.

Q: *What did he do in France?*

A: People told him to go in April. He worked in a factory in Paris. I didn't take him seriously when he told me that he wanted to go to France. He said to me: 'You know, if I go, I won't come back for two or three years.' 'Oh, no,' I told him, 'come back every year!' So he left. In the beginning I got a letter every week, then every month. Afterwards he didn't write any more . . . four months went by with no news from him. His sister Nazha saw that I was very worried: I cried all the time. She went to France to see him. She had his address. She waited for him at the factory gates. When he saw her, the two of them began to cry. She went with him to the factory doctor's office, and he agreed to give him a few days vacation. He took his sister around to visit lots of places. Nazha had the key of an apartment that a woman friend of hers, a lawyer, had lent her. And he went to stay with her there for the week that she spent in France. Before leaving, she reproached him a bit for leaving his mother without news, telling him that he should write to me from time to time or telephone. She gave him the telephone number of some neighbours of

Farida, and he began to ring up every Saturday. I was very happy. It was as if I were seeing him. Then the people at whose house he used to phone me moved to Tiznit, and he must have phoned without finding anybody there. Then four or five months went by without news of him. I don't know if he will return soon for a holiday as most of the immigrant workers do. Last year he took a trip and sent us lots of postcards.

Q: *How old is he now?*

A: He's got to be twenty-one.

Q: *He's very young!*

A: When Nazha saw how he was living in France, she made me feel better by telling me, 'You could easily take him for a tourist.' He gets a good wage. He has a room in a hostel, eats in a restaurant, and dresses well. He doesn't miss out on the Saturday night dances; he deprives himself of nothing; and he is not concerned about anything, while I sit here worrying about him. He has always been like that, even when he was here.

Q: *Were you a little strict with him?*

A: Not at all! He would stay out as long as he wanted, sometimes until midnight, sometimes even until after breakfast. He would go directly to the kitchen and get something to eat. Then in the evening he would get up to go to a surprise party. Not a care in the world in France. He has found what he wanted.

Relations between mother and daughters

Q: *And your daughters, did you let them go out?*

A: They used to go out, yes.

Q: *How old were they when they began to spend the night with their girl-friends?*

A: Even now I don't let them spend the night elsewhere.

Q: *Really?*

A: Their friends used to come to sleep at our house. But as long as they lived with me, I didn't let them spend the night somewhere else.

Q: *Even at their girlfriends' houses?*

A: Salima, yes. Since she has been working, she often goes to her girl-friends' houses when they go out together on Saturday night. Sometimes they even take trips together.

Q: *How old is Salima now?*

A: Nineteen. She also goes to the movies, but only on Saturday.

Q: *Do you go with her?*

A: Very rarely. I go to visit my family at the other end of town. But I don't let her spend the night at just anybody's house. I don't put too tight a rein on her, but even so I don't let her do everything she wants to.

Q: *Did your first husband take you out now and then?*

A: No, and as I never loved him, I only went out to go to the Turkish bath, and even then only if it was rented for me. I didn't go out for a whole year, except at the end to go to Marrakech. I was pregnant, and he even refused to let me go to Marrakech. My father insisted, but in vain. My first husband couldn't ever accompany us anywhere, because he had his work.

Q: *You couldn't go out? He locked you up, or what?*

A: If it hadn't been for my mother who came to visit me . . .

Q: *And he, didn't he take you anywhere?*

A: Nowhere – except to the Turkish bath, and then only at night when there wasn't even a cat in the street! It was already midnight when I left the bath.

Q: *Twelve or thirteen years old, all alone, and all the time at home – how did you pass the time?*

A: There were some neighbours who came to see me, and my former classmates. They kept me company. My mother came sometimes with a friend of hers. They would spend the whole afternoon with me.

Q: *And how was it with your second husband?*

A: He let me go where I wanted to.

Q: *Did he take you to the movies?*

A: I went with him to his family; he came with me to mine. Sometimes, when he didn't find me at home, he would join me at my parents' house. We got along very well.

Q: *So, in your opinion, should your daughters choose their own husbands or not?*

A: Oh, yes! I believe that it's up to them to choose their husbands because I know what happens when a woman marries a man she has not chosen. If one of them wants to marry someone, I would not oppose it. That is what happened with the oldest one when she got acquainted with someone. She told me that someone was going to come to ask for her hand; I told her that that concerned no one but herself. The same thing happened with my brother. I was living with him. He had said goodbye to us and preceded us to al-Jadida. He had just bought a new car. He stayed three or four days at al-Jadida. He saw a girl on the beach. He liked her. He telephoned me at the grocer's to ask me to join him. It was only afterwards that I realised what he wanted: he wanted me to go ask for that girl's hand. I told him that if he had chosen her, I could only agree. She was barely fourteen years old. They did the paper work for the marriage and she came to join us. She stayed with us for two years until she finished school.

Q: *She stayed with you?*

A: Yes, she was with us; the marriage contract was signed. She went to school and when she came home, she sat down at the table with us. She went to the movies with her husband at the weekends and invited her school friends to our house. I stayed at home. I took care of all the housework and shopping and other chores. That went on for two years until they celebrated their wedding.

Q: *How old was your brother?*

A: He must have been twenty. They got married at al-Jadida. His wife stayed with us. She already had two children when they left us to set up their own household by themselves.

Q: *She stayed with you all that time?*

A: Yes. I didn't treat her any differently from my own daughters. She was very young when she arrived. Even now, when she wants to go on a trip, it is I who take care of her children. They often come to see me. You know, we are all close in our immediate family. A brother and a sister live in the same town as I do. They have houses very near each other. My daughter, too, doesn't live far away.

Q: *And your daughter who is not yet married? Does she talk to you about herself? About her life, her relationships?*

A: Nazha? Oh, yes. Sometimes we stay up very late talking. She tells me everything. One time she told me about someone who telephones her all the time. He wanted to ask for her hand. She talked to me a lot about her suitors, but I warned her: 'None of them is right for you; you are still too young.' And she also doesn't want to get married; she is young.

Q: *Did your daughters ask your advice before getting married?*

A: Yes. I didn't want them to marry someone who wasn't suitable. I would have blamed myself for the rest of my life.

Q: *In your opinion, what is not suitable in a husband? What would you want your daughters to avoid?*

A: Someone who was a drunkard or didn't behave well would not be suitable, or someone who was not from a good family.

Q: *But how are you going to know all that?*

A: When someone comes to ask for your daughter's hand in marriage, you try to find out about him through someone who knows him. You try to ascertain if his conduct is good. I would not give my daughter to a man just because he is rich. He must be mature, from a good family, educated. Am I going to see her marry someone who is not educated? He should be even more educated than she.

Q: *You wouldn't want her to marry someone less educated than she?*

A: That wouldn't work out well.

Q: *Did you let your daughters use make-up before their marriage?*

A: At eighteen years old, girls know what they want. They buy make-up, and they use it as they like. For special occasions, for example, if they are going out, if they are invited to a party.

Q: *Do you let them smoke?*

A: No, I don't let them smoke.

Q: *You don't smoke, and neither do they? [I knew that Nazha smoked.]*

A: Nobody smokes in front of me.

Q: *Your son doesn't smoke either?*

A: He has never smoked in front of me. Previously, he didn't smoke at all or just from time to time when someone offered him a cigarette. I don't know what he does now.

Q: *And did your second husband smoke?*

A: He smoked and drank.

Q: *And the first?*

A: My first husband only smoked. It was my second husband who smoked and drank alcohol.

Q: *And why did you never smoke?*

A: No woman in our family has ever smoked.

Nazha[6]

Childhood with mother and grandmother

Q: *Do you remember when you were a child?*

A: When my memories begin, we were living with some neighbours. We had a room on the first floor. My big sister often went to my grandmother's house because she lived all alone. Sometimes I went with her. My big sister was with my grandmother more often than with my mother. It was almost as though she brought her up because my mother was too young. She didn't even want to breastfeed her. She took more care of me, because by that time she had more experience. But with her first daughter, she didn't want to take care of her. They had to remind her to give the baby the breast every time and things like that.

Q: *Who did the housework and the cooking?*

A: My mother, of course. She was helped by my grandmother, and also by my big sister, who carded the wool and spun it with my mother and grandmother. I also helped out when I was young. I remember that we removed things from the wool. We combed it.

Q: *Did your grandmother also spin wool?*

A: Oh, yes, my grandmother couldn't remain idle. As she had lost her husband when she was very young and her son was a school boarder, she used to work because she had nothing else to do. And also she helped my mother raise the children.

Q: *And your mother? Did she do anything else besides the housework?*

A: She spun wool and made carpets. My grandmother and my mother worked together. It was a sort of pastime, and it also earned some pocket money.

Working with wool

Q: *Did they have one loom or several?*

A: They had just one loom. You know, several people can work on one loom. You can even put the children behind the loom to do the knots. The children played a part; my sister worked very well; she helped with cleaning the wool; she went with my mother and grandmother to the sea to wash it. Once the wool was cleaned, carded, and spun, they went to sell it at a *suq* in the town, at the wool *suq*. They sold the cleaned wool and bought raw wool in the same *suq*. They brought it back to the house to clean it and so forth. They got maybe 200–300 francs a kilo[7] – that's all. Those who worked very hard could process two to three kilos a day. The price depended on the quality of the product. Each quality had a name: if it was spun very fine, it was called *al-sada*; if it was goat's wool, it was called *al-sa'ra*; if it was very rough spun, it was *al-barwal*. The quality also depended on the instrument used – *al-qursal* or *al-mast*. The wool can also be spun short or long. Do you begin to get the idea?

Q: *And your father, what did he do?*

A: He worked as a chef for a navigation company. He would be away for two, three, four months. And my mother stayed behind waiting for him to return. So she had plenty of time for working.

Q: *Did you see him very seldom?*

A: Very seldom. Even when he was on land, he was totally taken up with his work as a chef. He worked in the restaurants that the navigation company ran in the port. He would come home very late at night. We hardly saw him.

Q: *Do you remember him?*

A: He loved me very much. He would take me with him to the restaurant where he worked. His bosses were very nice to me, and then, at that time I wore European dress, had short hair, and spoke French. We had received some education. My father spoke lots of languages; he was a very intelligent person. He spoke French, English, Spanish.

Q: *How had he learned those languages?*

A: In his work, that's how. He came from the country. He learned easily.

Q: *Who supervised your schoolwork?*

A: I started school very young, at four years old. I was still not toilet-trained. The principal accepted me because my mother spoke French and had previously been a student at that school. I was accepted provisionally. I was in a sort of nursery-school class. They gave me dolls to play with and things like that. I was, in effect, the playmate of the little girls of the teachers. It was, in fact, my mother who supervised our education. And my grandmother also played a big role in our education. The person we were most afraid of was my grandmother. She is the one we respected the most. My mother never spanked us, or very rarely. She would argue with us if we did something she didn't like, but that was all.

Q: *Do you have some very vivid childhood memories?*

A: My father loved fishing. He had a lot of French friends. He would go off fishing with them for the whole day. And I was always with them. I have one memory that is very . . . There was a young Frenchman named Toto. Every time I saw him or he brought me home, I would say over and over 'Toto *diali* ' [my Toto]. He used to take me to the movies. I didn't particularly like the movies but I loved the candy he used to buy me when we went there. He also used to take me to bars and cafés. When he would drink red wine, I would also want to drink something red, so they would bring me a grenadine.

Death of her father

Q: *Do you remember the death of your father?*

A: Yes, I certainly do. It happened one evening. I don't know what my mother had prepared for supper, but she didn't want us to start eating. She told us, 'We must wait for your father.' We played in the living room and amused ourselves. Then someone knocked at the door. It was a police officer. My mother must have told you the whole story. I recall certain details. I was very struck by the fact that at the beginning they wouldn't let my little brother and me see him. We went down a little narrow street to the hospital and then we saw the shroud. There was a police inspector who tried to comfort me by giving me a few pennies. I remember that we stayed there very late into the night. Then I remember the funeral ceremony. My mother was dressed all in white. After that, she didn't go out any more.

Q: *Then how did she manage?*

A: My father didn't leave anything. He was the kind of spendthrift who spent what he earned the same day. He spoiled us. We were well dressed, we ate very well. But he didn't put anything aside. You might say he had a premonition that . . . When he returned from his voyages, he brought lots of presents, heaps of things. Things to wear, gimmicks that weren't available in our town. For example, elastic suspenders, which you couldn't buy here before, and ties.

Q: *Did you move to a different house?*

A: The house we lived in didn't belong to us. We shared it with the neighbours. We stayed there because my mother couldn't afford to go elsewhere. But you know, we got on well with the neighbours. We never had any arguments with them. My mother was very amiable, very sociable. But we did move when my uncle quit school in order to go to work. It was six or seven months after the death of my father.

Q: *Was it a big change for you?*

A: Oh, yes. Life was more peaceful because we lived alone without neighbours. My grandmother and uncle lived with us. But despite everything, we felt a little bit like orphans. People would keep saying to us, 'Oh, you poor children, you poor children!' You know, it was people like that who made us feel like orphans. In fact, we had a very stable life. You see, we didn't have any particular difficulties. We were all together, a united family. We had to earn a bit more money. So my mother made carpets. It's true that at that time everybody pitied our lot. There were some members of the family who helped us, gave us little gifts.

Q: *And school?*

A: We continued to go. We didn't interrupt our schooling after the death of my father. We went in the morning and didn't come home at noon because we ate in the cafeteria. We only came home in the evening. All three of us went to school. Sometimes my brother would run away, so we had to keep an eye on him, keep close to him. When he went off and hid, we tried to find him. But apart from my brother, we didn't have any problems going to school. We liked going there.

Life of a young girl

Q: *What were your spare-time activities? What did you do when you weren't at school?*

A: Spare-time activities? We came home and spent the night with the family. Later on, friends asked us to spend the night at their houses. I had lots of friends – neighbours, cousins, and also classmates. I could spend the whole day with them, or they could spend the day at my house, but at night each one would go home. Even with members of the family, I was allowed to spend the night only at those houses where there were no boys.

Studies and first paid jobs

Q: *And what about the company of men – cousins or classmates?*

A: You know, I was a school boarder in Rabat. There was a local person there (a sort of guardian) who was supposed to look after me, but I never saw him; he never came to take me out at the weekends. So at the weekend the other boarders went out but I stayed behind.

Q: *On Saturday and Sunday you didn't go out?*

A: I didn't go out, but I didn't miss it. Even on Fridays I didn't go on the walks organised by the school because Friday I had the theatre club or the photography club. I also took part in sports, any sport. We had a good time at boarding school; there were records and we listened to them. We had a lot of fun, and besides, I worked an enormous amount.

Q: *You had a scholarship at boarding school. Was it enough?*

A: In the beginning, my uncle supported us. But starting with the third year, my uncle began to have some difficulties, some problems that prevented him from taking care of our expenses as he had been doing. Finally, I felt that he couldn't help us any more. So my sister and I began to work.

Q: *How old were you?*

A: I was not even fifteen. The first year I got a job as a typist.

Q: *But how did you learn to type?*

A: My uncle, who worked at the Ministry of Youth and Sports, was able to get me into an office where there was a machine available. I taught myself for three or four days, and then he pulled some strings to get me a job in another ministry. I was able to work as a typist for two and a half months, and then I returned to school. My sister liked working; she gave up school and started working in that ministry where she still is. After that experience, I developed the habit of working the whole three months of the school vacations. I saved the money that I earned and used it throughout the school year to cover my needs – my clothes, trips, books, everything.

Q: *How much did you earn?*

A: The first time I worked I earned 1,000 francs a day.[8] The second time I worked by the day and they paid me by the day. You know, they don't have the right to hire girls. But they hired us anyway under men's names. I was called Muhammad Ben Ali or something like that. So we worked by the day, and got paid every two weeks.

Q: *So you received 15,000 francs every two weeks?*[9]

A: No, much less, because they didn't count Saturday and Sunday. Only the days you actually worked. The third year I got a more interesting job in an appraisal company. I worked there for three months and I was much better paid. I got employee benefits, paid holidays, everything. I replaced an engineer's wife who was ill. I did the secretarial work, the accounts, and finally I became the secretary for the whole place. So I earned 180,000 francs.[10] They paid me in a lump sum.

Q: *Did you give part of it to your mother?*

A: Oh, yes. I bought some trinkets for them, and with the rest I paid for weekends in al-Jadida, because I was living in Rabat where I was at boarding school.

Q: *And where was that three-month job? In Rabat?*

A: No, in Marrakech. You know, my uncle had worked in Marrakech after he had been transferred, and it was in Marrakech that my sister and I got our first jobs, and we had kept our contacts there. I worked in a lot of different places, even in the mine credit union. It was my graduation year. I worked as a teller, and also as a typist. I think they paid me 50,000 francs a month.[11] As soon as I got my pay for three months, I returned to Rabat to go back to school. I stopped working on September 30 at six o'clock. I took the Marrakech-to-Rabat bus at nine o'clock in the evening, and arrived at school at nine o'clock the next morning. I kept on going like that the whole year. You know, for me, going to Marrakech was going on holiday. Even when I began my university studies, I continued to work during the three months of holidays. You know, I didn't always have a scholarship at the university. If your marks were poor, they took away your scholarship. But the year that I didn't have one, I managed. I worked in a boarding school: I was an au pair, that is, lodging and food for twenty-one hours of work. And to cover my other expenses I gave private lessons in mathematics.

Q: *Traditionally girls were pressed to get married young. Was that also true in your case?*

A: Ah! In my case, the essential aim was getting an education. With us that was always the priority. My mother knew what it meant to keep a child from finishing her education. She had had difficulties in her life because of that and didn't want me to experience the same problems. At eleven or twelve years old I began to have suitors. They were always sent away. My mother told them: 'She has to get an education.' Marriage was not something we were concerned about. My mother kept repeating to us: 'You must not get married young.' You know what happened to my mother in that regard. She was against the marriage of very young girls. She was not against marriage in general but against early marriage. You know, education – that was the major concern of my family. Just imagine. They didn't let me take the entrance exam for the sixth form because I was too young, they said. At the last minute, the principal opposed it. So that I wouldn't lose time, my uncle presented me as a free candidate for the primary school certificate. For three months my uncle sent me to a vacation camp at Ifrane, and on my return, he presented me as a free candidate for admission to the sixth form. Moreover, I got in. My uncle was so happy that he wanted to encourage me, and so he bought me a bicycle, a watch, and a lot of other gadgets. It was education that was the most important thing in life, you see. However, between you and me, I was not very, very talented.

Q: *And what about boys? Dressing up?*

A: Nothing about boys.

Q: *No boyfriends?*

A: No boyfriends. But dressing up! In the whole family, we were the ones who had the least money, but on holidays we were the best dressed. We had to buy our fabric in the market, not expensive stuff, but we would do it up, put trimmings on it. I don't know how my mother managed, but I always had very pretty ribbons in a rainbow of colours and handmade trimmings. She had very good taste. She chose very pretty fabrics, and, although she could sew well, she preferred to have our clothes made by a dressmaker. You know, by watching her take care of these things, I myself learned how to do it. I know now that if I felt like sewing or decorating an outfit, I could do it, but I would have to have the time available to do it.

Q: *Do you remember going to the Turkish bath?*

A: Oh yes. I liked that a lot. When I was a child, all the children arranged to go to the Turkish bath on the same day – the whole class would go. And the bath! It was a lark, a party, so much fun! We used to slip and slide and watch people getting dressed. It was a real treat!

Q: *When you were at boarding school, that is, when you were a student, did you use to go out?*

A: No, no going out at the weekend.

Q: *And boys? Surprise parties?*[12] *At boarding school, you used to listen to love songs and read poems, didn't you?*

A: Boys! There were little notes signed by initials. But I didn't get involved in those things. I was too busy with my studies. For example, I was not satisfied with just being on the honour roll. I had to be at the top. It was a problem for me. I wasn't really a swot; I was more the relaxed type. I never managed to memorise, to recite the lessons. I was very good at maths courses, I was first in all of them. But you couldn't find in my notebooks what the prof had dictated – never. I spent my time reading the encyclopedia of geography or any other encyclopedia. I also spent a lot of time with my friends, because I had many. I established close contact with people very quickly. For example, the girls easily confided in me. It was like living life through others. Do you understand? The door of the boarding school was always closed for me. So I fell back on the experiences of others. I took advantage of it. I put myself in their place when they confided in me.

Q: *What are your projects for the future? Do you have a precise idea of what you want to become?*

A: No, I don't have a very precise goal. I am not the sort of person who repeats to herself from the age of ten: 'I want to be a lawyer'; or 'I have to become rich.' No, I have never gone in for that kind of talk. I rather adapt myself to circumstances, to situations. I am just as much at ease among poor people as among very rich people. It's because I have known both extremes.

Q: *And romance, love, did you dream about that?*

A: That didn't happen until my graduation year. There were some students from Marrakech who were already at the university in Rabat. They used to return to Marrakech for holidays; they were also working there during the holidays. It was at that time that I met a boy. He worked with my sister. They were friends at work. We met at a surprise party organised by a girl who was celebrating her graduation. I thought that it was a party just for girls. As I hadn't lived in Marrakech for a long time, I wasn't up on the latest fads. However, it was a surprise party. At first, I refused to go in. I was accompanied by a cousin and I asked her to leave with me. I was annoyed. For me, going to a surprise party was crossing into the new world.

Q: *Did you know how to dance?*

A: But of course I knew how to dance. At boarding school we danced all the time. But it was girls dancing together. It wasn't dancing itself that bothered me–I had always danced and I still dance. No, it was the fact that it was a mixed party. I felt guilty toward my family. When I got home, I told my family that the surprise party had been mixed. And Mama started off by saying: 'But they should have told you that it was a surprise party!' And my sister went one better with 'Now that's it! If you begin going to such affairs, you will be labelled', and so on and so on. It was a big scene.

Q: *In the end, did you dance at that unexpected surprise party?*

A: No, I didn't dance. I didn't budge. [Laughter.] I kept saying I didn't know how to dance. I was very shy. My cousin who accompanied me was very relaxed. Every time somebody came to ask me to dance, I hid. Afterwards I went home. Two or three weeks later the girls came to ask me what I thought about the party. I told them I didn't like parties like that. 'Perhaps you didn't like it because there were too many people. We are going to have a small party, and you can choose the people you want invited.' So they organised a little party, and it was then that I met this boy. At first, he came over to talk to me, but he had nothing to say to me. Nothing at all. [Laughter.] Afterwards I went back to school in Rabat. Later a girl from Marrakech came to Rabat. The boy in question was in her brother's group of friends, and that was how we began to meet each other socially, to go out in a group. Sometimes we travelled together, always in a group.

Q: *No kisses? Didn't you ever hold hands?*

A: No, no, nothing. It was friendship. Besides, I was very impressed by his behaviour. I managed to forget that boys were 'wild', were 'terrors'. I was very impressed to see him so polite, so courteous; after a time you become trusting. [Laughter.]

Q: *Afterwards, how did it turn out?*

87

A: It was strange. It was a book that started things. The book was *La foire au cancres*. We were passing it around from hand to hand. Then, one fine day, the day before my departure for Marrakech on vacation, this friend came to fetch the book and made me a declaration of love. He was serious. I was a little bit prepared for it, because he was a very reserved, timid person who didn't talk just for the sake of talking. He didn't talk to just anybody. He didn't have the courage to speak out, and he was too nice with me for it not to be sincere.

Q: *How did you receive this declaration of love? Did it please you? Were you proud of it?*

A: For me . . . I was not particularly happy. I was used to stuff like that. [Laughter.]

Q: *Wasn't it something to tell to your friends with pride?*

A: No, on the contrary. I thought myself different from the other girls. I thought I was exceptional. And now I realised that I wasn't any different.

Q: *What do you mean? Did the question of beauty bother you?*

A: No, not at all. 'Beauty' never posed any problem for me. I always thought there were more important things than physical beauty. There are some good-looking people whom I don't like.

Q: *When you were a girl, didn't the question of beauty come up in your life? In my experience, I have the impression, in the circle that I have lived in, that for a girl there is only one single value – beauty. The girls of the family are graded according to that. It is the aim and frame of reference in the life of a woman.*

A: It was different in my circle. You never talked about a person's physical attributes. The important thing was seriousness about work. Moreover, they used to call me *al-awra*, because I had a squint. [Laughter.] The important thing was your work. My sister worked hard. For her primary school exams, she stayed up all night studying. I was not taken so seriously because I spent much less time on my books. When I came home at noon, I would ask for something to eat and I would eat enough for ten people. My mother used to say to me: 'I am amazed that you pass. The prospect of exams doesn't seem to worry you.' In our neighbourhood, there were a lot of Europeans. I used to spend my time bowling or bicycling. I never opened a book to revise. This was the reason they didn't take me seriously. When I was a boarder and only came home for vacations, they thought I never made enough effort, that I was always taking it easy. My mother didn't realise how much work I did. I never talked to her about my problems.

Q: *Never?*
A: I settled them by myself. She came to believe that I had a life without problems. I never spoke to the family about my worries because I knew they couldn't help me. It wasn't worth it to trouble them with the problems I was facing. I always tried to deal with my problems by myself.

Q: *And friendships? Couldn't you count on your friends?*
A: Not very much. In the end I found that friendship is fleeting. You can confide in your friends, but you have to know how far to go, because, if you don't, if you go too far, it always falls apart – or almost always. It is as if friendship doesn't survive problems. You know, I have a friend whom I know I can count on if I run into a problem, but I try to turn to her as little as possible, to count on no one but myself as much as possible. I do this, knowing that there are a lot of people who would help me if I had some problem.

Q: *Did you share your romantic, emotional problems with your friends? You still didn't tell me about that boy you met in your final year.*
A: That has lasted eight years! [Laughter.] I haven't got to know any other boys.

Q: *Do you love him?*
A: Yes. It began very slowly. You know, he is still a student.

Q: *Do you see each other often? Do you expect to live together?*
A: We see each other very often. As to living together, that is for the future. I don't know. You know, in eight years a lot of things have happened, and I have learned a lot of things. I don't regret letting myself get involved in this relationship. There have been difficulties, there have been times of tension.

Q: *He isn't jealous, is he, by chance?*
A: The gentleman is very jealous. But he can do what he likes, go out with other girls, because the gentleman is a man.

Q: *Would you want to marry him?*
A: No. Not for the time being.

Q: *Does he come and tell you about what he does with other girls?*
A: Yes.

Q: *Does he consider that normal?*
A: Yes, he considers it normal. He justifies it by the fact that up to the age of twenty he hadn't known any girls.

Q: *Did he go to brothels, as is commonly done?*

A: He was in boarding school, tightly controlled by the institution's codes and rules, but who knows? I have never tried to find out in detail.

5

Dawiya al-Filaliya and her daughters Latifa and Malika: a proletariat dreaming of humane factories

Dawiya al-Filaliya, born in 1913 in the Ksar es Souk region, was married at nine years old, according to the traditions of the area. She had her first child with her first period. But in the Morocco of the 1920s, the young girls of southern Morocco underwent some extraordinary experiences which neither tradition nor men had ever spoken to them about. Dawiya migrated, under the guidance of her mother, to the north. Her infant daughter under her arm, she went to work as an agricultural labourer in the market gardens around Salé. Later she tried to find work as a cleaning woman to be closer to her daughters, who were apprenticed to a *mu'allima* to learn carpet-making. She finished her work career in a spinning mill in Salé, while her daughters made their way to the carpet factories and workshops in the capital, and finally to their own workshop at home.

While Latifa, born in 1952, and Malika, born in 1954, were asking in astonishment why they had not had the right to the schooling, the training, and the advancement that the nationalists and officials of independent Morocco had emphasised, in Rabat people were drawing up, as the plan for the future, a return to authenticity, to tradition – a tradition which, apparently, no longer existed except in the fantasies of the planners.

Dawiya al-Filaliya

Leaving the countryside, early marriage, and divorce

Q: *Where were you born?*
A: In the Ksar es Souk region. My father was a peasant. We had our own

land. We had olive trees, date palms; we harvested the crops; we didn't lack anything. We had sheep and cows, and our house was very nice. I had five brothers and sisters. I was the oldest. The ones born before me all died.

Q: *How many children did your mother have in all, counting the ones who died?*

A: Twelve, but only five survived. I am the oldest. There were two girls and two boys after me. I was married at nine years old.

Q: *In the same region where you were born?*

A: Yes.

Q: *What did your husband do?*

A: He was also a peasant. He had his land and his olive trees.

Q: *What work did you do before your marriage?*

A: Nothing at all. I used to prepare some couscous, some soup. That's all we children did at my house. Nothing else, no carpet-making, no work with wool. It was the *ma'rabta* who did that.

Q: *Who are the* ma'rabta?

A: The *sharifas*; they carded the wool and wove it. All we did was eat and amuse ourselves. We waited for the meals to be ready to go and eat. Nowadays children go to school, but at that time we knew nothing about anything like that. Then later I began to work with my mother. I earned half a duro, which I gave to her. My little earnings helped her feed, clothe, and buy shoes for us. At that time, women got work by going to the *moquf*.

Q: *Did you also go to the* moquf?

A: Yes, I went.

Q: *And what work did you do?*

A: I stayed at the *moquf* with the other women until the proprietor of the *sania*[1] came to fetch us when he had work. When we got back from work, when the sun was almost down, we had to begin to do the cooking and make the bread. We ate what there was and saved some to take to work the next day. Then my mother married me off for the second time.

Q: *What happened to your first husband?*

A: My mother separated me from him.

Q: *How did she separate you from him.?*

A: She took me with her to Rabat. I had already had my first daughter, Aisha. My husband was working in Meknes.

Q: *Didn't your husband follow you to Rabat?*

A: No.

Q: *Why not?*

A: My mother vowed that I would not go back to live with him any more.

Q: *Why did she decide to do that?*

A: She was a very hard woman. As he had not come to offer condolences on the death of my father, she whisked her daughter away! She got her revenge on him.

Q: *Did she get a divorce for you?*

A: She got it, and legally, without my knowing about it.

Q: *And did your husband want a divorce or not?*

A: There was nothing he could do from the moment that she no longer wanted to see us together. So just as she had done with my marriage, she came and announced my divorce to me. 'That's fine', I told her.

Q: *Why? Didn't you love him?*

A: And even if I did love him, do you think that I could have said so to her? We didn't talk about that kind of thing in our family. I couldn't ask her why she had done what she did, nor tell her that I loved him or didn't love him. I stayed with her, and worked sometimes with her and sometimes with the other women, until the death of my father. It happened when he had finished harvesting on some other land that he owned and was on his way home. The vehicle he was travelling in overturned. We only found out about it two weeks later. We got a letter from the family with the news of my father's death. My mother, my uncle, and my cousin went there right away. I had just given birth to Aisha.

Q: *Was she from your first or second marriage?*

A: From my first marriage, of course.

Q: *You had two children with him then?*

A: I had a first child who died. I was eleven years old and got pregnant right away. The first one died. I was too young to bring up a child.

Q: *Was your husband there when you were pregnant?*

A: Yes, he was with me then. I was six months pregnant when I was divorced. I gave birth to the baby on the same day that the news of my father's death arrived. What an unforgettable day that was! My mother left with my grandmother, who was still alive at that time, and my uncle accompanied them to the country. When she got back, my husband wanted me to return to him, but my mother wouldn't hear of it. [2]

Q: *And your husband accepted your mother's decision?*

A: [Silence.]

Q: *And why was she so determined that you should separate from him?*

A: She was a very hard woman. She didn't want to hear any more about it. I waited three or four years. My brother, and then my sister, got married. I refused all those who came to ask for my hand – until the day that I married the one who was to be the father of my daughters.

Second marriage: no more work outside the home for Dawiya

Q: *How did you get to know your second husband?*
A: It was his sister who acted as the go-between. She knew my mother and was determined that I should become the wife of her brother, who was a widower. At first my mother refused. 'I don't want my daughter mistreated by a man', she told her. 'And besides she has a daughter.' In the end we got married. We used to argue because he didn't want me to work outside the home. I told him he was wrong, that all women worked. His unfailing answer was: 'As long as I live, I don't want you to work.'
Q: *He didn't let you work?*
A: No.
Q: *What work did he do?*
A: He worked in the market gardens of Salé.
Q: *He earned enough at that for you to live?*
A: Oh, yes. We lived very well.
Q: *And you didn't like it that he kept you from working?*
A: No, I didn't like it at all.
Q: *And why were you so bent on working?*
A: It allowed me to get out of the house, to meet people, to have some fun with them. I used to work just in the mornings, not like nowadays when you work until nightfall. So I used to have plenty of time to do things at home, just as if I didn't work outside. But when I remarried, my husband didn't want me to work any longer. I stayed at home to take care of my children and the laundry. He brought home everything that we needed: meat, vegetables. I had everything I needed. Every time I had a baby, we celebrated the *saba'a*.
Q: *How many children did you have?*
A: In all, I had seven.
Q: *All living?*
A: No, only four survived. Afterwards, I went through some hard times. My husband was hit by a car; his leg was broken and he stayed a long time in the Souissi hospital.[3] I went all the time to visit him. All my savings and my jewels were spent on that.

Q: *And what did you do when he died?*

A: I began to do housework. Sometimes I worked the whole day.

Q: *Did you still go to the* moquf *to get hired?*

A: No, I worked for people I knew.

Q: *And did you work every day?*

A: That depended. Sometimes it was for a week, sometimes just for a day. I had to leave Zainab with some people who adopted her. And then they proposed that I should work for them. I did the washing, the cooking, the floors; but they always told me that if I found a better job, I could go to it during the day and come back to spend the night at their place.

Q: *And who were the other children with?*

A: They were with my mother and my grandmother.

Q: *And didn't your mother work?*

A: Yes, she did.

Q: *Where?*

A: In houses – the houses of the country people in Tabriket. She always worked for them.

The insurance money

She didn't work for anybody else. She milked the cows and also did the housework. Sometimes she also went to work in the market gardens, or even to do housework for someone all day and come back at night. About this time we no longer had to pay rent. My mother should have received the insurance money for my father's car accident. But the government didn't give it all to her. She got 10,000 francs. [4] For the *'Id* [religious holiday] we bought a sheep, like everybody. My mother went to see the *qadi*. She told him: 'I have some fatherless children. I want to go back to the country and buy a piece of land or a house. I would know what to buy there.' 'I would very much like to give you what is due you', the *qadi* replied, 'but I want to be certain that your brothers don't take it all away from you.' 'My brothers are all for me. I want to be with them. I want to give the power of attorney to them', she replied. Finally they settled the question of the power of attorney. A *wakil* was appointed. Every Friday they went with him to the auctions where houses were sold. At that time there were no house agents. People went to an area near the great mosque and announced the price of houses: such and such a house in such and such a neighbourhood, you heard them calling. At the end of the auction, you asked to see the house, you visited it, and if you didn't like it, you went back to the auction. People began telling us that the *wakil* was going to take all the money. So my mother went to see him. When he saw her, he received her saying, 'You have come, daughter of Mulay Ali Sharif.' 'Yes, I have come', she replied. 'I am going to find a house for you that you will like this very day.' He accompanied us to look at one. When we arrived at the house, he asked my mother to knock on the door. When it was opened, he asked the people to let my mother visit her future house. The proprietor had just repainted the whole house because he was expecting to celebrate a wedding there. As they went out, the *wakil* turned to my mother and asked: 'Well, daughter of Mulay Ali Sharif, do you like the house?' My mother told him to decide: 'I am not from here; I don't know what to buy or to sell. I will be fine where you decide to install me.' 'You will be fine here', he said. 'You and your children. And moreover, it is a neighbourhood where there are only people of good family. You have nothing to fear.' They bought the house, and we no longer had to pay rent. What we were paid at the end of the day could be used to live on. Then my mother gave my sister in marriage to someone in the country.

Q: *Which of your sisters?*

A: Khaira. She married a cousin of Beni Hassan, but she couldn't stand life in the country. 'If you don't want to stay in the country,' my mother told her, 'you can come right back to us in the city.' And so she in turn got divorced. We lived together a good long time before I remarried.

Q: *Did your sister also work?*

A: Yes, as a cleaning woman, she too. We were cleaning women.

Factory life

Q: *How did you begin to work in a factory?*

A: There was a *sharif* who came to see us. It was the day of the feast of the Prophet's birthday, and we chatted with each other. At that time, my two daughters, Latifa and Malika, were already working in the factory.

Q: *At what age did they begin working?*

A: At six or seven they were working with Mu'allima Fatna. She didn't pay them. The important thing for me was that they learn a trade. I took responsibility for providing for their food and clothing. With the aid of another woman, I worked at preparing semolina for couscous. The boss gave us a quintal of farina and we worked the whole night.

Q: *Where did you prepare the semolina? At your house?*

A: No, at the house of the factory boss. We spent the night preparing semolina. We steam-cooked it, put it out to dry, and in the morning the boss took it to sell in the stores. I worked at this to earn the money for my daughters' clothes, and their father took care of the rest.

Q: *Did you begin to work during the life of your second husband?*

A: When I began to work at preparing the semolina, he said to me, 'As long as it is a house where you are working and not outside, that's all right.' We were a team of four women: two for preparing the semolina and two for cooking it. So I continued to work with these women until the *sharif* whom I spoke about came to visit us on the day of the feast of the Prophet's birthday. We talked a while, and he asked me where I was working. I answered that I had been doing house-cleaning in people's houses up until now and that I hadn't found better work. Then he asked me if I would like to work in the spinning mill. I told him yes. He said he would go and try to find work for me. Three days later he came back with a job for me. I went to the factory where I found a Frenchman; a Moroccan manager said to him: 'Here is the woman I spoke to you about.' The Frenchman told me to come back the next day. At eight o'clock the next morning, I reported to the foreman and he assigned me to the washing tubs: 'Just watch how the other women do it and do the same.' They gave me an apron and I set to work. I stayed there until the day they told me I didn't have to work all the time at the washing tubs and said I should move onto the machines. So then I learned to work at the machines.

Q: *How long have you been working in that factory?*

A: About six years.

Q: *Do you like factory work?*

A: Yes.

Q: *Do you work in the day or at night?*

A: One week I work in the day. I go to work at eight in the morning and get out at seven in the evening.

Q: *Do you go there alone?*

A: No, with the other women. We take our food with us. We work until noon and then start again at two o'clock.

Q: *Do they serve you something to eat at the factory?*

A: No! We take everything ourselves.

Q: *Do you make tea?*

A: We have a hot plate at the factory.

Q: *What do you take to eat?*
A: Cooked meat with sauce in a container. We heat it up on the spot. We eat in groups.
Q: *Do you take turns bringing the food?*
A: No. Each one brings her own, and we share everything. There is a lot of variety and each one eats with her friends.
Q: *How many friends do you have?*
A: Four.
Q: *How long have you known them?*
A: Six years.
Q: *Are they older or younger than you?*
A: They are all ages.
Q: *Are they married?*
A: They are all widows like me. There is one, the youngest, who is also a widow, but who is not a good person.
Q: *How is she not good?*
A: She works at the factory, but she also goes around with good-for-nothing types.
Q: *How is that?*
A: She works at the factory and afterwards goes looking for pick-ups. One Thursday, when we were working at night, they came looking for her at two a.m.
Q: *Right at the factory?*
A: The guard asked them what they wanted. 'We want Sa'diya', they answered, 'her mother is dying.' In fact, they were just looking for her. The guard very nearly reported it to the boss, but we begged him not to say anything, because she has a whole family to feed and she is the only one working.
Q: *And did you say anything to her?*
A: What would you want me to say? She is working for her family.

Life in the factory: workers' solidarity; wages; unions; pay

Q: *Why do you like work in the factory?*
A: Because we women have a lot of fun together.
Q: *Are there only women in that factory?*
A: There is one whole section for women and another for men.
Q: *And when you are ill, do they help you out a little?*
A: When I am ill or worn out, they hide me in the piles of wool to be washed, to keep the foreman from knowing what's going on.

Q: *They hide you?*

A: Yes. We do the work of the one who is unwell and hide her in the middle of the wool; you can only see her head. The foreman is a nice man anyway.

Q: *Does he also help you?*

A: Yes. He doesn't want any problems with the women workers. When he wants to go out, he tells us: 'Arrange things among yourselves but see that the boss and the manager don't know anything about it. I am just one of you.' So one of us tries to do the work of the one who is unwell. If she is very ill, the boss takes her to the doctor.

Q: *Do you have a doctor at the factory?*

A: No, outside, but the factory pays. But only for the trip to the doctor. We have to pay for the medicines ourselves.

Q: *How many days holiday do you get?*

A: We can ask for two weeks if we want to. Now we no longer get a holiday. We get a few days for the feast of the sacrifice.

Q: *How much money do you get for the feast of the Prophet's birthday?*

A: We get 350 dirhams.

Q: *How many hours do you work a day?*

A: I earn 1.40 dirhams an hour.

Q: *What hours do you work?*

A: From eight a.m. to noon and then from two to six p.m.

Q: *Those are the hours of the day shift, but what are the hours of the night shift?*

A: From six p.m. to four a.m., with a break from ten to eleven. I say four a.m., but if the guard is a good guy, we stop a little early in order to sleep a bit at the factory.

Q: *What time do you leave the factory?*

A: At six a.m.

Q: *They let you sleep if you finish early?*

A: Yes.

Q: *And so where do you sleep?*

A: Well, in the wool, like sheep. We make jokes until we fall asleep.

Q: *Are the workers nice?*

A: Very nice. There isn't a single one who isn't nice.

Q: *You never have any arguments?*

A: Yes, there are some arguments, some insults. Some people throw around epithets like 'whore' and so forth. But others try to intervene to re-establish peace.

Q: *How many hours do you work a week?*

A: Twenty-eight hours.

Q: *How much do you get a day?*

A: I get 8.8 dirhams a day.

Q: *Do they pay you once a week or every two weeks?*

A: Every two weeks.

Q: *And if you are ill? If a woman is pregnant?*

A: She has sick leave.

Q: *How much?*

A: That depends on what work she does.

Q: *And how much do women get paid these days?*

A: There are some who get 400 dirhams and others who get 350 dirhams. That is, if they get their pay in a lump sum once a month.

Q: *And what about those who have children?*

A: Those who have children, like my daughter, for example, get nothing extra for their children.

Q: *And for retirement?*

A: I don't think there is any pension. When you stop working, you get 1,000 dirhams. [5]

Q: *And don't you demand your rights?*

A: We demanded our rights and made a big ruckus in the factory. Some people even armed themselves with sticks, but we didn't get anything.

Q: *And the union?*

A: I never joined a union; I don't even know how it operates.

Q: *Why?*

A: Because I was new at the factory and I didn't know what you have to do. We are ten in my group.

Q: *And why didn't you act together?*

A: We didn't know if it would result in something or not.

Q: *Who goes to union meetings?*

A: Some women and some men. People from Zemmour.

Q: *People from Zemmour?*

A: All those who work in this factory come from Zemmour. It is they who sowed the seeds of trouble. They slandered the foreman, saying he had stolen a carpet. It was a real free-for-all. The police intervened. Some killed each other, others fled.

Q: *Were some people fired?*

A: Yes, and some were even imprisoned – as much as a year and half for five people.

100

Q: *Men or women?*

A: Men. As for the women, four were laid off for a month.

Q: *Young people?*

A: Yes, some young people.

Q: *Are the union meetings held in the factory itself or outside?*

A: Outside. They can't hold meetings in the factory; they are afraid of the boss. The boss told them: 'If you had informed me and asked my advice, I would have been with you, and you would have been given your rights. But since you wanted to break everything up, go and see the government. I will put into effect what they decide.' And since then there has been no more union, no more anything.

Q: *When did all that happen?*

A: Four years ago.

Q: *And for the First of May International Workers' Day, what do you do?*

A: We drape the portrait of the king with flags; we prepare tea and cakes. Everybody is happy; everybody has a good time and jokes around. We play the tambourine and they bring musicians. Everybody has a good time. It goes on all day.

Q: *Don't you go to the procession?*

A: One time our manager ordered a bus and took us to the Tuareg quarter,[6] to present us to the king. There was singing and dancing.

Q: *As far as work goes, is there a difference between the younger workers and those who have been longer at the factory?*

A: No, in terms of work, there is no difference. But we, the older ones, work more than the others, while they spend most of their time joking and having fun.

Q: *In your opinion, should a woman work or not?*

A: In my opinion, they can have women's work! It would be better if a woman works in her own house, except if she has no other choice. Especially in the factory, young girls . . . If at least they had a good job . . . But the factory is not good. There are a lot of no-goods who mistreat young girls.

Q: *Oh, yes?*

A: Yes.

Q: *And when you go to work at night, does someone accompany you?*

A: I go early, around five in the afternoon. I meet up with another woman who lives on the same street as the factory. It is still daylight when we arrive. We wait at the factory gate until six.

Q: *And at night? Do you go out at night?*
A: No, I never go out at night.
Q: *Doesn't anybody leave work while it's still night?*
A: No. Those who finish their work sleep until five a.m. And then it's already daylight when they leave the factory.

Injuries on the job

Q: *There is something wrong with your feet. One might say . . .*
A: There was nothing wrong with my feet until I began working. But the hot water, the soap, and sodium damaged them. We used hot water; the floor was hot, and I used to flounder around in hot water and soap and sodium. My feet were reduced to pulp.
Q: *Didn't you put something on – medicine or salve?*
A: We just put on mercurochrome – that's all. My feet were all red from it. That went on until we went to speak to the manager: 'If you please, our feet are in terrible shape. We need some shoes; we can't work like this.' So he came and asked each one her shoe size. Some were size 40, others 41. When it was my turn, I was embarrassed, because I have tiny feet, size 34. I could not bring myself to say that, so I said, 'I have very large feet – size 35'. He began to laugh. 'Where do you think we can find size 35?' 'I told you 35, but I only wear size 34.' He went on laughing. 'Work it out for yourself', I told him. They brought them to us the next morning.
Q: *And what did they bring you?*
A: Boots, and each one of us put hers on. They came up to here. He gave me a pair of boots and asked me to try them on. It was the right size. What did they expect to happen to your feet in that hot mash before they gave us boots? It was only yesterday we got them. We put them on. You should have seen us! We looked like shepherds.

Dawiya's daughters

Q: *There is one thing you didn't tell me about: why didn't you send your daughters to school?*
A: My daughters – that's a long story! For example, Zainab, the oldest: I wanted very much for her to go to school. I placed her with some people on the condition that they enrol her in school. The lady I left her with told me: 'You have two daughters. Leave one at my house, so that no harm will come to her.' I was afraid; I feared an evil spell. They were Alawite

sharifs, supposedly descendants of the Prophet. And then I had already lost three daughters. Death was stalking me. I repeated to her that I wanted my daughter Zainab to go to school. She replied to me: 'I am ready to raise her and send her to school.' And at the beginning, she did go to school. Later, the lady's husband used to go on a lot of trips (he was an inspector). I was afraid that Zainab was not going to school. The lady reassured me, but I turned to Zainab and said to her: 'Listen, my daughter, come with us. Your father doesn't want you to stay with these people.' But she wanted to stay with the lady who was raising her. 'It's she who is my mother', she said. So she stayed with them and didn't go to school at all. She did the housework for them – that's all. That's what happened to Zainab. It's another story with Latifa. She was six years old, and I had just put her in school. At that time, I was doing housework for Lalla Fatima of one of the big families of Salé. One day she told me to leave Latifa with her, saying she would see to her schooling. I agreed. She took her to school and registered her, because she was the principal of the school. She used to take her to school and bring her back, while I was working.

Q: *Who were you working for?*

A: For her. She was very good to me. Latifa went to school for two years. Then I fell ill and was unable to work for two months. 'Keep the house key', she told me. 'You will come back when you are better.' She took Latifa to school with her and did the housework herself. One day the husband of her niece, who lived in Rabat, proposed that I let him take Latifa to his house and he would send her to school in Rabat. I agreed. I said to him: 'You are an educated man. You will know how to supervise her studies. I am happy for her to go to Rabat.' But then he separated from his wife, and I took my daughter back. When she came back to me, she no longer wanted to go to school.

Q: *Why?*

A: She didn't have a head for studying. She didn't do well and her cousins made fun of her. She didn't want to hear any more about school, and so I looked for work for her. And that's why she never finished school. As for Malika, the last child, I never enrolled her in school.

Q: *You never put her in school?*

A: Never.

Q: *Why?*

A: She never had that opportunity. I didn't know that it was important for her to go to school. I didn't think it would help her find a job. I told myself that it was more valuable for her to learn a trade. I thought there was nothing better than mastering a trade.

Q: *Do you still think the same?*

A: No. Now I have changed my mind. I know the value of an education now. I am not as foolish as before.

Q: *Do you think that getting an education is important for a girl?*

A: Oh, yes. A girl who has an education is somebody. A trade is also useful, but an education is more important.

Future prospects

Q: *Do you intend to continue working?*

A: What would you want me to do? I have to work in order to eat. I have neither a son nor a husband who can work for me. I have only God. So I am condemned to work.

Q: *Don't you believe you could get a pension?*

A: I don't think so. I haven't worked long enough at the factory. Barely six years. Perhaps I started too late in life. If I had been working for ten or twenty years, but six years, what are they going to give me for that?

Q: *Are there women who have been working for twenty years in your factory?*

A: Oh, yes, there are some.

Q: *Do they have a pension plan?*

A: No. They have just received their work card. We are in the same situation. Previously one went to look for work for three and a half francs per day.

Q: *Is there a difference in wages among you?*

A: No, none. Nobody gets more than anybody else, except for those who work in the washing tubs. They get a little more.

Q: *And are there trucks that bring you to work and take you home?*

A: Only for the women who live far away. There are trucks that bring them and take them home. There are three or four that take them to Chellah and Bettana.[7] And there are some that come from Sidi Moussa near Salé.

Q: *And what did your sisters become?*

A: The one that has children works as a cook – for parties. She has a lot of mouths to feed. She is a very good cook and works at the houses of rich people.

Q: *In your opinion, if the government were to do something for all those women who have children and who work outside the home, what would be the most useful?*

A: I would ask them to help us by giving us flour and oil. It's that sort of thing that the poor need: clothes, flour, oil, sugar, soap. That's the most important thing for a poor person.

Q: *Does your sister live with you?*

A: No, she lives alone.

Q: *In a rented house?*

A: Yes, a house that she has rented for a very long time. She has six or seven rooms.

Q: *Do you ever return to the country from time to time?*

A: I went back only once.

Q: *That's all?*

A: Just once. My parents were still alive. They did everything for the boys, but the girls counted for nothing with them.

Q: *Why?*

A: My mother told us that we, the girls, since we never came to the country, should leave the ownership of the land to our brother, and he would cede the ownership of the house to us. 'Don't do such a thing', I told her. But she wouldn't listen.

Q: *And then?*

A: And then we agreed. We ceded everything to our brother and he allowed us the house. But my mother remained there with us like 'Joha's nail'. [8] She got the better of us, because she kept her share of both the house and the land.

Q: *And where does she live now?*

A: She is with me.

Q: *She doesn't work?*

A: No, she is too old. She is in the process of getting false teeth. But she still holds up very well and still makes all family decisions.

Q: *Is she still able to go to the country?*

A: No, she is no longer able to go there as often. But not too long ago, she went to get some dates and oil. She helps us a lot.

Latifa and Malika [9]

At the mu'allima

Q: *Let's start at the time that you went to the* mu'allima.

A: I was eleven years old and my sister Malika nine, when we began going to the *mu'allima*.

Q: *What did you do before that?*

A: I went to the *msid* and my sister to the school. [10] I didn't do well, so my mother took me out of school to place me with the *mu'allima*.

Q: *To learn what?*

A: Carpet-making. She put us there so we would learn. It is there that we grew up; we stayed there almost seven years.

Q: *Did the* mu'allima *pay you or did you have to pay to learn?*

A: She didn't pay us for four years. After that, she began to pay us. The first four years were for learning. In fact, we learned very quickly. We didn't take a long time to learn. She wanted to profit from us. It was only afterwards that she began to pay us. She gave us thirty-five dirhams every two weeks.

Q: *Thirty-five dirhams each or for the two of you?*

A: It was seventeen and a half dirhams per week for the two of us. I sent the money to my father. Life was not expensive as it is today; things were much better. Sometimes we asked him to buy us something or other with that money – clothes or something else. My father shared the money with my mother, and it was she who saved it for us. When we needed to spend some, we spent it – for going to the Turkish bath, for example, or for buying a tambourine for the celebration of Ashura or the Prophet's birthday. At each feast day my mother would take us to a shop to choose what we wanted, and she paid for it. We bought dresses or caftans. At that time we were wearing pleated skirts.

[Malika whispers to her sister to tell how they got in an argument with the *hajja*.] [11]

Q: *Why did you have an argument with her?*

A: We began to understand a lot of things, you know. A woman had asked us how much we earned, and she told us that her daughters earned such and such an amount. It was clearly more than we were being given. Nevertheless we continued to work. Then one day the *mu'allima* found fault with my sister and began to insult and hit her. My sister didn't put up with it and insulted her right back.

Q: *What did she say to her exactly?*

A: The *mu'allima* said to Malika: 'Do you think your father has some sort of power over me?' It was not the fact that she hit her that made me mad, but the insults. I didn't wait a minute; I stood up and put on my coat to go out. It was raining. The *mu'allima* was about to go out also. So the other apprentices asked us to stay. It was almost noon. We agreed to stay, out of politeness. We left at one o'clock as usual, without anyone knowing if we were still angry or not. Once we got home, I broke into sobs. My father asked my why I was crying, and I told him the whole story. 'You don't have to go back there any more', he exclaimed. 'That woman goes too far because I let you work at her place; she thinks she can do anything. Don't go there any more.' And that's what we did. In the afternoon her foster sister came to call on us. 'Tell the girls to come back', she said to my father. But he was not satisfied: 'I can't let my daughters go to her place to be showered with insults. My daughters work for her and I get insulted.'

Q: *What did she say in the way of insults?*

A: That our father was not her equal, as a way of saying that he didn't own anything, that he was less than nothing to her. My father was uncompromising: 'My daughters will not go to her place any more.' The *mu'allima* had sent that woman, but told her not to say that it was she who had sent her. We found it out when she said to my father: 'If your daughters go back to the *mu'allima*, they shouldn't let on that I came to see them on her behalf.' My father had heard enough. 'All right', he said, 'if she doesn't even have the courage to acknowledge that it is she who is making the representations and soliciting help in getting my daughters to return to her, too bad! They will not go back. They will find other places to work.' We stayed at home without working for four weeks. One day I bumped into the *mu'allima* in the street. I greeted her and she asked me to come and get our pay, which was still at her place. We went back to work and she began to pay us forty-five dirhams for two weeks.

Q: *You went from thirty-five to forty-five?*

A: She started by giving us one dirham right at the beginning, then fifteen, and finally, after this incident, we got forty-five every two weeks. We knew how to do everything when we began to earn forty-five dirhams. So when she met me that day in the street, she said to me: 'I still have your pay. I am keeping your job open and also that of your sister. Come, both of you, and start again tomorrow morning. Don't go to work somewhere else.' I said, 'All right', but first I had to speak to my father. He was furious: 'My wife will no longer be my wife if you cross the threshold of that house.' My mother intervened, trying to make him understand that being at the *mu'allima*'s house was much better than working in a factory. My mother was not opposed to our returning, but my father persisted in his refusal.

Q: *Did she live very close to you?*

A: Yes, very close.

Q: *Did you eat at her place?*

A: No, we went home to eat. We began work at eight o'clock and went home around twelve-thirty to eat. Then we went back for the afternoon.

Q: *When did you go home in the evening?*

A: We left when we had finished working.

Q: *At what time?*

A: When we had finished working. It could be at two o'clock, or three, or even five, six, seven, eight. When we finished we left.

Q: *Before leaving, did you have to finish the piece of work she had given you to do?*

A: Yes. Each of us had something to do and left once it was done. If you didn't finish it in time, you had to stay – sometimes into the night in order to finish the work given you. And if on a Thursday, for example, you hadn't finished your work, even though you didn't ordinarily work on Friday, you came back on Friday morning to finish it. When I told my father about my meeting with the *mu'allima* in the street, he told me: 'Your aunt lives right close to her. If she wants to settle what she owed you, she can send it through your aunt. Or better still, she can bring it herself. She knows where we live. If you don't go back to her, contact your cousins. They work in a factory; maybe they could get you jobs there with them.' It wasn't a factory, just a house with three looms. [12]

The carpet factory

Q: *How many people work on a loom?*

A: There can be six or even seven, or only four. It depends on the size of the loom. There are big ones and small ones. So we went to see my cousins to look for work. They spoke to their employer. He told us to come, but, as he didn't have a place open for us, we had to work with our cousins on the carpet that they were in the process of making. So we stayed with them.

Q: *How many of you worked on the same carpet?*

A: There were four of them, and with my sister and me that made six, although it was a four-person loom. We had arranged it with our cousins in order to get us into the factory.

Q: *And what about money?*

A: We shared the money, too.

Q: *Were your cousins the same age as you?*

A: Yes, my cousin was the same age as me.

Q: *Were you friends?*

A: No. It was at that time that we became friends. Previously, we had known each other, but we weren't friends. We didn't go out together. In fact, their mother was not my aunt; she was not the sister of my mother but her cousin. We called her our aunt, they called my mother their aunt. When we began to work with them, we stuck together. We passed by to fetch them to go to work, and they did the same. And when we were paid, we were paid together.

Q: *How much did you get?*

A: We got thirty to thirty-five dirhams a week. That was better than the forty-five dirhams for two weeks.

Q: *Double, no?*

A: More. Double thirty dirhams per week would be sixty dirhams for two weeks, and when we got to thirty-five dirhams that made seventy for two weeks. It depended on how much work you did. So we worked there until the man who employed us had to move to Takkadoum. He asked us if we wanted to go work with him in Takkadoum. We had to consult our parents. My father thought it was too far away. Our boss, who had a car, told us that he could take us with him and thus solve the problem of getting there.

Q: *He had a car, but how many employees lived in Salé?*

A: There were only four of us in Salé: my sister, my two cousins, and I. The other girls had decided to look for work somewhere else. We were used to our boss. That was the reason he asked us to continue to work for him. But my father had refused. One day he came to see my father. 'Let Latifa or Malika come to do the housework at my house', he said. 'Take them', my father replied. In the end, it was Malika who went to work for him. But it only lasted a week.

Q: *Why didn't you want to stay at his place, Malika?*

A: I didn't like staying in people's houses.

Q: *Weren't they nice to you?*

A: They were nice, but I couldn't stand living far away from my own home. I just couldn't.

Q: *So you went home?*

A: Yes.

Q: *How did it happen? How did you let him know that you wanted to leave? Did you cry? Did you say something to him? What did you do?*

A: No, I didn't cry, but they noticed that I wasn't happy. So they understood that I wanted to go home.

Q: *So you went home?*

A: The boss asked if I wanted to leave. I told him yes. He paid me at the end of the week and I left. When she got back home [Latifa resumes the story], she found us, my cousins and me, in the process of looking for work again. We went to visit a workshop. We knocked on the door. The *mu'allima* opened it. We told her that we were looking for work. She asked us where we had worked before. 'With so-and-so', we replied. It turned out that she knew our former boss. In short, she showed us around the workshop and we left. That was a Thursday. We stayed at home on Friday, and on Saturday we began work at the new workshop. It was a traditional house that she had turned into a workshop. At the beginning, she wanted to separate us and put each one of us with other girls on different looms.

Q: *Why did she want to separate you?*

A: Because she didn't have a loom available at that moment for the four of us. She had to put us with other girls. But my cousin and I refused. We told her that we had become used to working together at the other factory. He had arranged for the four of us to have a loom together. In the end, we agreed to separate temporarily. They put us with other girls. It gave her the chance to appraise our work. Then she put us together on one loom. She told us: 'You will be three on this loom, and one of you will be on another with other girls.' It was my sister Malika who went on the other loom. The other girls were very nice.

Q: *How did she pay you?*

A: Three dirhams per *tarha*.

Q: *How many* tarha *did you do a week?*

A: That depended on the hours of work that she gave us.

Q: *Well, about how many?*

A: When I did ten *tarha* a week, I made thirty dirhams.

Q: *Did you eat lunch at the workshop?*

A: Yes. We didn't go home. We bought food to eat.

Q: *Did they let you go out?*

A: No, we sent a little girl to do the shopping for us. When she wasn't there, we went and did it ourselves.

Q: *Didn't you have a break or rest period?*

A: No, we worked all the time, but we found a way of talking among ourselves and laughing, and even going over to see some of the other girls.

Q: *Was that possible?*

A: When the *mu'allima* wasn't there, certainly. If she was, no one budged from her place.

Q: *Did the* mu'allima *let you talk among yourselves?*

A: Either you obeyed her or you didn't. If you didn't obey her, you could get up and walk around the workshop or anything else. And as we worked by the *tarha*, you did it at the expense of the finished work, and thus of the money you received.

Q: *But when you were working, you could talk among yourselves? Nobody told you to be quiet?*

A: No, unless there were visitors. If someone was coming to look at the carpets, the *mu'allima* would warn us: 'There is someone coming. Don't talk or fool around.'

Q: *Was the workshop heated in winter or not?*

A: No, nothing like that.

Q: *Could you make tea?*

A: No, we only had it if one of the girls who lived close by was willing to bring some at a mealtime.

Q: *Did she bring tea for everybody or just for herself?*

A: Ah, would she have had the nerve to bring it just for herself while the others were watching her!

Q: *But there were some who did it?*

A: There were some. But there were also some girls who brought a tea-pot and offered tea to everybody. That is, they gave some to the girls who worked on the same loom as they did. But not to the others.

Q: *Were you only friends with those who worked on the same loom with you?*

A: Each one was friends with those who worked with her.

Q: *So you became the friend of those who worked with you. Did you visit their house and they yours?*

A: No, they lived rather far from me. So I met them at their house before going to work, and they did the same.

Q: *You went to work together?*

A: Yes.

Q: *You didn't share other things, like going to the Turkish bath, for example?*

A: No, I didn't go with them.

Q: *And trips?*

A: No, I went on trips with my brother and sister.

Q: *And after working with that* mu'allima, *what happened?*

A: Well, we got into a dispute again. But this time not with her, but with her husband.

Q: *Why?*

A: He didn't pay us on time. He would let it drag on until the end of two weeks. Sometimes he was away on payday. We needed our money to pay our rent and other things. So we used to wait, only to hear the *mu'allima* say that her husband was not back yet or that he hadn't been able to get the money out of the bank, and that we would have to wait until the next day. We didn't like that at all. They didn't hesitate to make us work the whole two weeks, but they made us wait to get our pay.

Speciality weaving

Then one day someone from the same region as my parents came to tell my mother about a factory where we could find work. They were looking for girls who knew how to do speciality weaving. My mother told him that we were already working in a workshop and couldn't go anywhere else. He was ready to help us; he said all you had to do to get hired was show an identity card or evidence of your marital status. That very day we were supposed to get paid. The *mu'allima*'s husband used to pay us every Thursday. This was the day that we had an argument with him.

He asked us to wait for our pay. We waited, all right, but as soon as he paid us, we left the workshop. We went to visit the factory which the friend of the family had mentioned. It was some distance; it was the factory of Sidi B.

Q: *In Salé or Rabat?*

A: In Salé. Actually in Oulja. The man who had told us about it went with us. He saw the manager and asked him to hire us. The manager received us and asked us our marital status. He hired us and we began to work. It was a Monday when we began. No one worked on Sunday.

Q: *Previously hadn't Friday been your day off?*

A: Yes. It was Friday, but the *mu'allima* sometimes gave Saturday or Sunday to those who asked for it. So then we began working in that factory.

Q: *How was it there? Was it different from the preceding workshops?*

A: Yes.

Q: *How was it different?*

A: At this place we brought our lunch, while before we used to go home for lunch when we were not so far away.

Q: *How long did you have for lunch?*

A: Two hours, from noon to two o'clock.

Q: *Was there an area set aside for eating?*

A: No, we ate in the same area where the loom was.

Q: *You didn't leave your loom at all?*

A: Yes. We used to get up. We could heat up our meal. Beginning at eleven o'clock, we lined up to heat up our food. And at noon, those who wanted to go home went, and those who preferred to eat lunch at the factory did so. Since we lived some distance away, we stayed and ate there. My cousin and I took charge of preparing and heating up the food while the others cleared off the loom so that we could eat.

Q: *You ate on it?*

A: No, on the floor. The loom was there, right in front of us. We raised the beam so that we could sit on the floor, on the wool that we were working on. We took the napkin that our bread was wrapped in and put our plate on it.

Q: *And if you wanted to make tea?*

A: Well, we made it. But we ended up by no longer eating at the factory because it took too much time to heat up the food, especially in winter, when it was so cold.

Q: *Why?*

A: There was no heating in a big factory like that.

Q: *How many looms were there in that factory?*

A: Eight or more. The windows looked out on the sea.

Q: *And so?*

A: And so it was very cold. When we were still eating at the factory, my cousin, my sister, and I continued to eat together. We had to line up a long time ahead in order to heat up our food. The girls who went home to eat began to come back while we still hadn't eaten.

Q: *Was there just one bottled-gas burner for everybody?*

A: Yes, just one. So we decided to go home for lunch.

Q: *How long did it take you to get home?*

A: A half hour each way. We left the factory at noon and got home at twelve-thirty.

Q: *Did you walk?*

A: Yes, we walked. There was no public transport at all. Except if you took a taxi. But at that time it cost 1 dirham to 1 dirham 20 for a taxi. That lasted a while, and then we got fed up with that factory, in particular because of the problem of meals in winter. In summer, it was easier. We ate less – fried peppers or fish. We didn't need to heat them up. In winter, it was more difficult.

Q: *Were you paid well?*

A: We earned sixty dirhams a metre.

Q: *And how many metres could you make?*

A: You could barely make one metre. Each person earned sixty dirhams. But it all depended on how many were working on the carpet. On each carpet, there were five workers and each got sixty dirhams. But all five didn't always finish the metre at the same time. But they nevertheless noted down the metre that we had finished. They paid us by the metre, but a little time was still needed to clip the carpet before making the reckoning. [13]

Q: *What did you do with the money you earned?*

A: It was around that time that my father died.

Q: *When was that?*

A: He died when we were still at the workshop of the second *mu'allima*. One day her husband, Abd al-Rahman, decided to pay us less than before.

Q: *Why?*

A: He waited until payday to tell us: 'Now you will get less than before. You will get such and such an amount from now on.' None of us accepted that. It was at that time that my father died and we went to work at the factory afterward.

Q: *Was it there that you began to earn sixty dirhams each? What did you do with that money?*

A: We didn't have to pay a lot of rent at that time, so we lived on the money that we earned.

Q: *Did the house that you lived in belong to you?*

A: No, we were staying at my aunt's house. The rent was not high. We paid thirty-five dirhams a month for two rooms. So we lived on what we earned.

Q: *Who else in the family worked?*

A: My sister Malika and I were the two who worked.

Q: *And your sister Zainab?*

A: Zainab was still not living with us.

Q: *Where was she?*

A: She was living with the woman who brought her up.

Q: *But there was also your mother who worked and brought in money.*

A: Only sometimes, because she didn't work all the time. Most of the load rested on the two of us.

Q: *Who took care of the household budget?*

A: My mother did the shopping at that time. We gave her what we earned, keeping only ten to fourteen dirhams for ourselves.

Q: *To use for what?*

A: For going to the movies and going out.

Q: *What happened after you moved?*

A: We moved just after the death of my father. My grandmother came to our house. She said to my mother: 'Come and live with me; you won't have to pay rent any longer.' I must admit that we also wanted to move. The house we were living in was very old. My grandmother's was nicer, so we went to live with her.

Q: *Does your grandmother still live with you?*

A: Yes, she lives with us. It's a house that she inherited but she is not the sole heir.

Q: *Is that the house where you celebrated Zainab's engagement?*

A: Yes. It was my grandmother's house where you came for Zainab's engagement party. We had the large room. The little room was my grandmother's, and the corner room was my aunt's. They divided up the other rooms of the house by private agreement, without having recourse to the court. Finally, my grandmother rented out her little room for thirty-five dirhams a month and moved in with us in our large room. She ate with us. Sometimes she gave us the thirty-five dirhams, and sometimes she kept it for her son when he came from the country, or sometimes she even used it to pay for a trip to the country to visit him.

Q: *Did she still have a son in the country?*

A: Yes. She bought him clothes and travelled by bus with everybody else. When she wasn't out of town, she lived with us and ate with us. At the end, she played a trick on us.

Q: *How did she play a trick on you?*

A: She never stopped arguing with us, telling us that we had lived in a hovel before, and that, thanks to her, we now lived in a beautiful house. She ended up by throwing us out, and we had to find another place to live. And that's where we are living now.

Q: *How high is the rent there?*

A: We pay 180 dirhams plus water and electricity; it comes to about 200 dirhams.

Q: *How many rooms do you have?*

A: Two rooms and a kitchen.

Q: *And where do you put the loom?*

A: In the small room.

Q: *You live in one room and work in the other?*

A: Yes. We live in one room and work in the other. There are only three of us; there's no noise or anything.

Q: *After you moved, you didn't go back to the factory?*

A: No. We quit the factory and began to work at home.

Q: *Why?*

A: As a matter of fact, the only reason we moved was to be able to work at home. The house we were living in before was an old house and had more than one floor. We weren't able to work there. So when our grandmother proposed that we live with her, that suited us for working as well. It was better for us to work at home, and besides we were fed up with the whole business of travelling to the factory

Q: *What is the difference between working in the factory and working at home?*

A: At a factory, everything depends on what the *mu'allima* is like. There are some who don't create too many problems about the schedule. But others won't listen to you and insist that you arrive and depart on time. It doesn't matter if you have guests or other matters to attend to. They make a scene every time you arrive late. At home, there is no one to force you to work. If you don't want to work, you can take it easy.

Q: *How many of you work on your loom?*

A: It is a loom for three or four persons, but there are only two of us working on it at the moment.

Q: *Your cousins don't work with you?*

A: No. We are alone, my sister and I, since we began working at home. My cousins have their own set-up as well.

Q: *Did they make the same arrangements as you?*

A: Yes, and the same person who sends us work also gives them work.

Q: *Does that person furnish you with the wool?*

A: He furnishes us with everything that we need. It was a young man who worked with us at the factory who put us in contact with him, when he saw all the problems we had with getting to work on time. My mother was working then, and we had to prepare our lunch ourselves. And into the bargain, our boss was yelling at us all the time. We tried to explain that we prepared our food and made our bread before coming to work, but it didn't make any difference.

Q: *You did the housework all by yourselves?*

A: Yes, we had to! My mother had begun to work at the factory. My grandmother was too old to do anything at all. We got up very early in the morning to tidy up the house. While I cleaned our room, my sister prepared the bread and put it in the oven before we went to the factory.

Q: *What time did you leave home in the morning?*

A: Around nine o'clock, but when the days were short, we left at about nine-fifteen or nine-thirty.

Q: *And so?*

A: And so, the other girls got out at twelve-thirty. We left at noon. We had asked the *mu'allima* to let us leave a little early to have enough time to prepare our lunch, because we even had to do our shopping then. We ate and then straightened up the house a little before getting back to the factory around two or two-thirty. We found all the other girls already there. When they went home at noon, they found everything ready. They didn't even have to clear up the table where they had eaten. And the boss never stopped pointing them out as an example to us. So I said to the young man who worked with us: 'We're going to end up by leaving this place sometime.' One day he came over to me. When he saw that I was very upset, he asked me what was the matter. I told him that I was fed up with this place and that if it were possible, I would work at home. 'All you have to do is accumulate some capital', he told me. 'But we don't have the means to do that', I told him. 'What we need is for someone to give us work to do at home. That would be the best arrangement.' It was then that he told us about one of his friends who might perhaps be interested in our case: 'If you are serious about working, I can speak to my friend about it.' And we were delighted at the prospect.

Q: *What did you need capital for?*

A: In order to begin, we had to have money for enough wool to finish one complete carpet.

Q: *If you had had that much capital, would you have made your carpet yourself and sold it?*

A: Yes.

Q: *And why don't you do that now?*

A: If I begin a carpet, I have to have money to live on during the whole time needed to make and sell it.

Q: *And how much capital do you estimate that would be?*

A: Not much. I would begin with a small carpet, costing about 200 to 250 dirhams.

Q: *And how much would you sell it for?*

A: That depends on the market.

Q: *Are you certain of making a profit?*

A: I can lose just as easily as I can make a profit. It all depends on the market. If the market is good, I make a profit. If it is not, I can lose.

Q: *So that young man helped you to leave the factory?*

A: He spoke to his friend, who is a very responsible person, someone from the same region as we are, a *filali*. I finished out the week, and before leaving I told the *mu'allima* that I wasn't coming back to the factory any more, but that if she wanted me to work for her at my house, I was ready to do it.

Q: *And what happened?*

A: She refused.

Q: *And did the other person agree to equip you?*

A: Yes, he took care of everything.

Q: *Is it he whom you work with now?*

A: Yes, it is he whom I work with now.

Q: *You still haven't bought your own loom?*

The acquisition of a loom

A: When I began to work with this new boss, he advanced me a little money and I had to borrow the rest. I had to wait until I finished my first carpet and was paid for it before I was able to buy the loom.

Q: *How much did it cost you?*

A: Around 100 dirhams. I don't remember exactly; maybe it was 90. At the beginning we had a wooden loom. The one that the new boss installed for us is much better; it is metal. The wooden one broke down all the time. Sometimes I was able to repair it and I did it; but other times I wasn't able to, and the work was brought to a standstill for a whole day.

Q: *Describe for me how a normal workday goes.*

A: My married sister brings her daughter to us very early, around seven or seven-fifteen. We are barely up at that time. I get washed and then check little Lubna to see if her mother has changed her nappy; if not, I do it myself. I give her her breakfast before I have mine. My sister tidies up the room where we have slept, and then one of us goes to the kitchen to wash the nappies. I take the basket and go and do the shopping; when I get back we begin preparing breakfast. We get down to work when the housework is finished.

Q: *When do you finish the housework?*

A: That depends. Sometimes it takes all morning to do it. And sometimes even the afternoon is wasted. If a friend turns up, we have to spend a little time with her; we can't leave her and go to work. She would be very offended.

Q: *Even if she knows that you have work to do?*

A: She would get angry if we didn't pay attention to her.

Q: *Do you have to do that just for the members of your family or for your friends as well?*

A: We have a large family; we have half-sisters who come to visit us. They don't have anything to do, and their visits go on forever, and we lose a lot of time because of them. For that reason, work in the factory is more profitable. But work at home has its good side. It is more restful; if you get ill, you can take the time to get well again.

Q: *Can't you make up for a lost day of work by working at night?*

A: No, we can't.

Q: *Why not?*

A: Because of the neighbours. They object to it; they say it makes too much noise.

Q: *It makes a lot of noise?*

A: Yes, you can hear the noise from the street.

Q: *At what time do you usually stop working?*

A: At sundown.

Q: *Have your upstairs neighbours complained of the noise?*

A: They've never said a word to us because when we agreed to live in this house, we warned them that we make carpets and that that was how we earned the money for the rent. They asked us not to begin work too early and to take a break at two o'clock while they ate lunch and took a nap. Finally, they asked us not to work at night.

Q: *And what do you do at night?*

A: We go out to do the shopping.

Q: *At night?*

A: Yes. At night, so that my mother can take her meal to work with her the next day. If she works at night, she takes her dinner with her. If she goes to work at around 5 p.m., she arrives at the factory at six and doesn't come home until seven the next morning. We prepare the meal in the evening; my mother takes it with her, and we have what is left over for lunch the next day. So during the day we don't have to worry about doing any cooking. All we have to do is make bread and tidy up the house.

Q: *Which is your day off?*

A: Sunday, because my mother doesn't work on Sunday.

Q: *What do you do on Sunday?*

A: We do a thorough house-cleaning or the washing. In the afternoon we go out. When it rains, we stay at home.

Q: *When it doesn't rain, where do you go?*

A: When it doesn't rain, we go to visit our sisters. We used to go to the cinema, but now we don't go any more.

Q: *Why not?*

A: Times are harder now. We need the money we used to spend on the cinema just for living. Before, we didn't mind. We kept part of our pay for going there. Now we can't afford it.

Q: *Who manages the budget now?*

A: I do.

Q: *Is the budget based on your income together with that of your mother?*

A: My mother gives me all she earns, and I take care of everything. When I run out of money, I go and get an advance from our employer. And we settle accounts with him when the carpet is finished. Either he still owes me some money or I owe him. In the latter case, he deducts it from the next order.

Q: *What do you do when there is a holiday?*

A: Which holiday?

Q: *The feast of sacrifice, for example.*

A: At the feast of sacrifice, our boss advances us the money we need. This year, for example, he owed me 350 dirhams for a carpet that I had just finished, and he gave me 100 extra. With my mother's wages we could buy the sheep and the other things for the feast.

Q: *What do you do in summer?*

A: From time to time we go to the beach, especially on Sunday. But we go less and less frequently.

Q: *Why?*

A: Because Sunday is the only day we have time to go to the bath. So if we decide to go to the bath, we skip the beach.

Q: *What about holidays?*

A: We don't have any.

Q: *Don't you ever go to visit the members of your family who live away from Rabat?*

A: No, never. We don't have any holidays. We work the whole year. We ease off a little when it's feast days. We manage things so that we finish a carpet just before. The feast days are like our holiday. We take seven days off.

Q: *And what do you do during those seven days?*

A: The first few days there are household chores to do. Afterwards, we go and visit our sisters and other members of the family to wish them a happy holiday.

Q: *Don't you ever go to stay with someone?*

A: No, never.

Q: *Do you ever go to visit your mother's family?*

A: We used to go a long time ago, when we weren't paying rent and when Zainab was still helping us with expenses.

Q: *Would you like to continue working after you get married?*

A: If it were some other work and if my husband agreed, I would gladly work, because it helps out. But continuing this present work, no.

Q: *What other work would you prefer to do?*

A: You know, I am not educated, so the kind of decent work available to me . . .

Q: *What do you call decent work?*

[From here, it is Malika who answers.]

A: Working in a doctor's office. That would be just tidying up the waiting room before the people arrived and opening the door. And then I could learn to give injections, even if I have not had an education. With practice I would begin to catch on.

Q: *If the man who asked for your hand in marriage couldn't get by without your working, would you marry him anyway?*
A: No. Why should I marry him if I have to continue to slog away? I have had several suitors who had a very precarious job or who were unemployed. I wanted none of them. They didn't have a satisfactory job. If my father was still alive and I had a well-paid job, I wouldn't get married at all.
Q: *You wouldn't get married at all?*
A: No, not at all.
Q: *So what made you decide to marry your fiancé?*
A: I am marrying him for his money, for his job.
Q: *Do you want to go and live with him in the town where he is?*[14]
A: It's a long way away and I don't have any family there. But I am fed up with the work that I do.

[Malika was getting engaged at the time of the interview. Before her engagement, I had heard that she would never marry a man who didn't have a sure future, as her sister Zainab had done, and that she would prefer to remain an old maid. Moroccan national statistics show a decline in the rate of women's participation in the labour force after marriage. Working conditions are so degrading for the young female worker that she aspires to give up working when she marries. See the postsript to this interview for what happened subsequently to Latifa and Malika.]

Q: *And if your present fiancé were not able to provide for you, would you marry him?*
A: No, I wouldn't marry him. I'm not going to put myself in the position of working for him, after all.
Q: *You don't want to work for a man?*
A: I prefer to work for myself and my mother.
Q: *What do you require of a man?*
A: That he be a good man, and not a drunkard. He can drink a little, but not get drunk and come home and beat me. He shouldn't lock me up. I don't want to be left at home while he goes out by himself.
Q: *He should take you with him?*
A: Not necessarily, but he should devote one day to me. If he doesn't work on a Saturday and Sunday, for example, we could take the time to go out and about, because I couldn't expect to go out all by myself.

Q: *How do the husbands of the women you know act?*

A: There are some who are all right, but there are also some who do not treat their wives well. There are some husbands who say to their wives: 'If you're not happy, get out!' That's what you have to think about before getting married. Because men change. They become different from what they were at the beginning when you first knew them.

Q: *And if your fiancé demanded that you stayed locked up in the house, would you accept that?*

A: No, I would never accept being locked up, even if he was rich.

Q: *And if he were very domineering, what would happen?*

A: If he gave me the freedom to go and visit my parents, we could work it out. Also, he could go out by himself. But if he forced me to stay at home, unable to go anywhere, while he went where he wanted and came back when he wanted, I would not accept that.

Q: *Have you talked about all that with your fiancé?*

A: Yes, of course.

Q: *What did he say to you?*

A: He talked about his family, asking me if I thought I could get along with them. It seems to me I could for the time being; later, I don't know . . .

Q: *He suggested that you live with his family?*

A: Yes, and I agreed.

Q: *And if he asked you to stop going to visit your family, and if he compelled you to put on a* djellaba*?*

A: I would not agree, but it would surprise me if he did. He likes me dressing in European style.

Q: *Did he ask you to wear European clothes?*

A: He likes it very much, yes.

Q: *Do you go out with him when you go to Oujda?*

A: We went out together only once when I was at his family's house, to buy some shoes he was giving me.

Q: *Is he nice to you?*

A: He is very nice now; afterwards, I don't know how he will be. I didn't go out when I was at his family's place in Oujda because they haven't any girls my age who could have accompanied me. They only have boys.

Q: *You stayed in the house the whole time?*

A: Yes, I didn't leave the house. You know, dressing in European style is a question of means; you mustn't forget that. You can wear a *djellaba* for a long time, but if you dress as a European, you have to change often, you have to have several outfits. If I had the means, I wouldn't wear a *djellaba* except to go to the Turkish bath or do the shopping. My cousins also prefer to dress in European clothes, but they can't afford to.

Q: *Whom do you visit, friends or your family?*

A: Only the family. You can't trust friends any more these days.

Q: *Why not?*

A: They are not reliable. People say that you shouldn't have friends. You have friends, and one fine day you discover that they are not all right and you have to break off with them.

Q: *Did you ever go out with a man?*

A: No, never.

Q: *Didn't you ever go out with the one who asked to marry you?*

A: No.

Q: *You went to visit his family?*

A: Yes, but without going out with him. I told you that I only went out with him that one time.

Q: *How was your engagement arranged? Did he ask for you in marriage when he saw you the first time?*

A: He had already decided to ask for my hand, but I didn't know anything about it. He is a family relation, although rather distant. My mother is related to his family.

Q: *He used to come to your house?*

A: He came on holidays.

Q: *And you didn't go out with him?*

A: Yes, we went out all together.

Q: *Where did you go?*

A: To his uncle's house.

Q: *Are you going to continue to help your mother when you are married?*

A: Of course. I will go and see her often, and if I can afford it I will help her. That will depend on my husband and his generosity. [15]

Postscript: what became of Latifa and Malika

In 1978 Malika married an employee of the Coca Cola Company in Oujda. She has two children: a boy and a girl. She has given up working since she got married. She has learned to embroider caftans with pearls in the Oriental style. But she only works for herself and her family. It's a pastime for her, a means of self-expression, rather than a source of income.

Latifa got married in 1980. Her husband is a fireman in the Civil Defence Force. She has a daughter, and she does dressmaking and embroidery at home. Her husband bought her an electric sewing machine with his savings. At the present time she lives with her mother Dawiya because of the prohibitively high rents in Salé.

6

Habiba the psychic: the supernatural in the service of the people

Morocco's resources are not limited to land, water, and trees, to phosphates and manganese.

One has to include the non-material resources without which mastery over the above is not possible. And that involves fabricating the past, designing the future, and occasionally conjuring away the present. Thus it involves, among other things, the manipulation of the past and of religion.

If the access of women to material resources is strictly supervised, their access to non-material resources is institutionally proscribed. To imagine that a woman could be an imam or a caliph is the purest blasphemy.

So, in order to have access to non-material resources, and especially to the use of religion (monopolised by the powerful), the less powerful had to go outside orthodoxy and establish religious areas judged heretical by the guardians of the monopoly. They set up shrines and erected tombs for their saints, trying in this way to resolve the everyday hunger for food and for dignity.

Women, veiled and marginalised in the mosques of the masters, slipped away among the outcasts and went to the courtyards of the shrines, where the supernatural is more approachable, where the spirits speak in the dialects of the people and accept the most humble of offerings.

Habiba, illiterate and handicapped, embarked at the age of fifty on a journey of initiation to the shrine of the saint Sidi Ali Ibn Hamdush. She returned confirmed in her vocation as a psychic. She built a temple in honour of Lalla Aisha Qandisha, where the yearnings of those who suffered were welcomed – those who suffered from not being able to work out a decent life amid the upheavals of present-day Morocco.

Habiba feels that she has really made a success of her life. She has created a career for herself by achieving mastery over the supernatural, which used to overwhelm her with seizures. And she has established a harmonious relationship with a husband who is a legless cripple and unemployed.

Habiba had no advantages in life; she had nothing but handicaps. But she transformed them into a source of life.

Habiba the psychic [1]

A peasant father

Q: *Tell me about your life from the time you were a child. Tell me what your father did, where the family lived, where you were brought up, and so on.*

A: When I was born, my father was a soldier. He had enlisted in the Spanish army.

Q: *Were you born in the Spanish zone of Morocco?*

A: When my mother died, we were still there. My father was fed up with his job. He left the army and came to live in this area [the interview took place in Rabat]. We were eight children.

Q: *Were you the oldest?*

A: No, I wasn't the oldest. There were six girls and two boys.

Q: *Your mother had eight children in all?*

A: Without counting those who died. My father brought us to this area and went back to farming.

Q: *Did he work on farms or did he have a little piece of land?*

A: He worked for other people. You know, my father always worked in farming. He always worked the land. Even when he was in the army, he was assigned to farming; he worked the land for the army. Then he brought us here and in order to support us, he worked the land. After my mother's death, he married a very good woman who was very kind to us. My father and my stepmother are dead now.

Q: *Did your stepmother have children by your father?*

A: Yes, she had three; one died and two are still living. We are all married, except one daughter who is handicapped. The poor thing, and God gave her no help! She also, like me, had seizures. [2] The seizures struck her during the wedding of one of our younger sisters. My father had married her off very young, when she was seven years old. He had put her in the care of a woman who was supposed to protect her until the age of ten, that is, to prevent the consummation of the marriage before my sister was ten years old, to prevent the husband from coming near her. But this woman did not keep her promise. At any rate, my little sister stayed with that man just long enough to persuade him to give her a divorce. Then she remarried and had children with another man. After that, it was my turn to get married. I was married before I met this man [the interview took place in Habiba's living room, in the presence of her husband and children].

Q: *How old were you when you got married?*

A: I was fourteen.

Q: *People got married young at that time.*

A: I got married without a licence, without anything. I got married just with the *fatiha*.[3]

Q: *In Rabat?*

A: At that time my father was living in Sidi Slimane in the Gharb and my husband in Sidi Kacem, not very far away. My husband was originally from our part of the country [that is, the Sahara]. But Allah did not let that marriage succeed. I had two children with my first husband, but the marriage quickly turned sour. My husband mistreated me, and I left him. I remained a divorcée for four years, and then Allah arranged for me to meet this man, and I married him. He is also from our people.

Q: *The second time, did you get married in Sidi Kacem?*

A: No, I got married in Rabat to this man you see here.

Q: *Your children are from your first husband?*

First signs of 'seizures'

A: Yes. Unfortunately Allah has not given me children by my present husband. As for my present condition, that began when I was a small child. My brothers and sisters would begin to tickle me and I would black out. I wouldn't regain consciousness until they put my hand in water or had me inhale something that had been burned in fire. If someone tickled me, I would run away from them like mad. My father, may Allah rest his soul, would yell at the children, ordering them to stop: 'Leave your sister alone, don't tickle her any more', he told them over and over.

Q: *How old were you when it began?*

A: I was ten or eleven. You see, I was very young. There wasn't much of a gap between us, and people used to believe that we were twins. There was an animal that had a terrible effect on me, worse even than the tickling: I mean frogs. I was terrified of frogs. It was enough for someone to say the word in front of me for me to go crazy. If I had something in my hand, I threw it; I became aggressive, chased other people. Yes, I became crazy. I began to scream like a mad person, screaming until I lost consciousness. My poor father tried to prevent this from happening, to protect me. He forbade my brothers and sisters to torment me. And because of all that, this thing that I have began to get worse. I remember one day when I was invited to visit my brother. My son Muhammad was still a baby. Someone said the word '*jrana*' [frog] in front of me. I fell upon my baby and I nearly killed him. I lost consciousness. My brother was so upset that he swore that from then on he would take to court anybody who tried to excite me: 'You know perfectly well that my sister has an attack when she hears that word, so avoid saying it in front of her!'

Q: *Was your first husband aware of the situation?*

A: Yes, I used to have attacks when I was living with him after our marriage, if someone upset me. But, you see, he didn't believe in it; he used to say to me, 'You are crazy.' He didn't have faith, he didn't believe at all in that. So when he saw me having a seizure, he would cry out, 'I think this woman is crazy.' In fact, he was rather inflexible; he didn't believe at all in the power of the djinns.[4] He was a very ordinary man; I never understood him. He had an odd manner about him. I stayed with him for five or six years.

Q: *He didn't believe in those things?*

A: He didn't believe in them at all. But when I had an attack, you see, I have to admit that he did take care of me. But he had a sort of pride, it was as if he was ashamed in front of others when this happened to me. We lived on a farm in the country, and he didn't want people to see me in that state or to know about it. When there were strangers in the house, he would lock me up and ask neighbouring women to take care of me.

Q: *And your second husband? What is his attitude about the djinns? Did you tell him about it before you got married?*

A: Yes, he knew all about it when he married me. You see, although he doesn't have any legs, he helps me when I have an attack. If the seizure comes upon me when I am near a puddle of water, he throws himself on top of me, tries to pull me away, and calls people to my aid. He gets them to carry me to a clean place; then he washes off my clothes, rubs me with benzoin,[5] puts my head on his shoulder, and calms me. Life went on like this until I got pregnant. I got pregnant two or three times with him, but it always came to nothing. You see, he had been married before meeting me. The parents of his first wife came and threatened me in order to make me leave him and thus force him to return to their daughter. They threatened me with a knife, and that incident made my seizures worse.

Q: *Did they attack you?*

A: Yes, they attacked me. They burst into the garage where we were living at that time in the Hassan neighbourhood of Rabat.

Q: *Was your husband there?*

A: Yes, he was there, but not in the same room. They locked themselves into the garage with me, where it was very dark. They attacked me once in the stomach with the knife and once in the neck. And then my condition got worse: I was beset on one side by the 'spirits', and on the other by fear. Just before my periods, my belly would swell up. I went to see a doctor and had an operation to make it possible to have a baby by this man, but up to now God has not granted our wish, and we continue as we are. You see, the djinns made a pact with me; they gave me to understand that I could never have children if I didn't pay a visit to the shrine of Mulay Ibrahim, and up to now I haven't been able to. [6]

Q: *You still haven't been able to go? Then how were you initiated into your work as a psychic? How did you become a psychic?*

The calling becomes clear

A: The day that I began to work, that was it. I became a *shuwafa*, a pyschic.

Q: *Were you with your first husband or your second?*

A: I was with my present husband. You see, we have been together for a good long time.

In short, before the time that I became a psychic, I had begun to have visions; it was on the eve of the Prophet's birthday. One of the most persistent visions that kept returning was that of a woman who had the feet of Aisha Qandisha.

Q: *She had cloven feet?*

A: Yes, like those of a sheep. Sometimes I saw a flock, a whole flock of sheep who spoke to me like human beings. I saw them in a procession, so to speak.

Q: *You imagined that or you saw it?*

A: No, I didn't imagine anything. All that appeared to me very clearly and unfolded before my eyes. It was all premeditated and part of a plan designed to lead me to a specific place.

Q: *That all happened here, in Rabat?*

A: Yes, everything I am telling you happened in Rabat. In this very room where we are, in this blessed house.

Q: *Right here?*

A: Yes, it all happened here in this house. As the Prophet's birthday holiday drew near, I felt I had to go and visit the tomb of the saint. My visions became more frequent. In one of them I saw a fire in one of the local shops, and three days later that shop really caught fire. My son was very upset: 'Mama, I think you are going crazy', he said. 'What you told us you saw is just too much.' One day, I had a seizure. A Senegalese friend was staying at my house and he remained with me for six or seven months. He called me 'Mama', because he felt so much a part of the family. We had three sheep in the house that we were keeping for the feast of the Prophet's birthday. A woman neighbour invited us to have dinner with her that day. She invited us at the last minute, and we had already eaten. But we went over to her house anyway. Towards the end of the afternoon, I was in great form, and I said: 'Bring one of the sheep, and we'll kill it right here and now.' And they killed the sheep, but they didn't give me any meat. It was possible for those who didn't know me to make a mistake about me; they didn't know that I had a compulsion to eat raw meat. I got up, went over to the meat, and ate my fill. Afterwards the spirits took possession of me, and I proclaimed to my brother-in-law that he was going to leave for Mecca. I told him: 'First of all, you are going to meet the king; you are going to kiss his hand and make a request of him; he will grant your request.' A few days later, what I had predicted took place. In the beginning, no one believed me, but then my predictions came true. My brother-in-law really met the king, and asked him to grant him the favour of sending him to Mecca, and the king gave him his wish. After seeing the king, he came to see me. It was raining that day. He arrived soaked to the skin, as though he had swum a river. He threw himself at my feet, with his hands linked behind his back. '*Al-taslim*', he kept saying. I didn't understand what he meant. '*Al-taslim a-lala*, submission to you, my lady', he kept repeating. 'What is going on?' I asked him. 'Tell me.' At that time, I had still not paid a visit to Sidi Ali's shrine.[7] I still didn't know that I was going to be a psychic. He told me that he was going to leave for Mecca: 'I met the king, just as you predicted, and he has sent me a ticket. A government officer came looking

for me in the area and brought me a ticket.' I admit that I was very happy
to hear that. I was delighted to see the gift that God had given me become
a reality. It was a very strong sensation. I felt myself stiffen, and then I
fell into a light faint. Someone gave me something nice to smell, and I
came to.

The journey of initiation

As soon as I could, I made the pilgramage to Sidi Ali's shrine. I said to
my husband, 'I must go.' 'But where are you going?' he asked me. My
older sister was supposed to accompany me, but she let me down at the
last minute.

Q: *Did you give up the idea of leaving then?*

A: No. I left, but all alone. I went out of the house and I began to ask the
way. I came to the place where they sell bus tickets, and I bought one.
There was a crowd at the ticket window. It was the height of the pilgrimage season. I hesitated, and then I decided to leave even if I were never to
return. Was I perhaps going to be doomed to wander from one saint to
another? I would follow the decisions of Allah, whatever they might be.
So I left. I arrived at the shrine of Shaikh al-Kamal.[8] There I found the
ritual procession going toward the shrine of Sidi Said, may God increase
his glory![9]

Q: *Did that happen the same day that you left Rabat?*

A: Yes, the same day. When we arrived, with the pilgrimage in full
swing, the town-crier came on to the bus to announce to us: 'Beware!
Don't wear black. You might have trouble.' I was dressed entirely in
black from head to toe. My *djellaba* was black, and my veil also.

Q: *You hadn't known about it?*[10]

A: No, I really hadn't. It was the first time I had heard of it. And just
imagine: I have always loved wearing black. When I see people dressed
in black, I stare at them and can't look away; I want to jump on them and
take their clothes. When the bus arrived, I got off, but I didn't know
where to go, what direction to take. I met two young men, one about the
age of my son and the other a little older. I said to them: 'I beg you, take
me to the saint; show me the way.' They told me that I should wait there
for another bus which would take me. So I remained there until nightfall.
The taxis which usually carried people for two and a half dirhams began
to double their price. They took advantage of people's impatience. While
I waited for the bus, I heard people around me saying that every year

during the pilgrimage there is a bus that is cursed and breaks down, never gets repaired and never gets its passengers to their destination. It seems that somebody had once committed a shocking act during the pilgrimage. Having heard these rumours, I looked around me. I spotted a man sitting there, and I approached him and asked him where he was going. 'To Sidi Ali', he answered. He told me that he lived nearby. When the bus came, I boarded it at his side; he was the only person in the group in whom I felt any confidence.

But when we were settled in the bus, they asked us for five dirhams. Everybody then left the bus, except for that man and me; we were the only ones who agreed to pay double the normal price. When we arrived at Sidi Ali, it was already quite late at night. He asked me where I was going and if I knew where the shrine was. I begged him to take me to the door of the shrine, telling him, 'I don't know where I am. I have never before left Rabat to go further than to Kenitra. Please help me. I am a stranger here; I don't know where to go.' He agreed, and then added, 'If you want to stay the night at my house, you are welcome.' I accepted with pleasure, and went to his house. He had brought a table and some utensils with him on the bus. He walked along and I followed him. It was a very dark night. To tell the truth, I was very afraid of him. I said to myself, 'He is going to lead me somewhere and cut my throat.' But, on the other hand, I was deeply convinced that I was following a preordained path and that no harm could come to me. My objective was right and good: to visit the saint's shrine. So I followed him. Along our route someone greeted him, calling out, 'Good evening, *sharif*.' 'Well,' I said to myself, 'he is a *sharif*, so nothing can harm me.' When we arrived at his wife's house, she caused quite a scene. She woke her children up and said to them, 'Come and see what your father has brought from the market; he has brought a woman. He forgot to buy the things we needed because his mind was on something else; he has brought back a woman. That's what interests him the most!'

I was very humiliated and upset by this scene as it was on my account that the man had got into this quarrel. I turned to the woman and said to her: 'Give me a sheepskin, I beg you.' She asked me who I was, and then prepared a very unappetising meal for us. I couldn't swallow a mouthful of it, but I told myself that if I didn't eat, her suspicions would grow. So I took some eggs out of my bag and laid them on the table with half a loaf of bread and some cakes. I also gave the mistress of the house some money – ten or fifteen dirhams, I can't remember exactly. I told her,

'Please accept this contribution for the food.' In spite of all that, I still kept on my *djellaba*. The mistress of the house showed me a place where I was supposed to sleep, then went with her husband into another room to sleep. Before I fell asleep, she came to me and asked: 'Do you intend to rent?' I answered, 'Madame, I will do what you want. If you want me to rent [the sleeping space], I will rent. You see, I have come to visit the saint. It's the first time I have come, and I don't know what is customary.' The next morning I got up, washed, and said my prayers. Since the daughter of my host and hostess was leaving for school, I asked her to take me to visit the saint's shrine. I left all my things at their place: my bag, the blanket I had brought from Rabat, my towel, my sheet – in short, I left everything I possessed at that woman's house. I told her, 'I am leaving all my things with you; if I succeed in finding this house again, I will fetch them; otherwise they are yours, you can keep them.' She asked me again if I intended to rent space in her house, and I answered that I didn't know yet what I was going to do. 'I have to go to the saint's shrine to find some people that I know.' In fact, I didn't know anybody; I wasn't supposed to meet anybody. I just said those words, like that; I don't know why.

Pilgrimage to Lalla Aisha

So I left that house and went down with the daughter toward the saint's shrine. She pointed out to me the grotto of Lalla Aisha:[11] 'There is Lalla Aisha, if you want to visit her, and the saint's shrine is at the foot of the stairs.' I thanked the little girl and gave her some money. Then I 'visited' Lalla Aisha. But people told me, 'This is not the time for the visit to Lalla Aisha! This is not when they hand out the henna.' They asked me why I had come. 'I am a person possessed and I have come to visit.' A woman then advised me to come back at sunset: 'That is the time for visiting this place, when hens and cocks are sacrificed here.' So I went on to the saint's shrine. I pressed my head against the wrought-iron grille and broke into sobs. All the events of the previous night came back to me – the humiliations, the insults of that woman. I was overcome with sorrow as I remembered it all. I had been weeping for some time when a woman approached me and said: 'Why are you crying? Don't cry any more.' For a long time I couldn't say anything. I shook my head like a mute person, as though I were telling her to let me take care of myself, to let me cry, and I continued crying until I felt better. 'What's the matter?' she resumed. 'Well, Madame', I began, and I told her all that had happened the night before, finishing by saying, 'I came, and now I no longer know where to turn.' 'Welcome', she told me. 'My husband is the *muqaddam*.[12] We are camping in a tent, and we eat at the *sharif*'s table. Our food is brought to us from the *zawiya*. You are welcome to join us.' 'Where are you from?' I asked her. 'I am from Rabat, and where you do you come from?' she replied. 'I am from the Sahara.' She welcomed me with open arms. Her husband had two other wives. One of them had stayed at home, and the two others had accompanied him to the shrine. Her husband decided that I should be welcomed as a guest; he forbade me to do any of the housekeeping chores. They gave me food that was all prepared, and all I had to do was eat it. I wanted to do the washing up; sometimes I tried to wash and cut the mint bouquet, but each time someone stopped me. Allah is great. The blessing of the ancestors and saints was with us. I stayed with them until the last day of the pilgrimage. On only one evening did they let me pay for the cost of dinner; otherwise I was completely taken care of. One of the wives of the *muqaddam* was a psychic. We went together to perform the ritual dance of possession. The day of the ritual procession, we went to the saint's shrine, taking the *dabiha*. Each group had its own special ritual. So we left with the procession going to Sidi Ali Ibn Hamdush, then to Sidi Ahmad Dughughi. We walked the whole route of the procession in bare feet.

Q: *Were there just women, or men and women together?*

A: We marched in the procession together. The announcers called out to the crowd: 'Barren women, enter the shrine!' They entered and stretched out on the ground, and the procession marched right over them. Some were very well dressed, wearing a caftan of thick felt, but they lay down like the rest. To all those who had a malady they wanted to be cured of, the *muqaddam* called out: 'Come forward, ye who are halt and lame; approach, ye who have pain in the back.' The *muqaddam* got so excited that his saliva sprayed out. The march was accompanied by the music of bagpipes. Meanwhile, if the crowd of those performing the dance of possession saw someone passing with a goat, they wrested it from him, brought it into their midst, tore it into shreds, and ate it raw.

Q: *The goat?*

A: Yes, if it was a goat. It could also be a sheep or any animal, and it was torn away from its owner and eaten raw. If anyone was marching with his shoes on alongside the dancers, the latter rushed at him: everyone had to be barefoot. We marched along, hand in hand, without *djellabas*, without anything. The wives of the *muqaddam* who had offered me hospitality also gave me an *izar*, which they draped around me. They invited me to join them in the ritual. I followed their every movement. When they stood up, I stood up with them; when they sat down, I sat down with them. When they got up to dance, I got up with them, but then everyone danced according to his or her own rhythm. I could only dance according to my own.

Q: *You have to wait for your own rhythm?*

A: Yes, you must wait until the musicians are playing your rhythm. When I heard mine, I got up and danced until I went into a trance. My hosts, the *sharifs* who had shown me hospitality, insisted that I stay with them until the seventh day, when the two banners are brought together, that of Sidi Ali and that of Sidi Ahmad Dughughi. The sharifs, descendants of those two saints, ride out on horseback from their respective shrines, surrounded by banners, and embrace each other beside a palm tree. Everybody does the same, while some emit ululations, and others invoke the name of the Prophet. Almost everyone is in a state of trance by this time. Some crack their heads with a hatchet, others break earthen pots on their skulls. You see blood spurting and running down their faces; they are covered in blood both back and front. Others devour mud, and still others swallow spiny cactus – all according to their own rhythms.

Confirmation of the vocation

A: Now where was I?

Q: *You stopped at the point where the woman offered you the bread.*

A: Yes. When I was going down toward Lalla Aisha Qandisha's shrine, a woman offered me bread. When I took it, I realised that it was warm. Someone said to me: 'You must give us a bit and take the rest back home.'

Q: *Did you understand at that moment what that was about?*

A: Yes, I understood at once. There was a group of us women standing in the saint's shrine. They had chosen me to be given the bread. They said to me: 'Well, take your bread.' God, may he be blessed and exalted, had given me the bread – that was the meaning of that incident.

Q: *Were there many women who, like you, came to ask for the bread?*

A: Yes, obviously. The sanctuary was full of them, standing there.

Q: *And you were the only one to receive the bread?*

A: A woman stood up in the midst of those present and said: 'Sharifa, here, here is your bread.'

Q: *She gave it to you?*

A: Yes, to me. A woman next to me whispered, 'Take your bread. It is given to you by God and Lalla Aisha.' I took the bread and performed the ceremony. I cut it in morsels and handed it around. You know, when the man was in the process of cutting the bread, I had the impression that he was slashing my heart. I was distressed at the idea that all the bread would be distributed and there would be none left for me to take home. It was strange. As we left the shrine, a man came over to me. I had met him earlier during the march; he was a *buhali*. I was with another woman to whom he said: 'It is not you that I want to speak to.' And, pointing to me, he said, 'It is to her that I have things to reveal.' He continued speaking to my companion: 'This woman has come to receive her bread. You have already received all of yours. But she who is accompanying you is far from that point. She has come from very far in quest of bread.' Then, speaking to me, he said: 'You have come from very far. You are going to succeed. You are going to get what you want.' I placed a candle like everybody else. The man said to me: 'Go forward, march on. You are going to begin to work and you will not want for anything. You will return many times to this shrine.' He kept on speaking and speaking, and I listened as if everything he said was going to come true. I had confidence in myself; all that was going to happen.

Q: *And did you begin to work after your return?*

A: From the moment I got back to Rabat I began to work.

Q: *How did it take place? One morning you woke up and began to 'see' things?*

Doing the work of a psychic

A: No. I began to see things after having made the 'blood sacrifice'. I bought a cow for 800 dirhams without giving a thought to the price. I invited the *muqaddam*, who came accompanied by fourteen people, not counting the women.

Q: *Where did the* muqaddam *come from? From the shrine of Sidi Ali?*

A: No, he came from Kenitra. The first time he visited me, he had said, 'You must prepare yourself. When you are ready, come and tell me, and

I will arrange the celebration, the *laila*.' So they came and they stayed at my place for seven days. We danced for seven days, and I never got enough of it. The day they wanted to leave, I threw myself on the ground in front of the door. I didn't want them to leave me. They began to pray.

Q: *They stayed seven days with you?*

A: Yes, seven days eating and drinking, thanks be to God. The *muqaddam* stayed a whole month with me. He left very satisfied.

Q: *You began when he left?*

A: He left me after my inauguration. His wife came to join him; she herself was a *muqaddama*, an initiator. They put the banner on my door. [13] The *muqaddama* made a *tabaq* for me.

Q: *I have visited lots of psychics who don't have a banner. Have the ones who have a banner on their door, like you, carried out the celebration and made the sacrifice, or what?*

A: Of course. There has to be a blood sacrifice. You have to receive the approval of the *muqaddam*. You see, afterwards, you must make blood sacrifices on specific occasions: in the month of *Sha'ban* and for the Prophet's birthday. If you don't, you go in fear of your life. You don't have to observe the Hamdushi celebration; you can do the Ganawi or the Jilali, if you prefer. Each person must dance for their own master. Each can operate through a saint who is particularly close: Mulay Abd al-Qadir Jilali, al-Ganawi, al-Hamdushi, al-Issawi, or al-Sarqawi. You know, there are several kinds of spirits. We leave people free; we try to be flexible with them; but in fact each person is possessed by their own *malik*, their own master spirit. Each one of us, the possessed, dances their own dance: one handles fire, another pours water on the head to feel well, and still another must tear their clothes to find relief. Another, seeing a person they don't like, runs after him and hits him. That's the way it is in our world. When I had carried out the celebration and danced and cured some people, I began to receive others. For the next Prophet's birthday, I paid the expenses of a Ganawi celebration. The tray that I offered to Lalla Malika [14] cost me 200 dirhams; I had to put on it a variety of things, such as *siwak*, watermelon seeds, figs. The piles of things must be placed on this tray so that there will be *hajba*.

Q: *What does* hajba *mean?*

A: *Hajba* means that the tray must be isolated in a room which no one goes into, especially children. You cover the tray, which has been very carefully arranged. If someone enters the room and takes something without permission, they put their life in danger. One of my nieces, who was seventeen years old, was touched that night. She didn't know what was going on, the poor thing. Now she is touched, she too.

Q: *She went into the room where the tray was?*

A: No, it happened when we put the scarf on the horns of the cow.

Q: *When the cow was being sacrificed? At that moment?*

A: Yes, just then. When she saw the cow with the scarves, she let out a crazy laugh. Then 'they' struck her. Now she dances more than I do. I stopped after a certain time; she, the poor thing, continues. I have really tried to intervene with 'them' to free her, but in vain. One time a participant at the Hamdushi ceremony that I had organised got up to dance. In twelve years Lalla Aisha had never made an appearance to her. That night Lalla Aisha came. I begged her to free my niece: [15] 'Why has my niece been chosen? [16] She is only a child. It is right for you to choose me, who is beginning to age, who has lived a long time and has accepted life's hard knocks. But she is a girl; she still knows nothing of life.' She replied to me: 'We want our family to grow. You don't want to be our only kin, do you? That's why we are going to keep her among us.' So my niece was obliged to pay all the expenses necessary for the ceremonies; she had to finance all the activities for healing, and today she is still possessed. She 'sees' everything. She sees everything just as I see everything. [17]

Q: *Does she practice as a psychic, like you?*

A: No, she doesn't 'see' for others. She sees imaginary beings. Sometimes she sees Lalla Aisha beside her; she sees herself travelling with Lalla Aisha, accompanying her everywhere. As soon as she sees her, she laughs in her face. She has never recovered, the poor thing.

Q: *Didn't you ever take her to see someone to help her?* [18]

A: We didn't take her to see anyone. She went to pay a visit to Sidi Mi'mun, in God's name, at El Ksar, and her mother arranged a blood sacrifice – she made all the arrangements for the black cermony. [19]

Q: *And is she better now?*

A: She is better when she dances. For example, after the *Sha'ban* ceremonies, [20] she feels better during the following months. But she quickly relapses again into her old condition. She just has to see someone crying and she has a seizure. You know, this is not acting.

No, it's not acting. You know, one day I was visited by a client, a young woman who was very self-assured and full of youth and health. I thought she didn't believe at all in our world. She had to come to see me because she had some problems. I conducted a séance for her. The *jawads* told her everything: 'You were once engaged, there was a dispute', etc. That day I had the *muqaddam* and his wife at my house, and there were some ceremonies in progress. The young woman appeared at the door and she didn't respect us. I thought that she didn't believe in our world, that she must be laughing at us. Well, do you know what happened to her? She fell down right in front of the grocer's across the street from my house. They picked her up; her foot was sprained, her toes twisted; she couldn't walk. The grocer and the neighbours, who knew me, understood what had happened. They told her: 'Go back to the *sharifa* and ask her for forgiveness.' She returned to my house, limping, and said: '*Sharifa*, I am limping . . . ' 'My daughter, ask to be forgiven, make obeisance, and never again laugh at us, at all these people, the *jawads*.' I pulled at her toes, and then she left, walking on both feet, as if nothing had happened. Afterwards she became a *habitué*; she came and brought everything that was necessary. She is a wonderful young woman.

Q: *How long have you been practising as a psychic?*

A: Three years.

The visit of the young black man . . .

Q: *You began by charging two dirhams for a séance?*

A: Yes, exactly. The day that Allah willed that my resources be augmented, I saw a young black man, black as that young man there across from you.[21] He was like him, very similar in appearance, except that his hair stood on end.

Q: *Did you see that young man in a dream or in reality?*[22]

A: I saw him in a dream. Latifa, a 'teacher' like me, was here. She had just come to tell me that someone was at the door and wanted to see me. I opened the door and found myself face to face with this young black man. We greeted each other, and then he said at once: 'Are you the woman who uses the *ladun*?'[23] 'Yes', I answered. Then he put me to a test: 'What do you do for someone who comes to you sick?' 'If you want to see what I do, then come in. I will show you. If you are a believer,[24] you are welcome.' I was very afraid of him. 'Why are you afraid?' he asked me. 'Master, people are afraid of me, and I am afraid of you. In the name of God, who are you?' 'I am the Master of the *Ladun*.' I grabbed him by his clothes and pulled him with all my strength to the sofa where I pushed him down. 'How do you use the *ladun*?' he asked. 'I give it to my visitor to hold in the hand; then I throw it in the fire, and then in cold water.

140

Afterwards I look into it, and I see.' 'Next time do the same thing, but on the head of your visitor, like this', he said, acting out his words. Then he ordered me to 'do' the *ladun* on him. I began by passing the *ladun* over his head with my right hand. He grabbed my hand in his, saying, 'Very good, seventy rials [three and a half dirhams], and you really deserve it.' You know, I remember every detail of that dream. It was five months ago that I met that man in my dream, but the dream remains engraved in my memory in its smallest details.

. . . and its consequences

The next day I didn't dare announce the new fee to my visitors. At the beginning I used to accept any donation at all, even just a bit of benzoin. I was embarrassed to announce this rise in my fee to my visitors. I could already hear what they would say: 'You know our Morocco.' Once their tongues were loosened, if they decided to attack me, they would not try to look for the reason that had impelled me to act. So the day after that dream, I was unwilling to announce the rise to my clientele. That same evening a black woman appeared to me in a dream. She wore three rings, one in her nose, another in her ear, and a third was hanging from her lower lip. She made them clang against each other and lashed out at me: 'You refused to obey orders. You refused to announce to people that your fee would be seventy rials from now on. You will see what is going to happen to you now. You will suffer the consequences of your act. We are going to burn you. You were more afraid of people than of us. We are going to burn your mouth. Your wound will linger for a year.' I was terrified. I had already been suffering for a year from a wound in the foot that wouldn't heal. And now I was supposed to have committed an offence against 'them'! I had already lost a finger in this business. So, with these threats, I was terrified and had to announce the new fee to my clientele.

One day, at eleven o'clock in the morning, there was a knock at the door. There was no one there, just thirty rials on the ground. I called to my daughter, 'You are irresponsible, dropping coins with the face of His Majesty Hassan II on the ground.' But it was not she who had put that money there. I realised then that it had to be the spirits, because the thirty rials was the amount of the rise in my fee. So I announced my new fee to everyone. To those who protested, I said that I was not going to put my life in danger and there was nothing I could do for them. I showed them the marks of the three burns on my leg, three scars as big as a rial, which appeared after the dream. I still have those marks. Here, look. [Habiba then showed me her leg, where the traces could actually be seen.]

Now people come to me from all over, from all sections of the city. The other day a woman came. She had dreamed of Lalla Aisha. She had had an accident – a moped had crashed into her in the street because she was on her way to attend some séances without having done her ablutions and anointed herself. Her face was all swollen. The people in the street told her to come and see me, to come and light some candles for Lalla Aisha. She came and brought some henna. She put it right here and lighted the candles in honour of Lalla Aisha. That very evening Lalla Aisha visited her. You know, I built a shrine for Lalla Aisha.

A shrine for Lalla Aisha

Q: *Where did you build the shrine?*

A: Right here in this house. The day that we began to dig the foundation, the *muqaddam* and his aides, who were in charge of the ritual of the installation ceremony, sacrificed a cow before setting to work. They found the spot where the blood gushed hot from the beast. I asked the *muqaddam* the meaning of this, because it was my sister who was helping him dig, and it was she who had seen it. The *muqaddam* answered: 'That means that God has made you rich. You can build a shrine to Lalla Aisha in your house.' We bought the necessary bricks and cement, and a black bird that was offered in sacrifice at that same spot.

Q: *Did all that happen right here in the house?* [25]

A: Yes, right here in the house. I regularly placed the henna. People came to visit the shrine; they came from far away with their problems and asked Lalla Aisha for her help. But you have to believe in it, obviously, if you want this to work for you. If you believe in it, Lalla Aisha comes to visit you in a dream; she tells you what has to be done, how to begin, and the order of the steps to be taken. Lalla Aisha tells you to come to see me; she will make your wishes come true through my mediation. [26] Do you know that a woman who had never heard of me came the other day from Tabriket [Salé]?

Q: *Then how did she know your address?*

A: She had come once, but she didn't know that the shrine existed. She dreamed that it was as it is. She told me: 'I saw the door with a green plant falling over it.' 'Come see if this is the door you saw in your dream.' She followed me and recognised what she had seen in her dream. She brought some benzoin, bread, olives, and candles, and made her wish. She wanted to 'find a key', that is, she was looking for an apartment. She has not yet found what she wants. But she came from Tabriket without knowing the route and by asking along the way.

Q: *What did she ask?*

A: She asked the people she met: 'Do you know a black woman who has made a shrine for Lalla Aisha?' One child told her that he knew a black woman living in this neighbourhood, but he didn't know if she had built a shrine or not. 'Only Allah knows. You will have to go and ask her yourself.' When she came to my door, I had her come in and led her to Lalla Aisha. She broke out in sobs: 'I was looking for this place without knowing the address.' I did for her what I could. You know, some people refuse to pay the seventy rials. It happens and I can't do anything about it. It is not my fault. When I see that a woman is really poor, I let it pass. I even give her back part of the money for bus fare. You see, when a woman is very poor, I have to reduce the fee. I can't let her be lost.

An illiterate woman writes charms

Q: *And writing charms, how does that go?*[27]

A: It depends on the age of the client. If it's for a sick child, I write it for 200 rials. If it's for a grown-up, I charge double, 400 rials. Sometimes people simply have to burn a selection of things in a brazier at home; the smoke is supposed to be purifying and dissipates the *thiqaf*. They give me money – it is not a fixed sum – and it is I who then buy them the necessary items. The other day two men came to see me.

Q: *For a charm?*

A: Of course, for a charm. I have a *faqih*[28] who writes for me, but just in the evenings. I never write a charm during the day, except in very urgent cases, for someone very ill who is really suffering. In that case, I write the charm during the day. But normally, it is the *faqih* who writes for me.

Q: *How is it done? Do you write while awake or asleep?*

A: I write while awake, but in fact it is not I who writes. My hand moves by itself, as if it were connected to a machine, in the space of a few minutes. I can write forty or fifty charms very easily. But it is not I who writes. All I do is carry out the orders of my *faqih*, whom I obey and in whom I have total confidence. It is he who writes for me. I write charms for different problems: to help a young girl get married, to solve work problems, etc. I write charms in the evening. It is my *faqih* who instructs me; he reveals things to me, shows me things I don't know about.

Q: *So, a person orders a charm one day and then comes back to get it the next day?*

A: Yes. You know, not everybody necessarily needs a charm. It depends on what the *jawads* demand. For some people they demand the *tabkhira*, for others the *kitab*, and for still others the *ladun*, for a certain period of time – three to seven days – and your problem can be solved. Sometimes it happens that people come back a few days after having visited me to tell me that things are going better. A woman went out just before you came in. She told me: 'I dreamed about you two nights in a row. So I decided to come. The last time – just yesterday – I said to myself, ''I must go to see her.'' ' If you don't believe me, ask my husband, ask anybody.[29]

7

Khadija al-Jabliya: from peasant to citizen of the world

While Khomeini and the fundamentalists and Muslim lawmakers fantasise about veiled women and women secluded and hidden in rooms with barred windows, the women themselves are leaving them locked in their dream and are escaping into the life of the great world. Proletarian women succeed better in this escape, because they don't read what the men think about them and what they are planning for them – because they are illiterate.

Khadija al-Jabliya represents this generation of North African women proletarians who, like the men of their machine-invaded villages, seek prosperity abroad. Khadija was born in 1952 in a mountain community north of Fez, where the soil is not particularly fertile, life is hard, and the labour of all, both young and old, is absolutely necessary for the survival of the group. Through her life as an adolescent and then an adult woman, we witness the disintegration of that domestic economy and the rural exodus – first the seasonal departure of the men, and then that of the women and young people. Khadija's life is emblematic in that it reflects all the upheavals that have shaken the society: the disintegration of the rural economy under the impact of capitalism and the introduction of machines, the rural exodus to the cities, and the international migration even of the women, especially those born during the 1950s. She is also emblematic because she seems to have succeeded in realising the impossible: becoming a citizen of the world and of Morocco at the same time, without deluding herself about either one or the other. Through the experience of travelling and living abroad, the possession of a passport as an unheard-of opportunity to enlarge the horizons of her life, the chance to meet a caring man, and the occasion to judge other cultures and to evaluate her own by comparison, Khadija's life offers a lesson to be pondered by the middle-class intellectuals who long to return to the past, and by the male politicians who still cling to the veil of their grand-mothers.

Khadija al-Jabliya[1]

Life in a mountain douar

Q: *You were born in Mernissa?*

A: Yes.

Q: *In a village or a douar?*

A: In a large *douar*.

Q: *About how many people live there?*

A: About 200. It has two mosques and several saints' shrines.

Q: *Two mosques, and how many saints' shrines?*

A: Four.

Q: *Whose?*

A: There are those of Sidi Husain, Sidi Taha, another of Mulay Abdallah al-Sharif, and another of Mulay Abd al-Qadir Jilali. Each saint has his own speciality. Sidi Taha is for *riahs*, for those whose body is possessed; Mulay Abdallah al-Sharif is against the evil eye; Sidi Husain is also for those whose body is possessed; and at the shrine of Mulay Abd al-Qadir Jilali one gives alms. It is also a place to visit. There are two mosques: one is where they teach the Koran to children, and the other is for the *khutba*; that's where the prayers are said.

Q: *Do women also go to the mosque?*

A: Yes, just like the men.

Q: *For the prayers?*

A: Yes, for the *khutba*. It's nice there.

Q: *And what do people do for a living?*

A: They have olive trees, date palms, fig trees. They farm.

Q: *Do they also raise animals?*

A: Yes, some cows, but not a lot, as they do in the Gharb . . . Every-one lives according to his means. Some are very rich and others com-pletely without possessions – they have to go to the *suq* for every little thing.

Q: *And how was your family situated?*

A: Their possessions were rather few. My grandfather and grandmother had some livestock and were very well-off. But they didn't have anybody

146

to do the work; there were only three of them – my grandmother, my grandfather, and my father.

Q: *They only had your father?*

A: Yes. A brother had died, and he had a sister who was married. It is her son Muhammad who is in Kenitra now. My aunt lived with my grandparents and helped her father, because her husband worked with the *qaid*. He went everywhere with him; he was a kind of assistant; he never came home. My aunt and her children lived with my grandparents. My father was not yet married.

Q: *Was your mother his first wife?*

A: No, he had already been married, but his first wife only stayed with him a year. After that, he married my mother.

Q: *And why didn't he stay with his first wife?*

A: It was not fated that he should stay with her. And besides there were problems with her family.

Q: *So he married your mother?*

A: Yes. His first wife's family did everything to bring about the separaton. He got a divorce and married my mother. My aunt had five children when my father got married. It was he who took responsibility for them. He worked outside, and my aunt took care of the house with my grandmother. The two women fed the animals, sowed the grain, and did all the chores; the oldest of my cousins took the animals out to pasture.

Q: *And your uncle?*

A: He died. He was a *talib*. He was married, and when he died his wife left, because in our family you marry the wife of your dead brother. But my grandfather didn't want my father to marry her.

Q: *Why was your grandfather opposed to it?*

A: He said that if she wanted to stay with us she was welcome: he would take care of her.

Q: *Because according to tradition your father was expected to marry her?*

A: Yes, according to tradition. But my grandfather wouldn't hear of it.

Q: *Why not?*

A: My father was too young, and marrying a woman older than himself didn't appeal to him. She could have stayed and lived with us; she would lack nothing just as before. But she didn't agree to that and left.

Q: *Didn't she have any children?*

A: No. She didn't agree to stay. So my father got married. He married my mother and I was the firstborn. After their marriage a year passed without children and everybody thought she was sterile. 'You should repudiate her', they kept telling my father. 'You will spend your whole life taking care of somebody else's children', and other such things. My father didn't give up hope, and he had me, his firstborn. We continued living with my cousins. Then my mother had my brother Abd al-Qadir – he is the one who works for the government now. She had a third baby, but he died. Afterwards, she had a girl, then another boy, who is still in school. I grew bigger and began to help around the house.

Q: *What did you do?*

A: I did housework.

Q: *Tell me a little about your day. You got up in the morning . . .*

A: Yes.

Q: *What did you do – you, your father, your mother?*

A: When we got up, we prepared breakfast and ate it.

Q: *Who prepared breakfast?*

A: My mother.

Q: *What did you eat for breakfast?*

A: Coffee. We had milk. We didn't buy it at the shop. We had milk at the house, and bread and butter, or bread and olive oil. We ate breakfast before going to work.

Q: *And where did you work?*

A: If it was the season for the olives, the men went to pick them. If it was . . .

Q: *Did you have a lot of olives?*

A: Yes, a lot. In fact, we always had a lot. We didn't have enough people to pick them; we used to pick only some of them.

Q: *Who did the picking?*

A: My father and the people that he paid for working with him. When it was the harvest season, everybody in the house worked: the men did the harvesting and the women prepared food for them to eat. We brought food to them in the fields.

Q: *Was it far away?*

A: Yes, very far. It was as far as going from Rabat to Bouknadel, fifteen kilometres more or less. They brought back the olives on muleback.

Q: *Did you tell me who brought food to them?*

A: The children – a girl, or a boy if they had one. If not, someone else. If there were a lot of people to feed, it was a man or a woman who took the food to them – potatoes and . . .

Q: *Boiled potatoes?*

A: Cooked potatoes.

Q: *Cooked how?*

A: Cooked with a piquant sauce, like you make for salads. We took them yoghurt. In the daytime we took eggs, milk, coffee, eggs scrambled with tomatoes or in oil without tomatoes. In the evening they came to eat at the house. We killed a sheep or a lamb or a goat or something else.

Q: *Did your father go to work by himself or with his children?*

A: No. What I was just telling you about was when we had a *tawiza*. When he worked by himself, he had breakfast at home before going out, worked until the time for prayer, came back home, said his prayers, rested a bit, and had lunch. Then he went back out to work until evening. We didn't take food to him in the fields, except when he had someone working with him – then we took either lentils or beans or potatoes or fish or buttermilk.

Q: *So you were saying that in the morning when you got up . . .*

A: We prepared breakfast, and then we went to mow the hay.

Q: *Whom did you mow the hay for?*

A: For the cows.

Q: *Who did it?*

A: I did.

Q: *Where did you do it?*

A: Quite far away, about two hours from the house. But I didn't transport what I mowed on my back. I had a mule. I tethered him with a rope. If the load of hay wasn't heavy, I rode him. If there was a lot, I walked back leading the mule. At harvest time, I also went harvesting.

Q: *When did you go?*

A: Very early in the morning.

Q: *With your father?*

A: No, all alone.

Q: *Where did you go harvesting? Were you paid like the others?*

A: No, it was our grain that I harvested.

Q: *Your grain?*

A: I didn't need to harvest other people's grain. I harvested ours. When you have your own grain, it's like having a farm. If you have a farm, you don't need to go work on someone else's farm. I harvested our grain, the others did theirs, and so forth. It is those who own nothing who work for other people. A woman who is divorced and poor goes to work for someone else. She harvests with them and they pay her.

Q: *You took part in the harvest?*

A: Yes.

Q: *With your father?*

A: With my father and my mother.

Q: *Your mother also worked in the harvest?*

A: Yes.

Q: *What did you harvest?*

A: Grain. But they don't do it that way now any more.

Q: *Why not?*

A: Everything is modernised.

Technology and the struggle for the ancestral land

Q: *How do you mean?*

A: Nowadays, it's men who do the harvesting, and if there is a lot of land, it is a machine that does it. They farm with a tractor. That's what happened to the land which used to belong to us but which a *qaid* confiscated from us during the period of colonisation. After independence, the *qaid* died and his children tried to claim that land as their inheritance – but later his children moved to the city, abandoning the land, and tried to sell it, not to local people but to people who were strangers to the tribe. Then the local people exercised the right of pre-emption of the land and denied those who claimed to be the new owners access to the property. We had first rights on that land. If people from elsewhere wanted to enter into partnership with us, that was a possibility. But to sell the entire holding to them was not an option. Two of the sons of the *qaid* sold their share of the land to some people who were not local, and the other heirs, a daughter and a son, sold us their share. The local people decided to plough the whole property to sow beans, peas, and other things. Those who had bought a share also came to plough. The world and his brother came with their ploughs, their mules, and their tractors – it was chaos.

Q: *How so?*

A: We had exercised the right of pre-emption of that land, and we wanted to plough it. And those who had bought a share also wanted to plough.

Q: *With a tractor?*

A: Yes, with a tractor and two mules. The result was total confusion! They telephoned the authorities – the *khalifa* and the police. Our people did the same. When the government people arrived, they took everybody off to jail, saying that henceforth no one would do any more ploughing:

'You tried to sow disorder by each one ploughing his own way and you will end up by killing each other.' They locked everybody up.

Q: *Those who had bought a share of the land and the others?*

A: Everybody.

Q: *Your father too?*

A: Yes. I had just got married.

Q: *You too? And your husband? They put you in jail?*

A: No, he was from another tribe. He wasn't with us.

Q: *Was your father the only one who . . .*

A: My father and his tribe.

Q: *His tribe was imprisoned too?*

A: Yes.

Q: *All the men were taken away that day?*

A: All the men!

Q: *The women, too, or just the men?*

A: Just the men, and if there were two brothers, only one of them was taken. The same, if there were two partners. They were all taken to prison.

Q: *And those who had bought a share of the land?*

A: They too. They were sentenced to twenty-five days in prison and to a fine besides! We heard about it through a lawyer, himself a member of our tribe, who also owned land. When he found out that people of his tribe were in prison, he couldn't tolerate it. He telephoned the police: 'Surely you will not put them in prison before bringing them to me here at Taza', is what he said to them. So they took them to the court at Taza, and the lawyer received them at his place.

Q: *He received everybody?*

A: Everybody – the people of his tribe and the others. He invited them to his house and gave a party for them. He told the others: 'You should get a lawyer too.' He prepared the necessary papers. The affair dragged on for four years.

Q: *And who worked the land?*

A: No one. The government impounded it. It was guarded day and night.

Q: *Without being farmed?*

A: The land is divided in two by a wadi. When the water flows through the wadi, the land is a veritable ocean of mud. The affair dragged on and on. No one had the right to go on to the land; now it belongs to no one. We only farm the land that we inherited, which is some distance from that land.

Q: *How many hectares?*
A: It is subdivided by hectares, by plots. A Frenchman came to survey it once. We didn't know who he was and asked if he was just a tourist. He took photos of each plot.

Girls work in the country, while men move to the city

Q: *Going back to when you were a child, whom did you cook for?*
A: For my brothers and sisters and my mother.
Q: *How many brothers and sisters did you have?*
A: Four. There were five with me. I made the bread. I baked it in the oven, our oven, a country oven. I knew how to cook bean soup, peas, lentils, potatoes, meat. We bought meat at the *suq*, except when there was a *wazza'* in the *douar*.
Q: *What is a* wazza'*?*
A: It was when they bought a cow or a sheep, killed it, and divided it up. Each person paid five dirhams – only those present. Those who went to the *suq* brought back meat once a week.
Q: *You ate it once a week?*
A: Yes, once a week. If there wasn't any meat, we got fish and prepared it. After that, I began working outside the house.
Q: *What did you do outside?*
A: I collected wood. I would go at seven a.m. and come back around ten. At eleven or eleven-thirty the others came home to lunch. We prepared lunch, ate, and then rested for a while until it was not so hot outside.
Q: *How many of you went to collect wood?*
A: Four or five of my friends. From time to time one of us would get married. We continued to go together. We used to rest a bit and then we came home at the end of the afternoon around four or five o'clock. Then we would mow the hay or do something else. We would go for a walk for a while. We didn't tire ourselves out a lot in the afternoon. Sometimes we played around in the fields or guarded them.
Q: *What did you guard?*
A: If there was a field of beans or ripe peas, we guarded them. The shepherds might let their flocks into the fields, so we guarded them. In the evening we came home. If our mothers were there, they prepared dinner. If not, we ate what was left over from lunch, some bread. You know, we made enough bread for two days. If you had a lot of children, you made ten to twelve loaves at a time, once you had the oven heated up.

Q: *How many loaves did you make?*

A: Ten, sometimes nine, or just six. It depended on how often we made it. I was thirteen years old when one of my uncles asked for my hand.

Q: *An uncle?*

A: No, a cousin. I call him my uncle. He asked for my hand. They formalised the engagement, and he left to work for the government. When my mother died, the last of my brothers was a year and a half old. My brother Abd al-Qadir was eight, no nine; my sister was four; and another brother six. The youngest then was one and a half, and I was only thirteen. I couldn't get married and abandon my brothers to a stepmother. So I gave up getting married. I already had enough worries; it was better to wait until my brothers and my sister grew up a little – especially the youngest one. I could get married later. That's what I told my fiancé in wishing him good luck – that I couldn't abandon my brothers and sister. We broke up and he married my cousin. She lived very close to us. I looked after my brothers and sister; they were growing; one of them went to school. Abd al-Qadir left school in order to go to work in Casablanca in a shoe factory.

Q: *Why did he leave school?*

A: He didn't want to go any longer. We tried to make him keep going. The principal of the school once sent someone to look for him. In the end he ran away, got himself an identity card and went to Casa to work in a shoe factory.

Q: *Is he still there?*

A: No.

Q: *Why not?*

A: He works for the government now. I am talking about Abd al-Qadir, but the other one continued going to school, and the youngest one too. When he was seven years old, I enrolled him in school. My father was no longer with us; he was in another town, working for other people.

Q: *Where?*

A: In Meknes. He worked in the fields. When there was no longer anything for him to do at our place, he left us and went to work there. I took care of the house.

Q: *What did you do?*

A: I took care of the animals, the cow, the calf. We also had a mule and about ten sheep. A shepherd took care of them during the day.

Q: *You didn't take them out to pasture?*

A: I didn't have time to do it.

Q: *Nor did your brothers?*

A: They were still too young. My brother went to school; I didn't want him to spend his time doing it. Nowadays you want boys to go to school, but not girls.

Q: *And why not girls?*

A: Girls don't want to study. They are not used to going to school. In the country it's not like in the city.

Q: *And why is it different?*

A: I don't know. They are used to doing the housework, helping out at home, and their mothers can't bear to be separated from them. So my youngest brother went to school, and my sister did the housework, and I worked outside.

Q: *What did you do?*

A: I took the mule and went out to mow hay. I picked beans and peas. Then I came home to milk the cow and prepare lunch.

Q: *What did you prepare for lunch?*

A: Whatever I found – yoghurt with a bit of bread or a little oil, or eggs in oil, with an orange or whatever was growing at our place. For the other things, we went to the *suq* once a week. We bought apples or bananas.

Q: *And how did you wangle the money to buy things in the* suq?

A: We sold oil and chickens. We had a lot of chickens raised on grain and also some rabbits that we had bred.

Evolution of women's roles

Q: *Did you yourself go to the* suq?

A: Yes of course, to sell oil, eggs, and chickens. I would buy vegetables – tomatoes, peppers, squash – when they were not in season. We grew all those in our own fields. Throughout the summer there were potatoes, onions, tomatoes, and grapes – lots of them. It was in winter particularly that I bought tomatoes and squash in the *suq*. We ate lentils or potatoes while waiting for market day. I paid with the money from the oil, the eggs, and the chickens. I bought sugar, tea, vermicelli. If I ran out of high-quality flour, I bought it in the *suq*, because we only had whole-wheat and rye flour at our place. I would buy vegetables and, sometimes, also something for myself.

Q: *For example?*

A: A scarf, or a *sarwal*, some shoes, a *dafina*, a *shamir*, or some cloth to make a sheet or a skirt when I had enough money. If not, I only bought what I needed. I couldn't buy everything I wanted. But when my father was there, it was he who went to the *suq*.

Q: *Why?*

A: I stayed at home and he went to the *suq*. I only went when he was not there.

Q: *Did the other women go to the* suq?

A: There were lots of women who went, especially older women, but the young ones didn't go.

Q: *Not even those who were married?*

A: No, just those who were older. I couldn't go to the *suq* when my father was there. I only went when he left to work in Meknes.

Q: *And when did he go to work in Meknes?*

A: When there was no longer any ploughing to do.

Q: *And when did the ploughing finish?*

A: At the beginning of winter. They waited until the ground was well soaked with water before beginning to plough. That was when the olives were ripe. They still hadn't finished the ploughing when we began to pick the olives. Some of the olives were pressed and we kept the rest separately in a room. We waited to press them until the ploughing was finished, in order not to have too much work to do.

Q: *Did everybody work?*

A: My father went out to do the ploughing, and we picked the olives.

Q: *Who was that? Some others with you?*

A: Sometimes I went alone, or with my brother. Sometimes I took some girls with me, and in the evening I gave a basketful to each of them. They would rather have olives than money.

Q: *You paid them like that?*

A: Yes. They picked with me, and in the evening I gave them some. We carried the olives on muleback. I gave them two measures of olives, or one and a half when the olives were larger. And then later the men shook the trees to make the olives fall. Before that all we did was pick by hand the olives from the branches we could reach, the low branches. And we spread out a sheet under the tree and shook the low branches to make the olives fall. We filled the baskets and sacks after picking out the leaves that fell with the olives. Afterwards, the men shook down the olives from the highest branches. They were very high; we couldn't reach them. At this point, everybody worked together, men and women; the parents made the olives fall and the children picked up what fell. And if someone from the family didn't have any olive trees at all, he came to help. We didn't keep the whole crop; we sold part of it. After that there wasn't any more work for the men to do – after the ploughing was done and the olives picked, they were free. Some went to Meknes, others to Fez. Those who had fields went to work on them. There was nothing more to do at that time, except to collect wood.

Q: *Where did you go to collect wood?*

A: Into the forest. It was guarded because the forests belong to the government. We sneaked in to look for wood.

Q: *Without the guard seeing you?*

A: Ah, yes. The guard was right on the road, so we piled the wood we collected close to the road or we left it in the fields.

Q: *Didn't you take a mule to carry the wood?*

A: No. We carried it back in bundles. We only took the mule to carry the large trunks, like those you use to make charcoal. We made the bundles up of small branches, to use for heating the oven. We cut them when they were still green and let them dry near the road. Like that, the guard couldn't find them at our place.

Q: *Where did you hide them?*

A: In the fields or not far from the *douar*, until they dried. Nobody touched them; they were safe there. Once they were dry, we began to bring them, bundle by bundle, for heating the oven when we baked the bread. Each one of us had her pile of wood. We might go to get it in a group, as we did for the collecting, but each one only took from her pile.

Q: *Did the boys from the* douar *go with you?*

A: Yes. If a girl was engaged, her fiancé came with us and spent the day with her or watched her from a distance. When he saw the girls go to collect wood, he watched whom she went with, whom she talked to. It was only decent men who accompanied us.

Q: *Did they also go to look for wood?*

A: Yes, some married men. They loaded the mules with large trunks of wood with which they would make charcoal. When we got back home, it was laundry time if there was washing to be done.

Q: *Where did you do the washing? And where did you get the water?*

A: From the spring. It was like a fountain, but it was a spring. We didn't lack water. In the fields, very close to the house, everywhere you went, you found water, wadis full of water. I washed my things and those of my brothers and sister. Afterwards I made the dinner: a salad, some yoghurt, or something else. Or I heated up the leftovers from lunch. If there was no bread left, I made some. I cooked it in the stew kettle. If I had enough time, I heated the oven and rested a bit. It was in summer particularly that I had a lot of work.

Q: *In summer? Isn't it spring that's the busiest season?*

A: In spring it's the women who have a lot of work.

Q: *What do they do?*

A: They winnow grain. Some go to mow the hay for feeding the cows. We ploughed all the land – without leaving the least bit of ground where the cows could graze. We kept the straw for winter. When the hay begins to grow, we begin to mow it.

Q: *Is it the women who mow the hay?*

A: Yes, the men have other things to do. Some are busy with the olive trees; when it begins to get hotter, the work increases. There are others who work in the kitchen gardens tending the squash, the potatoes, the onions, the tomatoes. All those things that will be ready in the autumn must be taken care of in the summer. Then the harvest begins. We used to go to the fields for the harvest. We took our lunch with us, sat down under an olive tree and rested a little; we ate and then had a siesta. I would lean against the tree. If I didn't sleep, at least I rested, and when it cooled off a bit, we went back to work. At five or six o'clock we went back home.

Q: *Did you go back in a group?*

A: With friends, the daughters of friends. One day they harvest with you in your field, and the next day you harvest in theirs, in order not to work alone. The men bring the grain to the house; they bring all they have harvested in big sacks on muleback.

Q: *Don't they do any harvesting?*

A: Yes, they also do harvesting, but they have to transport the grain if they don't have anyone else to do it. They bring it right up to the house and make a large pile until the time for threshing. It's at this time that the *dakkar* are ripe.

Q: *What are the* dakkar*?*

A: They look like figs, and they have some ant-like insects inside. We collect these and stick them on each fig tree. These insects get into all the figs, which then begin to fall by themselves. We collect them, together with those that have not fallen, and dry them by spreading them on dwarf-palm leaves or on marjoram branches. When they are dry, we take them and thread them on a string of dry straw. We keep some for ourselves and sell the rest. At the end of autumn, it's time for the olives. They begin to ripen and we make *arwana* oil.

Q: *What kind of oil is that?*

A: We pick olives that are still green, not yet ripe like those you buy here, in order to retain the juice. We put them to cook in the oven and then we crush them in our press. We place it like that, just like you have placed your tape recorder. There are two pieces of wood, one which goes up and one which goes down. We press them together and the oil drips out of the cooked olives. We eat it before the olives are ripe. That's how we do things in the country.

Q: *And what about your father?*

A: My father, when he finished the work in the fields, went to Meknes. He came back to see us from time to time – once a month or every two months. He gave us a little money to buy what we needed, and then he left. There was nothing for him to do at the house, and he can't stand not working.

Q: *Are there a lot of women who go and work in the city?*

A: No, very few. Only those who don't have a large family are able to go; it's not possible for the others.

Q: *So the women don't go?*

A: No, not the women. Country women can't work like those who live in the city?

Q: *Really?*

A: Yes. A woman can't go and do the washing for another woman. She would find that humiliating. She wouldn't agree to go to work in another woman's house. If it was a woman who was going to give birth, she would go to help her, but she wouldn't go and work for her.

Q: *Couldn't a woman harvest for another woman?*

A: No. Only if she was divorced or an old woman with a lot of troubles. Then she has to work; she can't worry about what people will say. She is old and needs to work to live.

Marriage

Q: *Tell me about your marriage.*

A: I stayed on, taking care of my brother until he was nine years old and going to school.

Q: *You waited eight years after the death of your mother without marrying?*

A: Yes, I didn't get married. I couldn't. My father refused to take another wife.

158

Q: *Why?*
A: He said: 'If I take another wife, she will mistreat my children. You won't get on with her.' As for me, I didn't want to get married either. I didn't feel the need for it.
Q: *Why? Haven't you ever loved a man?*
A: No. At that time I didn't love any man.
Q: *Have you never loved?*
A: No, I have still never loved anyone.
Q: *Didn't you go to parties, to community dances?*
A: Yes, in summer . . .
Q: *And didn't you ever meet someone there?*
A: Oh, it's not like here. It's not like in the city where a girl can meet a boy who interests her, who speaks to her of his intentions, and whom she begins to like. There is none of that in the country; she can't do that. If her family catches her doing that or if they hear about something, or even if the neighbours do – if, for example, they catch a virgin girl speaking to someone, or even a married woman speaking to someone, anyone can chastise her, her uncle, her cousin, anybody at all. It's not just her father or brother who would not tolerate seeing her speak with a man.
Q: *So the girls who are still virgins don't speak to anyone?*
A: Right. A virgin girl doesn't speak to anyone; just to the one who comes to ask for her hand. Moreover, it is his parents who come to ask for her in marriage – it isn't the boy himself. Likewise, they can't see each other, get to know each other during the three or four months before the wedding ceremony – impossible.
Q: *And how did your husband ask for your hand?*
A: He is the son-in-law of my aunt.
Q: *The aunt who lived with you?*
A: Yes. He lived in the city. He was married when he asked for my hand. My aunt told me: 'Marry him.' I answered that it was impossible, because he was already married. I said that I couldn't be his second wife, that I wouldn't be able to get along with the first wife.
Q: *And why didn't you want to become his second wife?*
A: Because I knew women who shared a husband. It is no life at all; they don't get along well. It's just endless arguments; they never live peace-fully. 'If he who wants to ask for me in marriage is already married, I refuse him.' That's what I said to my aunt. 'If he wants to have another wife because the first one hasn't had any children, let him divorce her; then I will agree to become his wife. If he doesn't want to divorce, I will

never marry him.' My aunt wouldn't listen to me; she wanted me to marry him. The other women said to me: 'Aren't you fed up living with your brothers? When you are old and sick, it's not they who will take care of you, but your own children', and lots of other nonsense. In the end, I said all right to them, but I asked them to speak to my father about it. They went to see my father, who refused, claiming that he couldn't be separated from his daughter. My aunt, however, didn't give up. She told me that my father wouldn't ever be able to do without my work, since I took care of his children while he went off to work elsewhere, and that I would never get married. I let myself be convinced by my aunt. I must say I loved her dearly and couldn't refuse her anything. It was she who had brought me up. I told her: 'All right, but let him divorce his first wife.' She was an old woman, while I was still very young. I was afraid she would do something to me,[2] and then what if later he got along well with her? No, I couldn't do it. My aunt said to me: 'All right, he will get a divorce if that is what you want.' He got a divorce. But even before divorcing her and marrying me, he asked his brother to watch over me and, if there was a wedding around here, to stop me going to it. I couldn't go to the *suq* any more, and if I went anywhere at all, the brother was always there following me.

Q: *Did his brother work in the country?*

A: Yes. If he saw me with girls, he came over and argued with me; wherever he found me, he harassed me. I really liked talking to the girls and boys – with a girl and her fiancé, for instance. We used to laugh and have fun. He didn't want me to speak with other girls while his brother was in the city. I told him I was still free, and that if he continued to annoy me like that, I wouldn't marry his brother, and that I was no longer very keen to marry him anyway.

There was a boy who was hoping to become engaged to one of the girls. He wanted to marry her. So he waited until my fiancé's brother was watching, to approach me, to start talking to me, just to annoy him. The brother got mad and upbraided me for talking to that boy, even though he was going to marry another girl. One day – it was Throne Day – they were having a celebration near the tomb of Sidi Abd al-Malik, not far from the road. They were going to have dancers and everything. It was the *qaid* who had arranged for them to come. Every household had donated a carcase of beef. A big celebration! Right? And all the girls were going to the celebration. I wanted to go too. I went to see my aunt and said to her: 'Even those who are engaged are going to the celebration. Why not me?'

She answered: 'Listen, my girl, Muhammad will see you and he won't want you to stay there; he'll argue with you and bully you.'

Q: *Was your fiancé's brother married?*

A: Yes. So I went to the celebration. He came and argued with me and afterwards went around saying that he had seen me smoking and laughing with some boys, that he had seen me with the husband of so-and-so, and that I was no longer . . .

Follow-up

The rest of this interview was mislaid. In 1979, the second time that I met Khadija, I got the following information:

She married another man after having managed to get rid of the first one. She had a child. Then her husband married his sister-in-law, who had just lost her husband. That is the traditional thing to do in that region. Khadija refused to accept the situation, left her husband, and went back to her father. Her child died at the age of eight months. When she heard about the Green March,[3] she went to Kenitra to take part in it. On returning from the Green March, she looked for work in Rabat. She found work as a housemaid with a high government official in the capital. She left that job after three years because of a petty dispute. Then she went to Germany as a maid with the family of a Moroccan diplomat. She came back to Morocco a year later.

In September 1982 she went to Spain with the same family with whom she had gone to Germany. Before leaving, she interceded with the official for whom she had worked to get jobs for her brothers and cousins in the various security forces. She also supervised the marriage arrangements for her younger sister.

In answer to my question, 'Why didn't you remarry?' she responded that it wasn't because she didn't want to. 'You know, when a woman has neither beauty nor fortune and is not educated, which is my case, it is very difficult to find a man who treats you with respect. You know me: I can't bear humiliation. I have gone from one family to another because I will not accept being humiliated. I left my husband because I rejected humiliation. With a character like mine, life is difficult. You know, when I say hello to people and they don't answer me immediately and with the same enthusiasm, I get terribly upset. Sometimes I think about old age. I think about what my aunt told me: You have to have your own children to take care of you later. Yes, I think about it often. You know, my brothers don't think about me at all; none of them has ever given me anything, even a little present. But it's difficult for me to find a good man. I don't want to get married just for the sake of getting married. I support myself by working for others. I buy what I want, a caftan, a scarf. You know, since we last saw each other, I bought some gold bracelets and earrings. I would like to get married in order to . . . in order to . . . have a good relationship with a man. That would be nice. Sometimes I tell myself that Rabat is a city of crazy people. Look how many women live alone without a husband and how many men live alone without a wife. Why is it so difficult to get together? [She laughs.] It's all so complicated!'

In November 1982, Khadija came back to Morocco. She had left her job in Spain. After three months of unemployment, because she refused to work for a salary of less than 400 dirhams, [4] she left for Iraq to take a job arranged by the Iraqi Embassy in Rabat. She was promised a wage of 1,000 dirhams a month in addition to room and board. She left for Iraq on 15 February 1983.

Update 1986

My doorbell rings at an hour when visitors are not expected in Morocco, at seven o'clock in the morning, on a Sunday into the bargain. I open the door and there stands a woman with a baby and an expression of great sweetness on her face. She is wearing a blue *djellaba*, and the baby wears a little imitation ebony hand for protection against the evil eye and a smile that makes you feel happy with the world.

'Khadija al-Jabliya!' I exclaimed. 'Where have you come from this time? And where did you find the baby?' I had not seen Khadija since the winter of 1983. In Morocco, people don't write when they have emigrated unless things are going very well and they have grown rich.

Khadija laughed. She handed me the baby without a word. Without waiting for me to invite her to come in, she entered and preceded me into the living room. 'We have been travelling since four o'clock this morning. We took the bus. I leave the day after tomorrow for France to join my husband. He is a migrant. He works on a farm near Montpellier. I came to tell you hello and to show you my daughter. You must add her to the book.'

She didn't have time enough to tell me everything that had happened since February 1983: 'If I were to tell you everything, you could write a book, maybe two books. I'll come back again, maybe in a year. For the moment I've got too much on my mind to concentrate. Tomorrow I have to go to the French embassy to get a visa. I never had to get a visa before. Those blasted terrorists – they are creating an uproar in Europe, and it's the migrant workers who are paying the price.[5] Because of the terrorists, I have to wait for the bus for hours at the French border. I worry about the baby. I can't concentrate. I'll tell you everything another time. The important thing is that it is good for a woman today to have a passport and to travel, even if she is illiterate. If I had not had a passport, I would not have met the man I love. After Iraq, I came back to Morocco. I was out of work for six months. But I had my money. I bought a little land in the village. And then I left for France to look for work. And that's how I met my husband. He was already married – if you can imagine! He has another wife who is in Morocco. All my life I rejected the idea of polygyny. But I was younger then, and he is very nice. He respects me. We discuss everything and we make decisions together. Since I had the baby I don't work any more. I got fed up with working on the sly, because the French authorities wouldn't give me an official work permit. But France is a great country: I had my baby in hospital, where I was treated like a queen. But, as well, I acted like a lady: I didn't cry out when I was in pain. I didn't want to make a spectacle of myself in a foreign country. But when the baby didn't come after five hours, the nurse called an ambulance at four o'clock in the morning and they took me to a big hospital in the city. One of the doctors spoke Arabic. He had taught in Morocco. He told me how to breathe and I did as he said. When the baby came, the doctor ululated and said: "Bravo, bravo!" He insisted that I stay a week in the hospital. They kept the baby under observation because she had breathing problems. My husband's French health insurance paid the whole bill. France is a great country, because even if you are a foreigner you feel there that you have rights. Here in Morocco, I don't have any rights. I have to fight for everything. I work but I don't have any social security benefits. Maids in Morocco don't get social security. You know what I mean. They say that Muslims are good to each other. It's not true. If I had had my baby here, I would not have had such good treatment. Now I don't know what to believe any longer. The Christians are supposed to be bad, and the Muslims fair and just. But in my life that is not true.'

On Tuesday Khadija departed for France. She took a bus that left from Fez and, after crossing Spain, deposited her in the south of France. The trip cost 600 dirhams. Although illiterate, she has become a citizen of the capitalist world. She takes care of herself, her passport in her pocket and her Moroccan *djellaba* always carefully pressed on her back, as she travels the world in search of happiness. She understands that, for a woman, whose territory in the past was limited to her kitchen, the future offers scope to travel, to feel at ease anywhere at all, even in countries where she understands neither the language nor the customs.

8

Aisha al-Hyaniya: a ten-year-old housemaid remembers her country home

Born in 1969, in the Hyayna tribe, north of Fez, Aisha was seven years old when her father gave her to a family in Fez.

Mistreated, she left that family for another in Rabat, where she was working at the time of the interview in 1979.

She stayed there until 1981, when she returned to her father's house in the country to get married. She had just turned twelve.

The awkwardness felt by an adult interviewing a child, as well as the child's feeling of awkwardness, is evident in this interview. But I have kept it as it is. Aisha was ten years old at the time of the interview, and it is often difficult to distinguish reality from fantasy in what she says. It is perhaps this which gives this interview its special interest and charm.

Aisha al-Hyaniya

Aisha sings in her tribe

Q: *So you don't have any* shaikhas *in your tribe?*
A: No, we haven't any.
Q: *And what do you have instead? Who sings? Who plays the tambourine? Who dances?*
A: Well, the men do; and also we, the women and children, we sing and we play the tambourine. We dance to the drums and tambourines. A singer from the country of the Shluhs[1] sings:

> Ha la la al-afrita
> Walad buhamrun
> 'Asu kulhum[2]

Q: *And does that song make you laugh?*
A: Yes, that makes everybody laugh.
Q: *Why does it make you laugh?*
A: Because it says that all the children who had measles survived, that is, that none of the children who had measles died.
Q: *Do you know any other songs?*
A: The singer also sang:

> Oh, you who make the tea,
> Give me, the stranger,
> Give me a glass,
> Oh, my cousin, oh, my mother.

And then he turned to me, who was seated on the doorstep, and sang:

> You, little rascal,
> Get up from the doorstep.
> I could touch you
> With my scissors.

Q: *I could touch you with what?*
A: 'I could touch you with my scissors', because he was dancing with some scissors. And then he sang again:

> Oh, you who make the tea . . .

Q: *Why are you talking like that?* [Aisha was talking like a toothless old man.]
A: Because he didn't have any teeth! [She laughs.] Then he sang:

> Go tend your herd of cows.

A girl began dancing right in the middle of us all. He sang to her: 'Get going, go take your cows out to pasture.' That meant: 'Get going, you don't know how to dance.' It was a joke.
Q: *And do you know how to sing? Wait a minute. There is a song about a taxi that you sang to me once.*
A: I'll sing it to you:

166

Yaha, yaha, the taxi is in the fields,
Oh, my brother, it's Abdallah and Najat who are there,
Oh, my brother, yaha, yaha,
Oh, my brother, the horse is kicking against the traces,
Oh, my brother, he wants to cavort in the fields,
Oh, my brother,
Yaha, yaha, the one with the white horse,
Oh, my brother,
The rain is falling and the roses are blooming,
Oh, my brother, yaha, yaha.

Q: *Is it true that when it rains the roses bloom?*
A: Yes, because if it didn't rain, the roses couldn't bloom with just the sun. The rain is very important. When it rains, everything gets wet. The ground gets wet and the roses bloom and everything else.

Aisha compares the city and the country

Q: *Which is better, the city or the country?*
A: The city.
Q: *What region do you come from?*
A: I am from the Hyayna.
Q: *What is the name of your* douar?
A: Douar Walad Bushaib.
Q: *How long have you been in the city?*
A: I don't know exactly.
Q: *And you prefer the city to Douar Walad Bushaib?*
A: Yes.
Q: *What do you like in the city?*
A: What I like in the city is that everything is close by. You can find cloth, vegetables, everything. In the country, you have to wait for the *suq* on Sunday, and then it is far away. You have to wait for the *suq* to get vegetables and everything.
Q: *Is that all you like about the city?*
A: That's all. In the *suq* you can't even get a mouthful of water.
Q: *Why?*
A: You can only have one drink. It's a government order. Even if you pay, you can only drink once. You can give two dirhams and not get a mouthful more.

Q: *Why?*

A: Well, you get one drink for ten centimes, and that's all.

Q: *Have you been to the* suq?

A: Yes.

Q: *What did you go there to do?*

A: I went there just once with my father. I was in Fez where I was working. He came to see me on a Sunday, and I went to see a *suq*.

Q: *And what did you do there?*

A: I bought things for my sisters, my big sisters. I bought them, you know, cakes, three cakes. There were yellow ones, red ones, and black ones. So I bought them some cakes. And for my brother Muhammad, I bought a whole box of cakes, long cakes.

Q: *Who gave you the money?*

A: My father gave me some money and told me to buy myself something. But I didn't want to spend the money on myself. My aunt gave me the money for the long cakes.

Q: *You still haven't told me the difference between the city and the country.*

A: I told you that I prefer the city.

Q: *Why?*

A: You find vegetables easily. In the country you have to wait for the *suq* day, and then it is a long way away, and people get hungry at the *suq*. They are dying of hunger. Even if you pay for a teapot full of tea, even if you make tea in the *suq*, you get hungry straight away afterwards. And on the trip back home, people disappear along the way. It's very far, and it gets very hot in my part of the country. While here, there is everything you could want. In the city, everything is close by: cloth, vegetables, everything you could want. In the country there is none of that. If you need something, you can't get it if it's not Sunday. You have to wait for the following Sunday to get some vegetables. On the other days, there is nothing at all.

Aisha works at home

Q: *What do you eat in the country?*

A: Wheat. We grow wheat. We cut it with a sickle. Afterwards, we pile it up and bring the animals to thresh it. The grains of wheat become like flour; no, not the grains, I mean the wheat-ears. We use a *madra* for tossing the wheat; the cold wind of the Gharb separates the grains from the chaff, like you see on the TV.[3] It blows away the chaff and you just have the grain left afterwards. Then we put it in the storerooms; we have a lot of it. God be praised, I swear to you, Aunt Fatima, that once we filled a whole room with grain and two big baskets besides. We grind it for eating and often we still have some left the following year.

Q: *Do you only need grain in the country? Don't you eat meat and vegetables.*

A: We slaughter animals; we eat turkeys, sheep. We buy meat at the *suq* on Sunday. Then, there is a grocer's right close to us; if we need coffee or tea or things for the kitchen, we can buy them there.

Q: *What did you do in the country? Did you work?*

A: Yes. I did errands; I used to bring the pruning hook.

Q: *Did you dig for planting?*

A: Yes. We wait until it rains before planting. We put the seeds in the ground and wait for them to grow. They must be growing a lot now, very high.

Q: *Now?*

A: Yes. They must be growing. They must be higher than the house. We take very good care of our plants and trees, and they give us a good return. We collect the olives. We knock them down with a stick or a long branch. They fall and we gather them up. Once we have finished, we carry all of them to the house before taking them to the olive press. We go there, my father and I, and we bring back three, four, or even five jars of oil.

Q: *Is that all that you do? You help your father with the planting. Don't you do anything else?*

A: I lead the mule or the she-ass. I tie them to the olive press. They make the olive press turn while I collect the oil.

Q: *How do you manage to do that?*

A: I take some salt that I fetch from the house. I put an earthenware jar on my back and I hold it with my elbows. I sprinkle a little salt where the oil is. I sprinkle like this. I call upon the name of God and I sprinkle. I make the oil press turn. My father keeps an eye on it. When the olives are well pressed, it's like a well full of oil. We get four or five jars full. One year we even had five. God is great!

Q: *What else do you do besides helping your father with the planting?*

A: I also go to fetch water at the spring.

Q: *Why?*

A: For my father, so he can put it on the olives.

Q: *And besides working with the olives, don't you help your mother?*
A: Yes.

Q: *Doing what?*
A: I go to get water and bring it in jars on my back or even in pails. I water the mint so that it will grow well, but when it is hot in the afternoon, I wait until it cools off to do it.

Q: *Where do you go to fetch water?*
A: To the spring, very close to our house. Mint grows well at our house. I water it and leave it all wet, and the next day we find it grown tall.

Q: *Why don't you water it when the sun is shining?*
A: It burns and shrivels it if you water it when the sun beats down too strongly. Two days later it is all burned up.

Q: *And what else do you do besides all that? Do you help your mother?*
A: I fetch water; I wash the grain; I help with the washing; I make the bread for her.

Q: *You make the bread?*
A: Yes, and I get the oven ready. I light it, with my cousin Ghalia, who is older than me. I go to collect the wood, and come back with a big faggot on my back. She also brings back her faggot of dry wood, and we light the oven. I clean the house – all the rooms, the hallway – and collect the rubbish in a big basket that I put outdoors. I make bread, and also pancakes. It's my mother who taught me to do all that.

Q: *Do you know how to make different kinds of pancakes?*
A: Yes. I knead the dough – just a little, not a lot, enough to make two pancakes. I work it, I put water on it, and I make the pancakes like that.

Q: *Besides making bread and pancakes, what else do you do?*
A: I make *wagid*.

Q: *What is* wagid?
A: Cow-dung chips. You put them to dry in the sun to use for fuel. I collect the dung, filling a whole bag that I bring back home. I also go to collect firewood; every day I bring back two faggots.

Q: *Doesn't your mother go to collect wood?*
A: No. My mother hardly ever goes to collect wood. My father collects *qammar* from the palmettos.

Q: *What is* qammar?
A: It's what you find under the palmettos, beneath the ground. My father uses a pickaxe to dig them up, and I load them on the she-ass and bring them back home.

Q: *What do you do with them?*

A: We spread them out in front of the house and leave them in the sun for a month or two before we burn them. We use them especially during Ramadan and for feast days.

Q: *What else do you do?*

A: That's all. I don't do anything else.

Aisha, the shepherdess

Q: *What about taking the animals out to pasture?*

A: I sort of forgot to tell you about that, but I did do that, and my father used to kick me to get me to go further.

Q: *Why did he hit you?*

A: Because of the goats that climbed the trees! The owners of the property complained and took the goats to Menazla, and also brought us before the authorities.

Q: *You too? Did they bring you, too?*

A: No, not me. I let my goats just once go into someone's orchard, so my father hit me. But no one else but him saw me.

Q: *How did it happen that the goats went into the orchard, since you were watching them?*

A: It can happen, even if you are watching them.

Q: *How?*

A: Here's how: I try to collect all the goats, I get in the middle of the flock, and I keep watch. The minute I turn my back, there is a goat who gets into an orchard, and I go to fetch it. The another goes off, and I go to fetch the two of them. You go 'Tss, tss' to the goats. The billy goat has horns, and if you approach him, he charges you. You say 'Tss, tss' to him and he comes back. But if you go toward him, he butts you with his horns.

Q: *He butts you with his horns?*

A: Yes, he has very pointed horns. When I am afraid, I say 'Tss, tss,' and he comes back very quickly. To the sheep, you say 'Hay, hay, hay'; you frighten them by shaking a wolf's tail at them. Where we live, the wolf comes to eat the goats and sheep. So we do that to make the sheep come back to us. He pretends to butt me. Sometimes he looks as if he is asking me why I frighten him.

Q: *Do you go by yourself to guard the animals, or does someone go with you?*

A: I go with my sisters Latifa and Zubaida. Zubaida goes to fetch water, and Latifa, the youngest, plays with my little brother.

Q: *What time do you go out?*

A: At dawn. We go out just before the sun comes up.

Q: *Who wakes you up?*

A: Sometimes my father, at other times my mother. Sometimes I wake up by myself.

Q: *Do you leave without eating anything, or do you eat before you go?*

A: No. We don't eat anything. We take the flock out, and at lunchtime we bring them back to the house. We eat lunch, then rest a little, and then go out again with the flock. It's the goats that give us the most trouble.

Q: *How is that?*

A: They make us sweat because they go off in all directions and we have to run after them.

Q: *Which are more difficult to tend, the sheep or the goats?*

A: Well, the billy goat, for example, who chases a nanny goat. He tries to corner her in order to . . .

Q: *In order to what?*

A: In order to mount her.

Q: *In order to mount her? So do you separate them, or what?*

A: We try to separate them, but they don't want to let us do it. He wants to do it to her a little. We try to separate them, but nothing doing. The billy goat reacts by butting us and knocking us down. We go 'Baa, baa,' at him.

Aisha goes hunting and fishing

Q: *Do you ever do any hunting too?*

A: Sometimes, when I take the flock out, I hunt. I take a big stick with me, and every day I catch a partridge, or two or even three.

Q: *What do you hunt these partridges with?*

A: When I manage to catch them, I cut their throats and bring them back home. We hunt partridges a lot. We find lots of them.

Q: *What do you hunt them with?*

A: With a big stick.

Q: *With a big stick?*

A: Could be a big stick, could be a hatchet. Right at the moment when they start to fly, I hit them with the stick and they fall down.

Q: *You know how to do that? How many did you catch like that?*

A: I do it like that, on top of the head.

Q: *Do the grown-ups also hunt partridges?*

A: The grown-ups and the children, everybody hunts partridges.

Q: *Do you catch a lot?*

A: Those who are my age manage to catch them; the younger ones aren't able to.

Q: *How many have you caught up to now?*

A: When I was younger, when I was about the age of my sister Radia, I managed to catch two. One day I caught one with her babies. She had her eyes closed, and I trapped her. I caught the babies and put them in my basket. We kept them at home and fed them, and from time to time we would eat one.

Q: *And do you know how to fish?*

A: Yes, with a hook. I take a stick with a hook on it and some worms. I sit down at the edge of the water and let the hook down into the water. The fish think it is a scrap of guts; they try to swallow it and bite the hook. I used to fill a whole bucket with fish. My father used to catch big ones, like that.

Q: *Did you go hunting and fishing every day?*

A: Every day. One day, a partridge; another day, a bucketful of fish, just like the fish that you have at your house in the city.

Q: *But tell me. You have time to fish, to hunt, to tend the goats, to help your mother, to fetch wood. How do you manage to do all that?*

A: I didn't do it all at the same time. When I tended the goats, I just did that. It was afterwards that I began to do kitchen work and all the other things, when my sister began to tend the flock.

Q: *Before, did you tend the flock all alone?*

A: Yes, before, it was me. I would take the dogs and the sheep out there where there were neither orchards nor people. It was as far as going from here to Malika's house on foot,[4] and I ran after the fish.

Q: *The fish or the partridges?*

A: The partridges. I am always getting the fish and the partridges mixed up.

Q: *So, in the beginning, you took the goats and sheep out to pasture; and when you began to help your mother, who took your place with the goats and sheep?*

A: My sister did, and she also hunted partridges and brought home fish.

Q: *Who fed the animals? Did you also have cows?*

A: We had one cow and a heifer.

Q: *Who fed them?*

A: I did. I gave them vetch and lentils.

Q: *Lentils?*

A: No, not lentils. Vetch and wheat bran.

Q: *What time of day did you feed them?*

A: At night. In the daytime I took them out to pasture with the goats and sheep.

Q: *Did you also feed the goats and sheep.*

A: Yes.

Q: *What did you feed them?*

A: I only fed them in winter, because they were hungry then when there was nothing to eat in the pastures. The ground was white; there was no grass, nothing at all. We fattened up the cows and sheep and the others in summer, when there were plenty of things to feed them, and they grew fat. They ate grass, and I took them to the pastures where the grass was the most tender.

9

Tahra Bint Muhammad: making ends meet in a big-city shantytown

In her interview, Tahra Bint Muhammad distinguishes two periods in her life: the present, which is full of difficulties; and the past, her childhood, which was marvellous. Childhood for her was life in the country, in a cohesive community where the individuals, both men and women, had their place, their duties, and the possibility of expressing themselves either through excelling in economic work, or aesthetically in the design of a carpet or the rhythm of a poem improvised for the community dances at the village fêtes. For Tahra, having moved from the country, her present existence as a married woman and mother of children whose arrival she couldn't plan is a life with a limited horizon where a woman without education and without urban sophistication is unable to find her bearings.

Born in 1952, near Ain-Leuh, in one of the most beautiful regions of the Middle Atlas, Tahra migrated to Rabat, the capital of the kingdom, after her marriage. She became a worker in a carpet factory before her first confinement. She learned to speak colloquial Arabic, because up until then she had known only Berber. But for her, her feeling of exile was intensified by being an alien in the culture and language, as well as in the place. And her powers of adaptation were sapped by the difficulty of finding adequate birth control and the never-ending rise in the cost of living in an economy where she had to buy everything, where she no longer had cows to milk or plants to cultivate.

The difficulty of finding housing, the anguishing and anguished attempts at birth control, the turmoil and high cost of living seem to be monsters that devour her ability to deal with reality and weaken the defences even of a woman as clear-headed as Tahra. In contrast to Khadija al-Jabliya, who seems to conquer all by being always on the move and by continuously refusing to give in, Tahra experiences modern life, life in the city, as an uprooting which affects her psychic equilibrium itself. For a woman who has migrated to the city, is it access to a job – however hard a job it may be – that helps her escape the danger of the powerlessness that borders on madness? A comparison between the interviews with Tahra Bint Muhammad and Khadija al-Jabliya is absolutely necessary, not for developing grand theories about patriarchy, capitalist development, etc., but for posing, in all humility, all the issues that women's voices raise. Namely, that it is necessary to avoid generalising, to avoid projecting on poor women our own preoccupations and problems, and, above all, to do our work as intellectuals. By this I mean: to develop our listening capacity, to be sure that we hear everything, even those things that don't fit into our theories and our pretty constructs. And, above all, to abstain from positing a 'return to the past' as an alternative for women. For even Tahra, who seems to flounder and lose her country vigour in the face of the disorder of a city where she has no place, looks to education for her children as the solution for future generations. She only idealises her childhood, her past, in order to find strength for confronting the future, not for returning to it.

Tahra Bint Muhammad

Childhood in the vicinity of Ain-Leuh

Q: *How many brothers and sisters did you have?*
A: We were five. Lalla Fatuma, Lalla Zainab, Lalla Malika, Lalla Hashum, and I – and five others.
Q: *Half brothers and sisters?*
A: Yes.
Q: *Was your mother married twice?*
A: Yes. We were the ones she had from her first marriage.
Q: *Your father was her first husband?*
A: Yes.
Q: *Are they still together?*
A: No, my father died in an automobile accident. My mother didn't know what to do; she didn't receive any of the insurance money. We would have been able to live quite well with that money, but she didn't know about it. We stayed with my uncle; it was he who brought us up; he married my mother. She made her conditions very clear to him: she

would marry him if he was prepared to take care of us, of our education and everything else. He agreed. We were still very young. I don't remember my father. One of my sisters went to school at one point, but they took her out.

Q: *You didn't go to school?*

A: No, never. As for my four sisters, only one went. The others never set foot in school because they were only girls – it wasn't worth it. And besides, the school was a long way from our house. They told us it was more worthwhile for us to learn housework: 'They are girls, they will get married. It's better to bring them up well and teach them proper behaviour.'

Q: *That all happened at Ain-Leuh?*

A: Yes, at Ain-Leuh.

Q: *Is your family still there?*

A: Yes.

Q: *All of them? all together?*

A: Yes.

Q: *Do you remember at what age you got married?*

A: I must have been eighteen. I had already been engaged a first time – we had done the henna and the ululations[1] – but I didn't want anything to do with that man. I turned him down.

Q: *Why?*

A: I didn't want anything to do with him, because when he first asked for me in marriage, he said that he was getting a job, but I found out that that wasn't true. It wasn't that I was looking for someone very rich in order to lord it over my sisters, but I didn't want someone without a job. I wanted to marry a civil servant, someone who was educated. I would have preferred that to a rich man without an education.

Q: *Why?*

A: Because I am not educated myself. If I travel by train, for example, to go to visit someone, how am I to recognise the station where I am supposed to get off? I can't read the name of the town or street address at all. Still, even now, if I could go to school, if they accepted adults, I would go to learn at my age. I was never able to go to school; my parents never enrolled me.

Q: *Girls didn't go to school at that period?*

A: Where we lived, yes, they were already going. Some of them, even, who were older than me were already going. But there were only a few of them. It wasn't like today when lots of girls are going to school. And still, even today, few people in our area send their girls to school. It's only those who live in the village who do it. And even those who live in the village prefer to send their daughters to the Nadi.[2] You find barely half the girls in school and the other half at the Nadi, in carpet factories, and elsewhere. It must be said that in the country people respect us for our good upbringing. We didn't talk to men and never joked with them. We never went to weddings and you wouldn't find us fooling around with boys. If we happened to go somewhere, we didn't budge from our seats until someone came to fetch us.

Division of tasks

Q: *And did you work at home with your mother?*

A: Yes.

Q: *What did you do? Tell me what you did from morning to night.*

A: From morning to night . . . We got up very early in the morning. We milked the cows and the goats. We two sisters did that; my sister was a year younger than me; people always took us for twins. We began by milking the cows. I was more mature than my sister, and I suggested that we take turns at doing it. There was also my wet nurse who lived with us and who helped with the housework. Actually she lived very close to us, but she ate with us. She stayed with us until her death. We grew bigger, and my mother no longer had to do the housework; we took her place. We did everything. We had the best cows in the *douar* and our ox was very strong. After we had finished seeing to the cows, we made breakfast.

Q: *What did you eat for breakfast?*

A: Coffee and bread, sometimes tea and bread.

Q: *Bread that you made the same morning or bread from the day before?*

A: Bread that we made the day before. Where we live, we don't flatten it out as they do here; we leave all the dough, enough for ten or twelve loaves, in a pan for about an hour; afterward we flatten it out. We don't do it beforehand, like here in Rabat. We used to take turns doing that. Another chore was making the couscous, another was feeding the dogs. We began with those three things. You should remember that we also did the cooking; making the buttermilk was also our responsibility. We made the beds after everyone was up. We filled the kerosene lamps, and we went to fetch water.

Q: *You took turns doing all that?*

A: Yes, and there was also the washing to be done.

Q: *Did you divide up the work by the week or by the day?*

A: We divided up the work each day. One day, for example, it would be my turn to do the harder chores, and my sister would have the easier jobs to do. All right. Let's talk about me: I got up early; I went to milk the cows; then I made breakfast, and straight after I put the couscous on to cook. Then I rested a bit. Around nine o'clock, especially in springtime, was the time when the shepherd brought back the cows, and I had to serve him breakfast – he had already had one breakfast at dawn. This time he had couscous with buttermilk. In winter I served it to him with a sauce, some vegetables, and a little milk. Afterwards I went to feed the dogs, so that they could go out with the shepherd. These are the dogs that protect the animals from wolves. He has to have ten or twelve dogs with him and they are more mouths to feed. We feed them bran and dry bread. We also used to entertain quite a few visitors. If a doctor arrived at the *jama'*, it was we who entertained him; we killed two or three chickens. The *muqaddam*[3] was also one of our visitors. If there were letters to deliver to people of the *jama'*, he came to us to get information about such and such a person before going to find him. Just as you did now with me. You began with me before going to see the others, in order to do this work for the government.[4]

Q: *Was your house on the road?*

A: Not exactly. It was a short distance off the road. In fact, we still have the reputation we had during the years when we were well-off. We no longer have the same means, but everyone remembers what we once were, so they continue to come to our house. The least we can do for our visitors is to kill a cock and offer them some pancakes. We always have those on hand. We used to stock a special flour for guests.

Q: *A flour kept aside?*

A: Yes, very high-quality, sifted flour that we bought in the *suq*.

Q: *How many of you lived in the* khaima?

A: Three or four men in addition to the members of the family.

Q: *Who were those men?*

A: Shepherds.

Q: *Three shepherds who were not members of the family?*

A: Three or four.

Q: *Did they live all the time with you?*

A: Yes, all the time.

Q: *The whole year or just part of the year?*

A: The whole year. There were even more in winter. You also have to add the stable-boy who cleaned the cow barns, but he only lived with us three months in the year.

Q: *The family itself comprised how many people?*

A: The family? It consisted of my uncle and us – that's all. It was our third half-brother, who was older than my mother, who took care of us. My uncle had willed to my two half-brothers a third of what he owned so that they wouldn't waste it. The girls took care of the house until they got married. After we got married, everything changed at home. There was no longer the same orderliness, the housework well done, and everything else. It's not easy, you know, to keep the house clean in the country with all the dust there is; you have to continually sweep, wash, mop, even if the floor is not cemented, and sweep the dust off the doorstep. From the time she gets up in the morning, a woman has to wash the kitchen utensils, clean the goatskin bag and wait for two or three days before inflating it and scraping it to put it in proper shape. The high quality of our buttermilk was well known in the whole *douar*.

Q: *Do you wash the goatskin bag every three days?*

A: Every day or two. Then you inflate it, turn it inside out to scrape it with scissors, and then turn it back right side out again and put some salt in it. One of us takes charge of the goatskin, and the other has to go and fetch hay for the animals, and if the *khammas* isn't there, she has to cut the hay for the animals. She goes out to the fields and only comes back at night with a whole bagful. We only took charge of the housework, not at all of the budget.

Q: *Who took care of that?*

A: My uncle. He would go to sell one or two sheep in the *suq*, for 10,000 or 15,000 francs (100 or 150 dirhams) per sheep. He would choose one that was deaf or had ear trouble. Sometimes he sold it to the butcher or he would just sell the wool when it was shearing time. That's all that we sold; we didn't sell clarified butter or eggs. He always brought back tomatoes from the *suq*, and when it's watermelon season we always have some at home. Tuesday is the *suq* day. My uncle brings back the mule very heavily loaded – everything we need to eat for the whole week.

Q: *Until the next* suq *day?*

A: Yes, for five or six days, until there are no more vegetables in the house. Then someone else goes to fetch them. We keep mint in a dampened jute bag that we buy full, or we put it in a jar. My sister and I didn't see to the household purchases; all we took care of was the housework and the animals. Above all, you mustn't let them get thirsty; you have to give them water.

Q: *Is it the women who take care of the animals?*

A: No, the work is divided. The women only take care of the calves who stay at the house.

Q: *What do you have to do for them?*

A: Give them water and take them out for a bit before the cows come back.

Q: *Do you tether them?*

A: Yes, so that they don't suck. Also at night you have to smear the tits of the goats with dung so that they don't suckle the kids; then at daybreak, around five o'clock, you have to milk them. That's the way it goes.

Q: *And it's women who take care of all that?*

A: Yes, it's women, and they have to know how to do the job. If not, the calf dies, the cows don't give milk any more, and the goats suckle the kids. If a woman doesn't take good care of the calves, they get weak and become sick; the next winter you have to kill them off and take a loss. So a man who has a wife he can count on succeeds in everything he undertakes, whether it's raising animals or a business in town or anything at all.

Desire to create: carpet designs

Q: *Didn't you ever work with wool?*

A: We reserved the afternoons for working with wool, for weaving just what we needed at home – ropes for the animals and tents. We also made goatskin ropes to tie up the calves. It's tougher than wool. We made ropes for ourselves, for carrying straw in summer, and we made *hanbals* as well.

Q: *And do you know how to make carpets?*

A: Yes, I make carpets. Even if I don't know how to create a design, I can copy a design. I just have to see it to do it; you just have to count the knots. But when there is a drawing to follow, like for the Rabat carpets, I don't know how to do it. I don't know how to do fine ones like the Rabat ones. But I know how to make *marmucha* carpets. [5]

Q: *You just have to see a carpet to be able to make one like it?*

A: I count the knots. But I need quiet in order to be able to work. I can't have children coming to bother me. When there is someone to look after the children, I can work.

Q: *And have you made any carpets since you've been in Rabat?*

A: No, I haven't the money to buy wool. It's very expensive.

Q: *Didn't you have to buy it in the country?*

A: No, we had it at home. In Rabat, it's not the same; I have too much to do. I could have had wool sent from home, from the country; I could have made bed covers. There are city women who card wool, spin it, and make blankets that they sell to a shop; they also make mats. In the beginning, none of the women in my family knew how to make mats, neither my mother, nor my sister, nor I. My sister and I wanted to make one with lots of colours like those of the Zemmours. A lady showed us how to do it, so we tried; we had to sit on a pile of pillows to be at the right height. We counted and recounted the knots, copied two or three designs, and in the end we learned how to do it. We made one that was very beautiful – top quality. My sister took it with her when she got married; the one we learned on we kept at home. But since we got married we haven't made any more. What's good about mats is that they don't require a lot of wool; forty to fifty dirhams worth of wool is enough to make one.

Q: *Fifty dirhams to make a whole mat?*

A: Yes.

Q: *And do you still know how to make them?*

A: Yes.

Q: *And why don't you make them?*

A: With all that I have to do? What am I going to buy the wool with? Still, if I didn't have any children, I could buy some and build up a little capital, then buy some more wool, make some more mats and carpets, and go on like that. But I have children, who don't leave me any time or money to do that.

Q: *Isn't there anybody to look after the children?*

A: No, nobody.

Marriage and migration to Rabat

Q: *Tell me a little about how you got married. You told me that you didn't want your first fiancé.*

A: Yes.

Q: *Because he wasn't educated and a civil servant?*

A: Yes, educated and a civil servant. At least educated; if not, someone who has a store or some way of making a living. Otherwise, it's no kind of a life. Just making babies is not enough. If the husband doesn't have a job, he is reduced to stealing or he abandons you. Even though I am not educated, I think clearly and am far-sighted. There are some people who go into debt to get married and make the *tag-zdag*, *tag-zdag*, but that's

182

not what counts; it's what comes afterwards that's important. As for me, I don't want either any tambourines or wedding celebration. What I want is someone who loves me and who can be responsible for a household, not someone who at any moment might have to steal to survive or who would abandon me, leaving me with the responsibility for the children. I am not looking for wealth; I would even pass up a dowry. But I need to have someone that I can count on in the long term, who would help me get through these more and more difficult times. I would not cheat on him and he should not cheat on me either, until the children are grown up and repay us for what we did for them, if they are grateful. If not, we would at least have done our duty to them.

Q: *So, tell me, how did you get rid of your first fiancé? Did you reject him just like that?*

A: Yes.

Q: *And did your family agree?*

A: No, they didn't agree; they all reproached me. They told me that I would be cursed; they didn't at all like what I had done; we argued a lot. I went to stay with my aunt. I stayed a long time with her. I liked it at her house because she lived in town.

Q: *Where was that?*

A: At Ain-Leuh. My family finally understood that I had no desire to find myself divorced, with children from a first marriage, or instead be obliged to leave them with him to be mistreated by a stepmother. It's better to avoid all that. As the old saying goes: 'We haven't put anything in the pot that might stick.'[6] But I had never put on the clothes that he had given me, and we sent them back. Everybody in the *douar* was talking about it. I said that there was nothing wrong, that I just wanted to marry someone I loved. So I succeeded in breaking off that engagement. Afterwards I married my present husband, whom you have met. It's strange. Do you know that he asked for my hand before the other one?

Q: *Oh, no...*

A: Yes. I was not yet twelve years old when he asked for my hand.

Q: *Did he ask for it officially?*

A: Yes, but it wasn't destined to be at that moment. I still didn't know at that time what engagement and marriage meant. I didn't want to get married – that was all. I was still too young. I was somewhat giddy – I don't know – and besides, men didn't interest me at all. So I ended up marrying my present husband later, and it was he who persuaded me.

Q: *Did he have a job?*

A: Yes, but it was especially because of his family that I chose him. His family is Sahraoui, like mine. I wanted to marry a Sahraoui; you know, we Sahraouis are trustworthy, we are rather proud people. As he came from a pious family, I ended up by marrying him. We always end up returning to our roots, don't we?

Q: *He's Sahraoui, is he?*

A: Yes.

Q: *And you?*

A: My mother is Sahraoui. Not my father. I told myself that it was better to marry this man than anybody else. Everybody thought he would never get married. He had two girl cousins and both were educated, but he never wanted to marry either of them. He even went out with one of them before our marriage.

Q: *Before asking for your hand?*

A: Yes, and she continued to write to him after we were engaged.

Q: *Really?*

A: She sent him some drawings: a heart with drops of blood coloured red – you know what kind of nonsense I'm talking about. [Laughter.] I swear that she sent him things like that.

Q: *And did she know that he was engaged?*

A: She had never met me, she didn't know me, but she had wind that something was going on. She thought that since he had gone out with her, that was going to predispose him toward her. Isn't it crazy to think like that? If he had wanted to marry her, he would have said so when he went out with her. One time she wrote to ask him if he had married 'Miss Beauty'. I don't remember now what he answered. [Laughter.] I think he wrote her: 'Maybe it's not Miss Beauty whom I married, but in any case she is better than you. It's my heart she wants, and so she is better than you.' [Laughter.] She sent him another letter in which she asked who this 'Miss Beauty' was who had taken him away from her, who had made him forget her. Just imagine. She said that to him, who is very droll, a real joker. He knows how to burst your bubble with his darts. You shouldn't trust men nor write to them; you're just asking for trouble. So I got married. He told me that he would not be unfaithful to me; he assured me that he loved me very much. At the moment that we were joined he began to cry like a woman. You understand, a man for whom you sacrifice your whole family and everything, for whom you endure cold and hunger – if he is not grateful . . . I laid down certain conditions to my husband before having my first child. I told him: 'I can accept hunger and destitution; I can live with you in a dilapidated house, a house of corrugated metal, a tent if necessary. But if I see you doing – if I see you with another woman – or even if, for example, you decide to stay out late and come back to me afterwards, even if you have done nothing (and how would I know?) – that I would not put up with. If that is what is going to happen, better we should not have any children and should separate beforehand.' I have no lack of suitors; there are several who are still hoping, I assure you. [Laughter.]

Q: *About how long have you been married?*

A: You know, people who see me just casually underrate me. I don't say that I am beautiful – ah, beauty! – but I am not stupid and my behaviour is very proper. You know, among us, it is at weddings that girls are noticed with a view to marriage – it is there that one sees girls who never leave home. They are seen, they are heard singing. They can improvise songs full of innuendo and wit. That still goes on in the country, and men can't resist a woman who improvises songs with skill.

Berber songs and dances

Q: *And do you know how to improvise songs?*

A: Of course, I know how to sing.

Q: *How does it work? Do you sing responses back and forth to each other or what? Who begins?*

A: No, no, it's organised. There is someone who sings, who sings to you and tells you, for example – [she recites a song].

Q: *Sing me something so that I can see how it goes, if I like it.*

A: So that you can tape me? [Laughter.] No, never!

Q: *Please, go ahead.*

A: But we sing in Berber! [Laughter.]

Q: *So, sing in Berber.*

A: It's not in Arabic; you won't understand the meaning of the words; you won't be able to appreciate them.

Q: *Never mind. I am used to listening to Berber songs on the radio, and I have watched village dances in the country. I can dance but I don't know how to sing. But I enjoy it, you know; I am not an ignoramus. There is a row of men and facing them a row of women. A man steps forward to sing, then a woman answers him in the same way. Isn't that the way it goes where you live?*

A: Yes, that's the way it goes. As a matter of fact, the way we do it is not like the way you do it [that is, in the city]. In the city, often those who sing and dance are professionals who get paid for doing it – *shaikhas*. Among us, it is people like you and me who get together to sing. So we improvise songs full of allusions. There are some people who understand these allusions and others who do not – they go in one ear and out the other. Some people are satisfied just to sing, to repeat songs, to follow other people; but there are others who can place exactly which woman the singer is alluding to. They can decode the whole song. If, for example, there is someone who is going out with a girl, it is an opportunity for the singer to inform all the guests. If someone has refused a man a girl's hand in order to give it to another, the account is settled in public, at the time of a wedding.

Q: *Is he allowed to attack the girl's family in public?*

A: No. In his song the singer attacks the person who marries her, even if he is a good lad – it's a way of letting him know, if he doesn't know it already.

Q: *And are there still songs with such allusions at wedding feasts?*

A: Yes, very often that's what goes on at feasts, whether they are to celebrate weddings or births – on any occasion when people get together to sing. So you have to be well informed about everything that goes on in the *douar* to be successful at improvising, and also to understand what it's all about. Even if the people don't know each other, even if they have little information, they are able to understand what is implied; they can place who is being referred to in the song.

Q: *And do you still sing?*

A: I don't sing any more now; I have forgotten it all. I assure you that if I hear someone sing, I can barely follow. I have forgotten everything. I no longer know how to improvise.

Q: *Really?*

A: I have forgotten. I am no longer the same as I was before. Before, in the *douar*, they always made room for me when there were two rows facing each other singing.

Q: *A row of girls and a row of men? And they fire responses back and forth at each other?*

A: Yes, as though with guns. Sometimes it can go as far as serious disputes.

Q: *Really?*

A: Yes, people get into real disputes. Luckily there are always people to restore order. But what nasty remarks are exchanged! Real dagger

186

thrusts would be more bearable than some of the things you can hear at those feasts!

Q: *If someone provoked you in that way, would you respond?*

A: Certainly. But I never give them cause to do it. I don't go out with anybody, so I am blameless. Berber songs are full of meaning. You know, now I know Arabic and Berber, but I can only compose songs in Berber. I often listen to Arabic songs on the radio, but I don't understand.

Q: *One day we'll have to listen to the Berber songs together, and you can explain all that to me.*

A: There are some songs that have a double meaning, sometimes a triple meaning. Berber songs are always like that, full of meaning.

Q: *Yes.*

A: The songs tell about problems, they relate what's going on. There you have it – that's all I can tell you for the time being.

One pregnancy after another

Q: *So, when you got married, how long did you wait before getting pregnant?*

A: I waited – I can't remember any more – about eight months.

Q: *Eight months before you conceived your first child?*

A: Yes, for al-Abid.

Q: *And how long afterwards for your second child?*

A: I didn't wait long – four months. I was still nursing the first one.

Q: *You waited only four months. And didn't you realise you were pregnant?*

A: No, I attributed my tiredness and vomiting to illness. I had had problems with my uterus. I took my son and went to see a doctor – the government doctor where my husband worked.[7] I had to pay 100 dirhams for medicine. Never mind, I told myself, if it's to cure you. But I never for a moment thought that it was a baby that was sleeping in my belly. I waited a month. The doctor told me to come back if I didn't get my period. I did get it, and so I didn't go back to the doctor. It was a threatened miscarriage and not my period. I waited two more months, and then I took some herbs to abort.

Q: *Didn't you go see the doctor that time?*

A: No.

Q: *And did you get your period?*

A: Yes, but I got pregnant again. The poor little thing has waked up again, I thought. [8] I took some herbs, and I had another threatened miscarriage. And I had a lot of pain in the womb, really a lot.

Q: *And were you bleeding?*

A: Yes, a lot. My womb became very small. I told myself that it must be the cold. I thought I was cured. I took some more herbs, thinking I was pregnant. Finally I went to see a doctor who verified that I was three months pregnant. It was at that time that I stopped nursing. The baby I was nursing had nearly died with all that he had swallowed through me. I took him to the doctor, but it didn't do any good. Everybody told me that the medicines wouldn't help. He became as thin as a rail until someone recommended the turtle cure to me.

Q: *What turtle?*

A: We bought a live turtle and put it on the stove to cook until its shell was gone.

Q: *You put it alive on the fire?*

A: Yes, until the shell was gone. We boiled it as if it were a chicken. I put in plenty of spices, a little bit of everything. I cooked up the whole thing and I fed it to my son for three days. The first two days he liked it, but on the third day he didn't want any more. I made him finish it; I didn't give him anything else to eat.

Q: *And who recommended this cure?*

A: An *attar* from around here.

Q: *From around here?*

A: Yes, he is in Salé. And just imagine, that cured him. He had a very bad attack of diarrhoea afterwards. It wouldn't stop; it smelled very bad and lasted a whole week. Then he was cured. Luckily every month I was putting fifteen to twenty dirhams aside for him.

Q: *Why?*

A: For Abid. Otherwise I wouldn't have had any money to buy him a little rice. It was winter and I had to prepare food for him for two days at a time in order not to waste gas. Rice requires a lot of cooking. I cooked it and served it to him for breakfast, at lunchtime, and again in the evening – three times a day and the next day the same thing. I also prepared some semolina for him because it was less expensive – I made that for two days too. But when it began to get hot, I only prepared enough for a single day.

Q: *And didn't you give him milk at four months old?*

A: Yes, I gave it to him all the time. Do you know what I did? I bought milk in a carton – a litre or a half litre, depending on how much money I had. Fresh milk is better, even if it is a little expensive. And there were very few days when I didn't buy him any at all. It cost me about fifteen or twenty dirhams a month, and that was not enough for him! So I began to give him some of what we were eating – some potatoes boiled in water. That went on until I had my second baby.

Q: *Where did you give birth?*

A: In Salé.

Q: *In a hospital?*

A: Yes, I wouldn't want to deliver anywhere but in hospital.

Q: *Do you have group health insurance?*

A: Yes. I gave birth in our local health centre. I went to the maternity hospital once, but they didn't let me in. You have to go to your local hospital. I began to have contractions; I had had very strong ones since the seventh month, and I didn't know when the baby was going to come. Each time I told myself that it was going to be that day.

What kind of contraception?

Finally I had had enough of getting pregnant. Each time I told myself that after this baby I was going to enquire about getting some remedy or going to see a *faqih*. The pill was out of the question for me because I had had an operation for a cyst. And then I had a weak heart; I had never gone to see a doctor about it, but I was convinced that my heart was weak – it must be that. So I told myself that if I began to take the pill, it would kill me. And everybody says that when you take the pill, you have to eat well, either a banana or a little milk for breakfast. You see? But for someone like me, who, so to speak, has to diet, for lack of money, how was I going to be able to take the pill? That's the reason I didn't take it. I was ready to try anything, even though I didn't have a lot of confidence in the *faqihs*. I told myself that that would cost me twenty-five or fifty dirhams and I risked making myself completely sterile. And although I had no desire ever to have more children . . . So I did nothing, because of my reluctance. They told me that it was up to my husband to pay attention when he slept with me.

Q: *Does he use a condom?*

A: No, he doesn't use anything at all.

Q: *Who advised you about these matters?*

A: A friend of his or . . .

Q: *Or who?*

A: There is a woman who talked to me about it – the wife of a friend of my husband. During the last Ramadan, I began to feel certain cravings; I had just stopped nursing the second child. I told myself that I was willing to deprive myself of a lot of things to buy him milk. Because my milk is usually very good, my children are very fat when I nurse them. One day I will show you some photos. So anyway I stopped nursing and I bought a pill at four and a half dirhams to bring on a miscarriage. I knew what I was doing wasn't a good idea, but never mind.

Q: *Where did you buy it?*

A: At the chemist. But before selling it to me, the chemist's clerk asked me if I was pregnant. I told him no. I lied, may God forgive me. I strongly suspected that I was pregnant. But what do you want me to do? I was at my wits' end. I had no one to look after the children if I wanted to go to the Turkish bath; when I had these cravings, I couldn't get to sleep, I couldn't do the housework or washing. I couldn't bear to see the children with dirty clothes, nor my husband either. And then, when I am pregnant, I don't feel like going shopping. You know, I don't shop just anywhere. Even if there are shops very close to our house, I don't use them. I have to go a long way to buy more cheaply. In short, I was fed up and I took that pill so that the child would sleep for at least six months or a year. Better that than a miscarriage. I took it and I got my period. I continued to have them until not very long ago. A neighbour had just had a baby. It was at her house that I took some herbs. Some women brought them and prepared them.

Q: *What kind of herbs are they?*

A: *Ras al-hanut* and some others. They put them in cakes. They taste very good.

Q: *And then?*

A: Then I began to take the twenty-three pills. My period became regular every month.

Q: *How long did you take them?*

A: Only one month. After that I bought those that cost four and a half dirhams.

Q: *Also for one month?*

A: No. There are two kinds of tablet that cost four and a half dirhams. When your period is late, you take one kind for a month in order to have a stronger flow, while the other kind is for not having babies.

Q: *Do you have some? Can you show them to me?*

A: There are no more left. I threw them out. And here, afterwards, I had this child.

Q: *Did all this that you just told me about happen quite recently?*
A: Yes, very recently, four or five months ago, when my neighbour had her baby. She gave me some herbs that some friends brought her. They had made some cakes stuffed with those herbs.
Q: *And why did your neighbour take them? For what purpose?*
A: They are good for women in childbirth, so that they don't keep any of the afterbirth, so that they get well more quickly. Women take them during childbirth and they cost two dirhams. They take them with olive oil or with clarified butter. That gets them back on their feet right away. I didn't do that when I had al-Abid. I didn't have anybody to advise me. Afterwards I had a little heart trouble and was late with my period. Usually I get it on the twenty-fourth or twenty-fifth day. I got scared that time; I didn't get my period until the thirtieth day – after having taken a pill that the wife of my husband's uncle gave me. I took it and the next day I got my period – but a very heavy flow. I was very confused – I didn't know what to do. I wondered if once again I had had a miscarriage. My next period came after twelve days.

The problem of rent, the high cost of living, and the desire for contraception

Q: *Why don't you want any more children?*
A: Why? Well, because of lack of money, and also because of my health. If I had more money, I would get someone to take care of the children, a woman to whom I would give twenty to twenty-five dirhams at the end of each month. But I don't have the money. There is also the problem of housing. You can't live in a house with other people if you have a lot of children. You have to have your own house. If you live with others, they would have to be tolerant so as to avoid disagreements. That's the reason that I prefer to have few children – you need less space when you don't even have a place to live. You could find yourself out of a job or fall ill. Just the other day my husband became sick and it wasn't the first time that had happened. And what if they didn't want him any more where he works? Besides, how can we manage on the 150 dirhams a month that he earns? That's why we have to think about every penny we spend. How can you live like that? And with me, who is sick all the time . . .
Q: *How do you manage?*

Economies at every turn

A: You know, I economise. Instead of drinking coffee with milk for breakfast, I drink tea, even though I don't like tea. We only eat meat twice a week; we never eat sardines. We need a lot of oil – at least five litres a month. In the afternoon, we never drink coffee. Doughnuts cost 80 centimes a pound, so we don't have them. Fruit? Don't mention bananas or apples. We don't even buy oranges.

Q: *Even oranges?*

A: Yes, we even give up oranges sometimes. Sometimes we really would like a little rice with dinner – it costs 2.40 or 2.90 dirhams a kilo. If I buy just half a kilo, I have to get a carton of milk at 50 or 55 centimes. Add it up: 2.50 to 3 dirhams for a, let's say, light dinner. And so, I don't do it. Instead of going to the public bath twice a month, I only go once, and most often I take my bath at home. Instead of getting myself new clothes for each holiday or at least twice a year, I never buy any. I haven't bought any for two years. I avoid asking my family to come to visit me on feast days; I haven't seen them for four years.

Q: *Is it four years that you've been married?*

A: A little more, I think, maybe five years. But I haven't invited them since I had al-Abid. My mother came at that time, but I haven't been able to invite them. At that time, we got 150 dirhams a month and we paid 40 dirhams in rent – and don't forget bus fare. How much is going to be left over?

Q: *Is it your husband who takes the bus?*

A: Yes. We have just enough left to feed ourselves. But my big problem is lodging. If we had bought a house, we would have finished paying for it by now – despite the high cost of living. It costs a lot to live now.

Q: *How much rent do you pay now?*

A: We pay 15 dirhams for one room. Previously I had more work to do, but I got less tired. With just one room, I have too much work. At night you have to get out the mattresses, and in the morning put them back again. In the time left to you, you have to make bread and wash the dishes. I can't let them pile up, and besides I'm always afraid that someone might drop in to visit me. Then there is the cooking, and you have to wash the sheets – it's like that from morning to night. The simple act of drinking a glass of tea requires you to wash up the glass. Afterwards you have to mop the floor, and when the baby wakes up you have to put him on the potty. I tidy everything up very quickly before someone arrives and finds things in a mess. When I had several rooms, I didn't get as tired. I had a separate kitchen and a room for receiving guests with long cushions and tables, which I have sold.

Q: *You sold them?*

A: Yes, I had to sell them. My husband was ill and wanted to go back to the country. So I sold them for 150 dirhams. They were going to fire him from his job because he was ill so often. There was a certain Abd al-Qadir who didn't get along with him. He was just waiting for a chance to get rid of my husband.

Q: *And did you want to work at the beginning?*

A: What do you want me to say, my sister? Even if I didn't want to work, I had no alternative. And if my husband got fired again? I would just have to go to work. Luckily he recovered quickly, but my big problem is housing.

Q: *How much do you have to have to buy one?*

A: For two rooms and a kitchen with a metal roof you have to count on 4,000 to 4,500 dirhams.

Q: *And how much do you have available at this time?*

A: We have 1,500 plus 300 dirhams. That makes 1,800 dirhams and with this month's pay, let's say, 2,000 dirhams. And as we are still owed 500 or 750 dirhams back pay . . . You do what you can.

Q: *How much do you still need?*

A: With the back pay, it comes to 2,750. We are still about 1,250 dirhams short. My parents also send me a little money. If the harvest is good this year, which would surprise me, but if it is good, they could perhaps lend us 500 dirhams. As soon as we buy a house, we will pay off our debt very fast. At the end of each month we will pay off part of it, if they are willing to wait. I will make every sacrifice, I won't buy any clothes, or anything at all. We will have to borrow . . .

Q: *You need someone to lend you 500 dirhams to be able to pay for the house. Is that right?*

A: I will end up buying it, no matter how difficult it is.

Q: *And what did you do to save the money that you have?*

A: Every month I save a little bit, as if I owed it to someone. And even if I need the money, I don't spend it.

Q: *How much do you spend for food?*

A: It's too long to tell you the whole story. If I need to buy something for one dirham, I only spend 50 centimes.

Q: *And how do you manage to do that? Tell me in detail.*

A: No, I don't have any more time [it was five o'clock in the afternoon, and the interview had already taken up several days]. All right. Peas cost 1.30 dirhams. I don't buy them; I buy a kilo of turnips for 40 or 50 centimes. Potatoes cost 1.20 or 1.25 dirhams; I buy only those that cost 40 or 50 centimes a kilo. Cauliflower is expensive; so instead I buy cabbage at 30 centimes. As I don't have guests today, I won't use red peppers for dinner, just salt and pepper. Tea? I don't make it in the afternoon. Some people make tea for breakfast, then again at ten o'clock; they make some more for lunch, then after lunch as well, and at four o'clock in the afternoon. They also make coffee and buy doughnuts. If there aren't any doughnuts, they serve bread and butter. I don't eat any of those things. I haven't bought butter in six months. From time to time I buy a little jam and olive oil, but I don't eat any.

Q: *You don't eat olive oil?*

A: Very little. I haven't bought any for a month or two. That's the way I manage to economise and save. I can't invite my family because that would cost me 100 or 150 dirhams. When there is a feast day, I never go. Sometimes I would really like to buy myself a *djellaba* cut in such and such a fashion, but I don't do it. I only have one, while I know some people who have three or four.

Q: *And why are you absolutely determined to buy a house?*

A: Why?

Q: *There are some people who pay rent their whole lives!*

A: Pay rent, but what about afterwards? We have to think about the future. Suppose my husband no longer had a job. Who is going to pay the rent? He would have to argue with the owner of the house. It's out of the question for us to move out, but the owner deprived himself of everything to buy that house, or he inherited it, or he sweated blood and had plenty of trouble before acquiring it. As for you, you don't deprive yourself of anything and you don't have to move out of your place. Why? It's not fair. If the owner appeals to the government, we can't say that it's our house that we are living in. All the owner has to do is produce his title to the property for the government to restore his rights to him. What can you do when you can no longer manage to pay your rent? Beg? Steal? On the other hand, if you own your own house, you no longer have to pay rent. And even if you lose your job, you can accept any work at all just to be able to live.

The difficulties of finding housing

No owner can house you free of charge. He needs that money. And rents are very high now, especially in the big cities. Someone who has a house or two to rent doesn't have to work for the rest of his life, at the price rents are now – from 200 to 250 dirhams a month.

Q: *How much did you pay when you got married?*

A: I paid – I can't remember now how much. I paid 40 dirhams – that's it, 40 dirhams.

Q: *Where did you live when you first got married?*

A: In Salé.

Q: *For how long?*

A: Quite a long time.

Q: *Is that where you had your first child?*

A: Yes. Afterwards we moved here to Rabat; then we went back to Salé.

Q: *Why did you move?*

A: It's closer . . .

Q: *Close to your husband's work?*

A: Yes. And we didn't know anybody in Rabat. We used to spend Saturday and Sunday with friends in Salé. Then we went back there to live.

Q: *Do you know people in Salé?*

A: Yes. We have some close relatives there. We returned to live in Salé, but the rent was higher and that house didn't bring us luck. You know, there are some houses that are unlucky. The one where we live now has been lucky for us. I lost my engagement ring at the former one; it fell down the drain in the sink. My husband lost his wallet twice, and then he had a road accident. We didn't stay there for more than a year. I sold all my woollen things when my husband lost his wallet. I sold all my jewellery to help him buy a scooter, a Honda. I was a fool to sell my things.

Q: *When did he buy the Honda? The first year of your marriage?*

A: He bought it after I had Muhammad, the last child. But we have sold it. I told him that I was going to pawn it for 1,000 dirhams and why not use that as a down payment on a bit of land? A scooter is only a pile of metal; it's a luxury item for people with money. But people without money, like us, who don't have enough to buy food, how can they buy themselves a high-priced scooter and the petrol besides? When he lost his wallet, I got fed up and moved to Rabat. I was very cramped for room. When I wanted to have large mattresses, I moved again – it was still more expensive. When I had sold everything, I swore to myself to buy nothing more before I had my own house. That's why I haven't made any more acquisitions, not even one more blanket. Last winter we were dying of cold, but I wouldn't buy anything. How could I buy myself something before having my own place, without paying rent? It's not hard to buy things, whether on credit or at the flea market. In two months I could buy plenty of things, but as long as I don't have my house, I won't buy anything at all. Look at what I have on my feet – plastic sandals. Luckily for us, there are some people who help us out a bit.

Friends

Q: *Who helps you out? Your family?*
A: It's as if they were family.
Q: *But they aren't?*
A: They're from the same region as we are. We were brought up together – foster brothers and sisters. I call them 'my brothers and sisters' – they are almost family and they help us out. They do more for us than real brothers and sisters. They help us to buy all the things we can't afford to buy. Eventually we repay the money they lent us.
Q: *Did you live together?*
A: No, but when we first arrived in Rabat, they took us in; we ate and slept in their room with them.
Q: *Are they your friends or friends of your husband?*
A: They are from the same area as our family, from 'back there'. We knew three or four other people, but they weren't like these. We can count on these; they have given us a lot of help.
Q: *How long did you stay with them?*
A: Quite a long time.
Q: *Four or five months?*
A: Quite a long time.
Q: *A year?*
A: No, no, less. And when we found a place to live, we would always go and visit them on feast days, and we spent evenings together. I was working at that time.
Q: *Were you working when you got married?*
A: Yes.
Q: *Where did you work?*
A: In a workshop.
Q: *Close to home?*

A: No, far away.

Q: *What kind of a workshop?*

A: A carpet-making workshop.

Q: *Did you take the bus back and forth?*

A: Sometimes I took the bus and sometimes I walked – most often I walked. And I had lunch at the workshop.

Q: *How much did you earn at that workshop?*

A: Very little at the beginning. Later I earned about 100 dirhams. It depended on the tempo of the work.

Q: *How do you mean?*

A: In the beginning they paid us when the carpet was finished. Later they paid us by the day.

Q: *And how much did you get per day?*

A: It varied with the day. Sometimes it was very little – three dirhams, or two and a half. That was the minimum, and if you worked more, you could make it up to five dirhams. So I used to go to work, and when I got back home, sometimes I didn't have any shopping to do. We would go to eat with our friends. We didn't dare to go to their place all the time, but they would come to fetch us. Sometimes they bought our bus tickets; we were like brothers and sisters.

Q: *Were they married?*

A: Yes, yes, and his wife was one of us. His wife was also brought up with us.

Q: *Brought up with you or your husband? I don't understand. Were these women or men who were your friends at the beginning?*

A: It's the same thing.

Q: *How is it the same thing?*

A: We are from the same area.

Q: *And what did they do? Where did they work?*

A: At first they were in the country. They come from the same place as we do. When they arrived here, they got government jobs. They were two brothers, but each had his own house.

Q: *What work do they do?*

A: They work for the government. They are in the police.

Q: *The two brothers are in the police?*

A: Yes, both of them.

Q: *And didn't their wives work?*

A: No. And even if they had wanted to work, their husbands would have stopped them. They think that a woman should stay at home and not go out. And that's still the way it is. When there was a feast day, we would put aside a little money in case guests came – fifteen to twenty dirhams – as if I owed it to someone rather than having to borrow. The rent we paid immediately my husband got his pay, and with the rest we tried to make ends meet until the end of the month. I didn't have any children at this period. Above all, I didn't want to have any debts. I would prefer to go without eating rather than get into debt. If you buy on credit at the grocer's, the grocer will collect the money at your workplace, and that might be enough to get you fired. Why buy on credit? Do you think the government is going to raise your pay the following month! You have to manage to live on what you earn and not cause problems for yourself.

Q: *Tell me a little about your former job.*

A: I went in the morning and I worked until six o'clock in the evening.

Q: *Six o'clock in the evening, and you walked back home?*

A: Yes.

Q: *Who did the shopping, you or your husband?*

A: He did it from time to time. But as he had a lot of work at that period, he didn't come home often. So it was I who did it. And besides I didn't have any children, and I work very fast. I was never bothered by the housework; the house was always tidy; I did the washing twice a week; I fixed couscous or some other dish.

Getting settled

When my husband was at home, I cooked meals as if he were my guest – so that he wouldn't get angry and say, 'I do my job but my wife doesn't do hers.' And so that he wouldn't get tired of me. Yes, as if he were my guest. On Sunday I would fry a bit of sardine or I would buy a half pound of meat, and serve it with fried potatoes. It was fancier than what we had the rest of the week, fancier than what I made just for myself.

Q: *You say that you did that so that he wouldn't get angry with you?*

A: Yes, so that he wouldn't get angry with me. When we went out together, sometimes I wore a *djellaba*, at other times I didn't. We used to go out for walks until it got dark. We got along well together. He loved me, and I loved him even more. What I didn't like was when he went away on trips. I spent the whole time crying until he got back.

Q: *Did he travel a lot?*

A: Sometimes he was away for a whole month.

Q: *And you stayed alone all that time?*

A: Yes.

Q: *Was that just after you got married?*

A: Yes, and I cried the whole time he wasn't there.

Q: *And what did you do while you waited?*

A: The people I told you about used to come and visit me. They told me that they would see that I had everything I needed and urged me to come to them if I needed anything or if I didn't want to work any more: 'You are welcome. You are like our daughter.' And why do you think they talked to me like that? Because I was a serious person and not at all frivolous. That's why they liked me so much. If I had not been a good woman, they would not have liked me like that. That's the way I spent my time waiting for my husband to return. And if he didn't find me at home, he joined me at their house, just as if they were his family. He used to relax at their place, and he sometimes even spent the night there. And when we were sick of our house, we would go to their place with all our baggage until we found a new place. They were really like relatives to me. It went on like that until the beginning of my pregnancy. Then I left work and we found housing that was less expensive but rather far away. We paid 40 dirhams rent and we lived on the 100 dirhams that we had left.

Q: *You didn't work any longer?*

A: No.

Q: *What did you do with your money when you were working?*

A: Since my husband didn't earn a lot, we put everything in the common pot. I didn't keep any for myself. But I knew how to manage things.

Q: *So it was you who managed things?*

A: Yes. Then I had the baby; it was a very difficult birth. I wanted my mother to come, but she was ill. She didn't arrive until sixteen days after the baby was born.

Q: *When did you ask her to come?*

A: When I began to have contractions. But she didn't arrive until sixteen days later. I had the baby at the hospital. My husband was ill, which was a bit of luck because it meant he had a week off. He took me to the hospital. I had a neighbour who was very nice, an older woman, very kind. She washed the nappies for me for a week. She also went to fetch water from the public fountain, because we didn't have running water in the house.

Q: *So your neighbour really helped you?*

A: Yes, my neighbour, but also our friends. One of their wives came to help me in the afternoons. She didn't stay all night. Yes, once she did stay all night. The other wife also came with her husband. They stayed two days once and brought me what they could. There was also the wife of a friend of my husband and they brought us a gift. We didn't celebrate the baby's name day right away; I had enough money, but I waited until my mother arrived. Then she went back with my aunt. I tried very hard to get up, even when I wasn't able to. I had a very difficult delivery. Luckily I had decided to go to the hospital for the delivery; otherwise I don't know what might have happened. They had to give me two injections. No doubt it was because it was my first pregnancy.

Q: *Did it take a long time?*

A: A very long time. 'God forgive us for what our mothers go through.' I didn't completely recover; I think I haven't been well since.

Q: *You got up?*

A: Yes. There was nothing else I could do. I had a little pain in the womb. I still have it from time to time. Every time I tell myself that I should go to the doctor and have an X-ray, I wait, I wait to finish saving up money to buy the house.

Q: *Who showed you how to take care of your first baby?*

A: The wife of the friend I told you about. She showed me how to change nappies; she did it two or three times to show me. I used to know how to do it. I had learned a very long time ago when I changed my brothers' nappies, but I had forgotten. My neighbour also showed me how to do a few other things. I took very good care of the baby. I put a little kohl on the navel, and that made it heal faster. I also bought some talcum powder for the baby and put it between his thighs. I nursed him, and then I had to supplement with Muchacho condensed milk. I no longer had enough milk. I made him three bottles a day – one tin of milk every two days.

Ordeal at the hospital

With my second child, I wanted to give birth at home; I didn't want to go to hospital. There are nurses and doctors – too many people – around the woman who is giving birth, rather than just one person who takes care of you. I didn't want to go back to the hospital after my first baby, also because I didn't like them taunting me. I am like that. I can't help it. Even though the hospital nurses are women, we don't feel as though we are among women; they make fun of us.

Q: *The nurses made fun of you?*

A: Yes.

Q: *Did that happen to you?*

A: Not to me personally, but to others who were delivering at the same time as I was and who complained about it. When a woman who is delivering starts to cry out, or if it's a woman who has just come from the country, or if she doesn't understand everything they tell her – then the nurses make fun of her.

Q: *What do they say to you, for example?*

A: They say to us: 'You didn't think about crying before (that is, when you were making love), but now you are crying.' And other things like that. One nurse tells the story to another, and they joke at our expense.

Q: *The nurses?*

A: Yes.

Q: *And you hear them joking?*

A: Yes, but we don't know what to do. If it's a woman with some spirit, she argues with them. But if it's a woman who is a little timid or gentle, she prefers to keep quiet.

Q: *How many of you were there in the delivery room?*

A: Two. But as my delivery was very difficult, I didn't see my neighbour. I heard her screams, that's all. I myself had to have my baby at the hospital. It went on for a very long time. They pressed very hard on my womb.

Q: *Who pressed on your womb?*

A: The nurse. She pressed very hard, and after that the contractions became more regular. They gave me an injection, then a second one; they put my legs like this . . .

Q: *They spread them out?*

A: Yes, a lot. There were two of them holding me down as if I was a sheep they were helping to lamb. I screamed a lot. Afterwards I had to stay at home for a month or two to recover. During those months I was completely done in; I could scarcely move. With all that they did to spread me out and hold me down, I would prefer to give birth at home, but I run some risks. There are some women who get good care at the hospital – those who have National Mutual Aid.

Q: *Don't you have it?*

A: Yes, I have it. What I meant to say was that those who have National Mutual Aid have an advantage, and the nurses take a little better care of them than of those who don't have it, the poor things. So, I had the baby and I came back home. In this house here, I at least have running water and electricity. The rent is a little high. I would have been able to save some money if I no longer had to pay rent. But what can you do, when you can't agree about things? He insisted on his scooter – and with all the other expenses and all the guests! In the beginning we managed to agree about things. Although he earned very little, we were able to celebrate the baby's name day. But now that each one has his or her own idea, even though he earns more, we weren't able to do the same for our second child. He bought his motor scooter; we had to sell everything, and we didn't do the things we planned to do. I had to sell the four pieces of jewellery that I owned.

Q: *Why did he want to buy a scooter?*

A: For going back and forth to work.

Q: *Did you go for a ride on the scooter?*

A: From time to time. But I never liked that scooter. I didn't agree that he should buy it. I didn't want to get on it with him. He wanted to take me for a ride on it but I kept thinking about the petrol. You have to have money before allowing yourself such things. He ended up thinking like me.

Q: *So he sold the scooter?*

A: Yes. Now he listens to me, you know.

Q: *He does what you tell him?*

A: Yes, but after a lot of fiascos. If he had listened to me from the beginning, he could have spared us them. We would have had our house before having the children. Even with a salary of 150 dirhams, we lived as if we earned 500 with my way of managing things. But things are going better now, thank God.

Q: *Do you want a third child?*

A: It's not that I don't want one, but I haven't a house. I would love to have a daughter, but not more than three children, and then stop. We can't provide a living for more than three children, dress them, educate them. I don't want my children to behave badly and run around the streets, nor do I want us to have to place them as servants in other people's houses, where they could be mistreated. I want them to go to school, as well as to learn a trade on non-school days, Friday and Sunday, in case they fail in school. They could fall back on a trade, such as carpentry or hairdressing, so as not to be total failures. And if I ever have a daughter, I would also send her to school, but just to primary school, not more. Just so that she knows how to write a letter. I would have her learn a trade – maybe carpet-making. Or I would place her in a workshop. But if I don't have a daughter, if I buy the house and I have a third son, I will adopt a girl and raise her as my own daughter.

Q: *You absolutely want to have a daughter?*

A: Ah, yes, I really want a daughter. You know, you get old, you don't stay young forever; the children grow up; they can provide for your needs, and even if they neglect you, you can take them to court and they will give you enough to eat. But if I get old and fall ill, it will be my daughter who will wash my linen, who will come to see me; it won't be my son's wife. If she makes me something to eat, that's already quite a lot, if she is nice. But if she is not, she will surely say to her husband, 'I don't want to go and see your mother.' That's the reason I want to have a daughter. I could fall ill. You know, I have a son who is ill; he has seizures.

Sorcery and magic

Q: *What does he have?*

A: It's what they call the djinns. There are some women who have something bad in their milk, in their breasts, and their babies are sick all the time. That was the case with the aunt of my son, my husband's sister. She had it in her breast milk; she has two or three children who are affected. I went to see a *faqih* in my home town. I promised to go back and see him to give him something because he said to me, 'If your son gets well, will you give me something?' And I answered him, 'What God allows me to give you, a gift.'

Q: *Was that the* faqih *at whose house I met you?*

A: No, another one, the one we went to see and who 'read' on some bread, because for twelve days my son didn't want to eat. He would only play without asking for food; usually he ate breakfast and lunch with us. That night he asked me for a little bread.

Q: *What happens when he has his seizures?*

A: He only had a seizure once

Q: *What happened?*

A: He didn't have any more afterwards.

Q: *What happened the time that he did have one?*

A: May God protect us! You can't imagine! His face became all blue, his eyes rolled back, and it was as if he was being strangled. He gasped, 'No, no, no.'

Q: *He spoke?*

A: No, it was as if someone was strangling him. He ended up by vomiting. All that lasted a quarter of an hour.

Q: *You didn't take him to a doctor?*

A: No, because I know that a doctor can't do anything for that. There are many families who have tried. I know a family in the country. I was very young at the time. They wanted to move and they had two children, a boy and a girl, whom they neglected for a while. The children got violent attacks of diarrhoea, and when they recovered, they could only move about on all fours.

Q: *And then?*

A: Then they tried all the marabouts. Their father was very poor, but despite that he was ready to try anything. They got around a little better afterwards; now they limp. If they hadn't been ill, they would have been able to help their father. I think that one has recovered. Did you ever see those who drank poisoned oil?[9]

Q: *Mmmm . . .*

A: That happened in the same period, even a little before.

Q: *Does anybody else in your family have the same thing as your son?*

A: No. I myself had that seizure on two occasions.

Q: *How was that?*

A: Yes, I had it twice.

Q: *When? Were you already married?*

A: No, the first time was before my marriage; I had just had an operation. The second time was afterwards. You know, I dream a lot, and I have dreams that come true. For example, I dream that something is going to happen, and the next day it happens.

Q: *So, you had seizures on two occasions?*

A: Yes, on two occasions. Once when I had had an operation.

Q: *For the cyst?*

A: Yes. Women say that when you have spirits in the body, you shouldn't have anything to do with doctors. Despite that, I went to see one at the time that my husband bought the scooter and when I had given birth.

Q: *Were you pregnant when that happened to you?*

A: No, it was just after my delivery. When my husband went out on the scooter, I was left at home alone with the children, and I couldn't bear it. I nursed the baby and tried to quieten the children. There was no one to talk to. I got nervous. Then, when I went to sleep, it came over me.

Q: *How did it happen?*

A: I didn't wake up. I went into a wonderful deep sleep. When I woke up, my husband put perfume on me. You just have to put perfume on me . . . ,

Q: *Was it he who told you what happened to you?*

A: Yes.

Q: *What happened?*

A: The only thing I noticed was that my tongue bore the marks of my teeth. I nearly bit my tongue off when I had a seizure at the hospital; I had vomited up everything, and my tongue . . .

Q: *You had a seizure at the hospital?*

A: Yes, at the hospital. And do you know what the women who were with me did with my tongue? They put perfume on me and they said, 'If she dies, we won't tell the doctor, and if she lives . . . ', because they had tried several things without results, like water . . .

Q: *Without saying anything to the nurses?*

A: Without saying anything at all. They slapped me until one o'clock in the morning. It comes over me when I sleep very deeply. As the spirits waited until everybody was asleep, it lasted about half an hour. The ward was full for more than two hours.

Q: *And all that you know is that you slept?*

A: Yes, and I didn't wake up until the morning. I realised then that something had happened when I felt my tongue all swollen.

Q: *My God!*

A: It's true! I told myself that one day I would bite my tongue off.

Q: *Didn't you go to a* faqih*?*

A: Yes, but I went to see him on account of my fear – I am afraid when I sleep all alone at night. Now that I have the children and there are other people where I live, it's better. When I am alone, I imagine that there are people who are going to attack me, and I can't sleep until I have checked all around that there is no one under the mattress or in the wardrobe. I even open the little wardrobe and rummage around in it. I tell myself that someone is waiting for me to go to sleep to surprise me. On the nights when this fear grips me, I can't close my eyes. But if I do manage to get to sleep, I have a seizure. I don't know what seizures like this are called.

Q: *I too had experiences like that when I was an adolescent, but not so serious. You want to wake up and you feel that someone is pressing with all their weight on you and paralysing you.*

A: Yes, and I have the impression that I cry out, cry for help to such and such a saint . . .

Q: *Without being able to speak . . .*

A: I feel as though I am awake and that someone is strangling me. Then I invoke all the saints I know, this one, that one, weeping all the time.

Q: *And does that still happen to you?*

A: No. It doesn't happen any more since I have been living in this house. I always keep a knife close to my head. . . .

Notes

Introduction: women's Morocco

1. The Prophet is supposed to have said, according to one *hadith*: 'Ask the opinion of your wives, but always do the opposite.' One of those who invokes this *hadith* is Ghazzali in his famous *Ihya' 'ulum al-din* (Cairo: Al-Maktaba al-Tijariya al-Kubra, n.d.), p. 44.

2. See Fatima Mernissi, 'Women and the impact of capitalist development in Morocco', part I, *Feminist Issues* 2, no. 2 (Autumn 1982), 69-104.

3. Léon L'Africain, *Description de l'Afrique*, tr. A. Epaulard (Paris: Adrien Maisonneuve, 1956); A. Toufiq, *Al-mujtama' al-maghribi fi al-qarn al-tasi'ashr, inoultane: 1850-1912* (Matba'at Dar al-Nars al-Maghriba, 1978).

4. *Nafaqa* refers to the necessities of life (food, clothing, shelter, and medical care) which it is the duty of the husband to provide for his wife.

5. The eminently endogenous character of family planning as a fact of Moroccan culture is clearly shown by the place occupied by techniques for spacing pregnancies in our traditional medical practice and pharmacopoeia. See Jamal Bellakhdar, *Médicine traditionnelle et toxicologie ouest saharienne* (Rabat: Editions Techniques Nord-Africaines, 1978).

There is a whole medical literature in which abortion techniques are discussed as an important aspect of Arab medicine. See for example Abi Bakr al-Azrak, *Tashil al-manafi' fi al-tibb wal-hikma* (Beirut: Al-Maktaba al-Sa'bia, n.d.).

6. Robert Castadot and Abdelkader Laraqui, *Le Maroc* (New York: Population Council, 1978), p. 6.

7. Morocco, Division of Statistics, *Enquête d'opinion sur la planification familiale milieu urbain*, p. 5.

8. Castadot and Laraqui, *Le Maroc*, p. 14.

9. Pierre Bourdieu, 'Le champ scientifique', *Actes de la Recherche en Sciences Sociales*, nos 2 and 3 (June 1976).

10. ibid.

11. Morocco, Division of Statistics, *La consommation des ménages au Maroc*, vol. 1, p. 8.

12. See, for example, Table 6.5 of *La consommation des ménages*, vol. 1, p. 50.

13. ibid., p. 19.

Batul Binjalluna and Mariam Talbiya: young girls in a harem

1. At the time of the interview (1974) Batul Binjalluna was about fifty years old. She is married and has nine children. Her husband, a business-man, lives in Fez with his second wife, who was sixteen years old when he married her in 1970. Batul herself lives in Khemisset and takes care of her house and does embroidery.

2. A slave, in the present case, is a woman acquired by the master as a purchase. She often comes from the poorest class. Her life is ruled by the master/slave relationship, especially as regards concubinage and affiliation.

3. A free wife is a woman 'acquired' by the husband through a marriage contract. Often the free woman is the cousin of the husband/master, or at least comes from the same social class, that is, the well-to-do class.

4. That is, the age of puberty.

5. 'To go to the *mu'allima*', that is, to leave the paternal family in order to learn embroidery, was regarded as a progressive step and a breach in the sexual segregation that forbade young girls from leaving the paternal abode except for two or three times a year on exceptional occasions.

6. This was the situation before the sons started to marry. When they bought free wives and slaves attached to their service, more buildings were added and the women were then separated according to status: free wives in one house and slaves in another.

7. The fountain located in the middle of the interior courtyard, which formed the centre of the traditional domestic space.

8. This refers to the nationalist movement which rocked Moroccan society during the struggle against French colonialism and which officially began in 1912. The events related here took place during the 1940s.

9. Talbiya is the feminine form of the name of a sharifian family (descendants of the Prophet). Usually the name of the family has a particular importance in defining the identity of an individual, given the many connotations of class, region, and tribes of these names.

10. The Binjallun family is the family described in the preceding interview. Muhammad is the younger brother of Batul Binjalluna. In the 1930s it became practically impossible to 'supply' slaves to bourgeois families. Because of this, another type of domestic servant made its appearance: 'maids', who came from the same social class, that is, poor families. And Mariam's case history shows how the rural family was 'proletarianised' just as much as was the urban family, with young girls, who previously had been taken care of by the extended family, now being driven to earn their living.

11. Obviously French protection didn't exempt the privileged classes from obeying the basic social laws, but it was nevertheless believed that they were exempt by the people, that is, by those who didn't benefit from such an exemption.

12. At the time of the interview (1975) Mariam Talbiya was fifty years old and still a domestic servant.

Rabi'a: escape from the harem into the middle of the twentieth century

1. At the last interview session, Rabi'a was around thirty-three years

old, divorced, with two children. A member of the urban middle class, she had had some higher education. Her former husband was a doctor and was now remarried.

2.   The words most currently used in Arabic to designate a domestic old, divorced, with two children. A member of the urban middle class, employee are *mut'allima* and *khaddama*. Both words have a pejorative connotation. Perhaps the absence of more 'neutral' words in the vocabulary comes from the fact that this work is considered degrading by both the employer and the employee. Women of the poor classes, who have a choice between domestic work and factory work, prefer the latter, even if the conditions are more harsh, the hours longer, and the pay less.

3.   Traditionally the household tasks in an extended family were carried out according to a rotation system which required each of the women to participate in it (the favourite women or those who had a special privilege such as age were excused from it), alternating between a period of intensive work and a period of rest. The young women of the household were obliged to take part in this rotation system in the same manner as the maids or slaves, in order to train them for the management of their own households later on.

4.   This refers to the panties stained with blood which certify that the bride was deflowered by the husband and that she was a virgin on her wedding night.

5.   The *shaikhas*, with the advance of capitalism, are beginning to perform for a fairly modest sum. Due to the licentiousness that reigns in their presence, the *shaikhas* have become synonymous with prostitutes. They usually come from very poor rural families, while the men who pay for their services are usually rich and powerful.

6.   Ramadan is the Muslim holy month of fasting.

7.   The current *Mudawana* (Law of Personal Status), which was promulgated after independence in 1957, stipulates that the husband has the right unilaterally to dissolve the marriage by pronouncing the formula 'I repudiate you.'

Zubaida Zannati and her daughter Nazha: a thirst for education

1. Born in 1931, Zubaida Zannati is a widow with four children.

2. Under Islamic law, a marriage to a child-bride cannot be consummated until she has her first period. In Zubaida's case, she became pregnant immediately after the marriage was consummated.

3. In this context, a *faqih* is a male Koranic teacher.

4. This seclusion before the marriageable age of thirteen was common in the early days of girls' schooling. Zubaida's parents are faced with a difficult choice: if they allow her to continue her education beyond the age of eleven, when she ceases to be considered a child, the risks of her losing her virginity and of dishonouring her family increase, and her chances of getting a good husband are jeopardised.

5. Ben Youssef refers to King Muhammad V.

6. Born in 1947 at al-Jadida. Since the interview took place in 1974, she has married and has one child.

7. Around two to three Moroccan dirhams in today's money. At the time of the interview, the dirham was equal to about 40p.

8. Around ten dirhams in today's money.

9. Around 150 dirhams in today's money.

10. Around 1,800 dirhams in today's money.

11. Around 500 dirhams in today's money.

12. 'Surprise parties' (in English in the original) refers to a phenomenon which appeared after independence in the large Moroccan cities, especially Fez. Limited to urban adolescents, this phenomenon represented a flagrant breach with the behaviour patterns that had previously governed relations between the sexes. While sexual segregation was previously *de rigueur*, the first years of independence saw adolescents of both sexes getting together to dance (with each other) to Western music (mambo, cha-cha-cha, etc.).

Dawiya al-Filaliya and her daughters Latifa and Malika: a proletariat dreaming of humane factories

1. *Sania* is the name given to the market gardens in the vicinity of Salé.

2. The contradictions in Dawiya's account of her first marriage reveal a perception of time that is very different to a Western chronicological approach.

3. The Avicenne Hospital in Rabat in the section of the city called Souissi.

4. This is 10,000 old French francs, equal to about 100 Moroccan dirhams today. At the time of the interview the dirham was worth approximately 40p.

5. According to the latest news, Dawiya has left the factory and is retired.

6. Barracks of the former Black Guard, located within the confines of the Royal Palace in Rabat.

7. Chellah is a shantytown area of Rabat, and Bettana is the shantytown area of Salé.

8. Joha's nail refers to a well-known story about the wag Joha, who sold his house with the exception of a nail in the wall, and then chose the most inappropriate moments for coming to use it.

9. Daughters of Dawiya, born at Salé, Latifa in 1952 and Malika in 1956. They were not yet married at the time of the interview in 1977.

10. The word 'school' here refers to a modern government school.

11. The *hajja* she is referring to is the *mu'allima*.

12. Latifa's account seems to confuse two occasions on which they left the neighbourhood mu'allima, who was like an extension of the family. The first time, after the argument, they were not ready to jump into the world of the factory and so returned for a while. The second time they had explored alternatives and knew that they would be better off financially working in the factory. Joining their cousins made it possible to recreate family warmth and solidarity in the new production unit.

13. In informal, precapitalist labour relations such as these, it is

impossible to establish a definite relationship between wages, time and output. Despite my questions, the workers themselves could not work it out: the whole labour process is conducted on such a vague and confused footing that the 'surplus value' produced by the workers cannot be quantified. As a result the exploitation of these women is far greater than in the formal sector.

14. Oujda, a town known for its conservative attitudes toward women.

15. Malika, who has since had two children and lives in Oujda, comes to visit her mother twice a year and brings her suitcases full of presents, black-market items bought around Mellila, the Spanish enclave city situated on the Moroccan Mediterranean coast.

Habiba the psychic: the supernatural in the service of the people

1. Habiba was born in 1927 in a village in the Spanish zone of Morocco. This interview took place in 1977 in Rabat, when I undertook the study on psychics. The other interviews in this book date from 1974 onwards. Originally taped in colloquial Arabic, they were translated into French by Said Binjallun, with the exception of this one, which I translated myself. In order to make Habiba's story understandable, I have included some notes on the quasi-mystical vocation of a *shuwafa* (female seer or psychic). Some of these consist of my personal reflections based on visits I made to twenty-two *shuwafas* during the spring and summer of 1976, which I hope will lead to a future analytical study of sorcery.

2. The seizures are supposed to be due to the possession of an individual by spirits (*riah*).

3. Since the enactment of the 1957 Family Law, marriage has to be registered with the government. Recitation of the *fatiha* is no longer sufficient.

4. That is, he was not a 'believer' in the djinns, in order to neutralise what was thought to be their fierce, destructive power.

5. Benzoin is supposed to calm the spirits and please them. Under its effect, they release their victim, or, at any rate, loosen their hold on her.

6.   Mulay Ibrahim is a saint of the southern part of Morocco, and one of the patron saints of psychics.

7.   Sidi Ali is the patron saint of the Hamdushi sect. Like Mulay Ibrahim, he plays an important role in magic practices and initiations, and the activities linked to sorcery. He offers the advantage, for a woman living in Rabat, of being more accessible (because nearer) than Mulay Ibrahim, whose shrine is in the environs of Marrakech. Sidi Ali's shrine is near Meknes, 130 kilometres from Rabat.

8.   Shaikh al-Kamal is the patron saint of the 'Issawi sect. The pilgrimage to his shrine at Meknes takes place during the first week of the celebration of the Prophet's birthday.

9.   The shrine of Sidi Said is located a few hundred metres from that of Shaikh al-Kamal and is an important centre for rituals and processions.

10.   The ban on wearing black during Shaikh al-Kamal's ceremonies is well known even in circles which are not particularly interested in the world of the spirits.

11.   This refers to Lalla Aisha Qandisha, one of the most important female spirits in the supernatural world.

12.   In this context, the *muqaddam* is the local figure in charge of initiating the novices and conducting the ritual.

13.   The psychics whom I visited in the shantytowns surrounding Rabat-Salé and Casablanca often had a banner on their door to publicise their vocation. Those who lived in the residential quarters of the cities were more discreet. Habiba is an exception: she lives in one of those residential quarters, but she has a banner on her door.

14.   Lalla Malika is a spirit like Lalla Aisha, but each spirit has its own distinct speciality.

15.   She makes her appeal not to the participant who is physically present, but to the spirit that possesses her – in this case, Lalla Aisha Qandisha.

16.   That is, chosen as the victim.

17.   She 'sees' future events, as well as perceiving beings who do not have a physical existence. The gift of psychic powers is supposed to be

one of the compensations enjoyed by those who are possessed by the most powerful spirits and who, as a result, suffer the most violent seizures.

18.　I didn't dare say the word 'doctor'.

19.　Each important spirit has its own colour, black being one of the most violent. After the ceremony, the patient will have a particular rapport with that colour.

20.　The month of *Sha'ban*, like *Ashura* (the tenth day of *Muharram*), is a period of great importance for those who, in one way or another, deal with the spirits. This is true whether they are people who make use of the assistance of the spirits for earning a living, like Habiba; or whether they are passive victims, like her nieces; or whether they resort to them to solve a specific problem.

21.　The whole family was present during the interview, including two teenage friends of her son. Habiba was very dressed up for the occasion, wearing a green veil on her head. The family and all their friends were dark-skinned. In the world of the spirits, having a very dark skin is a great asset. Contact with the south, with deepest Africa, is a dominating factor and point of reference. Let us remember the Senegalese visitor at the beginning of the interview.

22.　This clumsy, but necessary question revealed to me that the fundamental distinction between the real and the imaginary has no validity in the world of the spirits. The beings in the dream are as present as the real beings. The borderline between dream and reality, between the imaginary and the real, is meaningless, unimportant in the structure of Habiba's world.

23.　The *ladun* is a chunk of lead that serves as a prop during the séance. The psychic gives the 'client' the *ladun* after the latter has deposited the amount of money agreed upon as a fee. The client takes the *ladun* in the palm of the hand, tries to concentrate on it and infuse it with his or her wishes, before returning it to the psychic. The latter then throws it into a brazier where it burns in a spectacular fashion. She then plunges it into a bucket of water, takes it out, and, while concentrating on the twisted shape of the burned metal, details the client's problems and anxieties. The *ladun* is very frequently used among the psychics of Rabat-Salé, the only ones whom I visited during my intensive research in 1974 (twenty-two in four months).

24. She means a 'believer' in the spirits, not in Islam.

25. I had become a little confused about space and time in Habiba's narrative. I was no longer sure which events had taken place in real time and space, and which belonged to the realm of dream or the imaginary, as mentioned in note 28.

26. Habiba agreed to be interviewed in connection with the making of a film. The interview took place while she was being filmed carrying out some typical operations. As I used to come to see her fairly often and as I was having the *ladun* séance done for me (the film producer had handsomely paid for it), Habiba very subtly tried to push me to get more involved and make some specific demands of Lalla Aisha through her, demands that cost some hundreds of dirhams. However, as she was afraid of losing me as a 'journalist', she did not insist on this, since she was already earning a lot of money as things were, with the additional possibility of more publicity. Her refusal to either describe or show me her shrine to Lalla Aisha seemed to be just a way of exciting my curiosity and of drawing me into a closer and more costly relationship with Lalla Aisha. In the end I never was able to visit the shrine. During the *ladun* séance, she told me that my emotional life left something to be desired and that I had an emotional block as a result of a previous magical operation. The prognosis of course involved intervention by the *siyadna*, 'our masters', as will shortly be seen.

27. The word for 'charm' in Arabic is *al-kitaba*, literally 'the writing'. A charm then is a written formula designed to bring about the desired result. The production of charms, like access to Lalla Aisha, brings in thousands of dirhams. The initial séance (three and a half dirhams) only identifies the problem and establishes the prognosis. The psychic directs this process by using the *ladun* or the *tabaq*. She asks questions which one must answer, and usually the 'client' gives all the information she needs in order to divine the nature of the problem. Often the rituals which accompany this séance (benzoin fumes, a veil concealing the head of the psychic, loud burping and other strange noises by the psychic) are only devices to put the client in a favourable mood for participation. As for what happened to me, I had to furnish her with the details of my marital status in response to three short questions. The séance ended (as was the case with each of the twenty-two psychics with whom I had a session as observer-participant in 1977) with a diagnosis of total failure on my part:

I was a failure in my professional and emotional life, and I had a block, a *thiqaf*. Once the failure was identified and the block duly noted, the séance was at an end. One then either chose to remain stuck in the dead end which the psychic had sketched out as one's life, as I did, or decided to take action, which amounted to asking her to do what was necessary to nullify the famous *thiqaf*. At that moment, one gets involved in the second stage, where the price of the operations is not fixed, where she is going to try to 'do something': write up charms or something which is even more costly and without any limits whatever, planning magic operations around Lalla Aisha and her shrine. These operations can stretch out over months or years and require prompt payments which can vary, according to my research during 1977, from 200 to 2,000 or 3,000 dirhams.

28.   *Faqih* in this context refers to a guiding spirit.

29.   At this point, Habiba's invitation for me to get a little more involved than I had been until then was no longer ambiguous.

Khadija al-Jabliya: from peasant to citizen of the world

1.   Khadija al-Jabliya was born in 1952 into the Mernissa tribe south of Fez. First a peasant, then a housemaid in the city, she was twenty-five years old at the time of the interview in 1977.

2.   She was afraid that the first wife would resort to magic to do her harm.

3.   The Green March was a 'people's march' organised by King Hassan II to assert Morocco's claim to the western Sahara.

4.   At the current rate of exchange, five dirhams equal one pound.

5.   Ordinarily, visas are not needed for Moroccans or French people to travel to each other's country. But after the terrorist attack in September 1986, France decided to insist on visas for Moroccans entering France.

Aisha al-Hyaniya: a ten-year-old housemaid remembers her country home

1.   For Aisha, the country of the Shluhs is the neighbouring area where Berber is spoken.

2.   Ha, ha, ha, little devil,
                            The spotted kids
                            All beat you.

3.   She is referring to a series of television programmes depicting life in
the countryside, particularly the details of working in the fields.

4.   Malika is a cousin of Aisha who lives in Rabat.

Tahra Bint Muhammad: making ends meet in a big-city shantytown

1.   The henna and the ululations are the rituals that accompany the
engagement ceremony.

2.   The Nadi are training centres administered by the Ministry of Youth
and Sport where girls and young women receive training in professions
ranging from dietetics and family planning to crochet and embroidery.
Recently other ministries and various associations have opened similar
centres. Despite their limited budgets, these centres play an important
role in the life of rural and city women of the lower classes who do not
have the opportunity for schooling.

3.   In this context, the *muqaddam* is the headman of a small community.

4.   This interview took place in 1977 in Douar Ma'did in Rabat. I
avoided using the *muqaddam* as a means of introduction to the families of
the *douar*. Instead I asked the dispensary for permission to accompany
their teams who were visiting families who had had a baby born not in
hospital, but with the aid of a traditional midwife (*al-qabla*). I wanted to
avoid being identified as coming from the administration, the government. Once the first doors began to open to me, I no longer had to use the
mobile teams of the Ministry of Public Health. If an interviewee liked
me, she would introduce me to her friends. So, after the first week, I
went alone to the *douar* and moved around freely, being introduced by
one family to another. But that did not stop them from sticking the
government label on me, despite long sessions in which I explained the
aim of my work (collecting material for publication). I always make it a
point of honour to explain the aim of my work, because I don't believe

that an interview relationship based on a lie will succeed. The results of an interview in which the interviewer hides his or her identity and objective can only be false and inconsistent. If the interviewer does not get involved in the interview and does not try to experience the relationship completely, to listen intently, to put himself or herself in the position of the person who is speaking, to try to feel what that person is feeling, the interview will show it. And all this is only possible if the interviewer reveals to the interviewee his or her true identity and objectives. You can't be truly involved if you have lied about your actual identity and true motives.

5. *Marmucha* carpets are from the Middle Atlas mountain area. They have a complex design with symbolic geometric motifs and stylised representations.

6. *Ma darna fi qadra ma yatahrak*: an Arabic proverb.

7. Her husband worked in the Rabat-Salé provincial police service.

8. The allusion is to the idea of the *ragad*, the sleeping foetus. It is a belief that the foetus can remain attached to the uterus for months and years without growing and then can suddenly awaken and start growing again from where it left off.

9. There was a famous case of adulterated oil during the first years of independence, which resulted in many deaths and lifelong disabilities.

Glossary

al-awra   the blind

al-hudub   a sort of silk lace made with knots

al-kitaba   a charm

amin   a trade union leader, someone who has the confidence of the members and to whom they delegate the power of decision

attar   a druggist from whom one can obtain a great variety of medicinal plants and prescriptions

buhali   a half-wit or holy fool, who is in contact with supernatural forces and whose bizarre behaviour sometimes expresses messages that one has to know how to decode in order to profit from it

dabiha   the animal to be sacrificed

dada   the maid who lives with the family and takes especial care of the children; in the context of the old society it meant slave

dafina   a long filmy gown worn over another gown

darb   street, but with a connotation of 'community' or 'familiar territory' where people know each other and have very close neighbourly relations

djellaba   a long robe made of thick material that is put on over indoor clothing when one leaves the house. Originally male attire, it was borrowed by women who adopted it in place of the *haik* during the 1940s. It is synonymous with the veil because the djellaba is supplemented by veiling the face

douar   an agrarian hamlet

220

faqih/faquiha   faith healer, holy man/woman, guiding spirit

fatiha   the first *surah* of the Koran, recited during the engagement ceremony and other rituals

Filali   from the southern province of Tafilalet which stretches to the Sahran part of Morocco, the Filali (or Sahraoui) are known for their ethical rigidity, hard work and honesty

gallasa   the woman in charge of the bride's belongings and who lookes out for her well-being during the first weeks she spends in her husband's house

hadith   a saying or action by the prophet (Mohamed) as reported by his disciples, the Sahata

haik   a very long shawl of heavy cloth which women wear over their heads

hajja   the title given to a woman who has made the pilgrimage to Mecca

hanbal   a type of rural mat or carpet

izar   a voluminous outer garment that covers the whole body

jama'   a rural community which in the past had a local council that was strong and effective enough to stand up to central government

jawads   good spirits

kanun   a three-legged charcoal burner on which one places a pot or pan

khaddama   domestic employee

khaima   literally 'tent', used in the sense of 'family' or 'household'

khalifa   a representative at the local level of central government

khammas   a farm worker who has entered into a relationship of *khammasat* with a property owner

khammasat   a type of agricultural association still very common today in the countryside, in which the *khammas* gives his labour in exchange for a fifth (*khamis*) of the harvest

khutba   the Friday sermon at the mosque

kitab   charm

ladun a chunk of lead used during a séance

laila literally 'the night', but here it means the ceremony which takes place from sunset to sunrise

Lalla a polite way of addressing women, particularly strangers or respected members of the family, which has now been dropped in the big cities, where its use can have ironical overtones

ma'dhur a handicapped person, one who is excused 'for not being fit'

madra a sort of shovel

malik master spirit

Mama an affectionate form of 'Ummi' (mother), applied to any female member of the family as an endearment

ma'rabta the ones who are descendants of the Chief/noble families

moquf a public place where those who seek work go (a sort of labour hiring site)

msid Koranic school

mu'allima craftswoman, a teacher who trains little girls in the techniques of embroidery and other traditional crafts (ornamentation, weaving, carpet-making etc.)

Muchacho a variety of canned milk as well known as Nestlé

muqaddam/muqdadama

mu'tallima domestic employee

qabla midwife

qadi a judge

qaid representative at the local level of government

qammar a gambler

ras al-hanut literally 'best of the store', a cocktail of spices expertly concocted

riah the evil spirits who are believed to take possession of the body causing seizures

sab'a   the ceremony that takes place on the seventh day after a child's birth, at which the child is assigned its given name

sadaqa   one of the funeral rites

sania   a 'garden' but a special one, which is used for vegetable growing. It is given great importance, it is considered more rewarding to work there than in a factory

sarwal   a pair of voluminous harem pantaloons

shaikhas   women musicians and dancers

shamir   a long dress

sharif/sharifa   noble, high born

shuwafa   female seer or psychic

siwak   walnut bark used for cleaning the teeth

siyadna   'our masters' referring to the most dangerous, possessive among the mysterious forces called spirits

suq   market

surah   the verse of the Koran

tabaq   a container usually used for making couscous or keeping bread. The psychic's tabaq is an instrument of work and is used in her séances, particularly for holding shells of all kinds. She 'reads' your future in the disorderly combination of shells and other objects obtained once the container is energetically tossed up and down in your presence

tabkhira   a combination of herbs or minerals or other elements that are burned in a brazier

tag-zdag   an onomatopoeic rendering of the sound of drums, here signifying a wedding

talib   a man with some education who by virtue of this, plays an important role in a rural community

tarha   a unit of measurement

tasmiya   the term for the naming ceremony (see *sab'a*) used in some areas, the equivalent of Christian baptism

tawiza a traditional form of mutual help. The heads of families decide to devote a day (or several) to help one of their number who doesn't have enough hands for the harvest. The latter then organises a feast for the occasion

thiqaf a magical procedure that was supposed to stop the development of the foetus at the stage at which it then was

wakil an agent with a power of attorney

wali a multi purpose word: the protector, it can mean the women's guardian or the saint

zawiya the lodge at the shrine, sometimes refers to the sect